About the Author

Roger Knowles was born in 1937 in Warrington and raised during World War II and the early post war years. He left school at 16 years of age and commenced work as a trainee quantity surveyor. He secured his qualification as a Chartered Quantity Surveyor through study using a distance learning course. In his late twenties he qualified as a barrister, again by means of distance learning course. He founded James R Knowles in 1973, a company of Construction Disputes Resolution Consultants offering a one-stop shop which was the first in its field. This became the only alternative method of formally resolving disputes in the construction industry, without the need to employ a firm of solicitors. The company became a worldwide phenomenon.

Roger Knowles

SOMEBODY UP THERE LIKES US

AUSTIN MACAULEY
PUBLISHERS LTD.

Copyright © Roger Knowles (2015)

The right of Roger Knowles to be identified as author of this work has been asserted by him in accordance with section 77 and 78 of the Copyright, Designs and Patents Act 1988.

All rights reserved. No part of this publication may be reproduced, stored in a retrieval system, or transmitted in any form or by any means, electronic, mechanical, photocopying, recording, or otherwise, without the prior permission of the publishers.

Any person who commits any unauthorized act in relation to this publication may be liable to criminal prosecution and civil claims for damages.

A CIP catalogue record for this title is available from the British Library.

ISBN 9781785541773 (Paperback)
ISBN 9781785541780 (Hardback)

www.austinmacauley.com

First Published (2015)
Austin Macauley Publishers Ltd.
25 Canada Square
Canary Wharf
London
E14 5LQ

Printed and bound in Great Britain

INTRODUCTION

According to Robert Burns, The Best Laid Schemes of Mice and Men Gang Aft A-gley. We all have ideas and make plans for their implementation, why is it that some succeed whilst others bite the dust? Good planning, timing and first class execution play a large part, but there is often another factor which comes into play and determines the success or otherwise of the enterprise. Some refer to it as the fickle finger of fate, others luck, either of the devil, the Irish or otherwise. Is the outcome pre-ordained, or is there an input from a third power and can it overcome bad planning or execution? After a lifetime of work and endeavour does Roger have the answer?

CONTENTS

PART ONE – THE EARLY YEARS

CHAPTER ONE: THE SECOND WORLD WAR

Born in Woolston near Warrington and later moved to Padgate. Main activities in the area were the RAF Camp and Burtonwood Airbase. The Munich Agreement followed by the declaration of war and the outbreak of hostilities. Wartime Britain and its implications for Padgate. Dunkirk and the Normandy landings and ultimately the end of the war and back to peacetime.

CHAPTER TWO: VILLAGE LIFE

Padgate C of E school and school life. Singing in the school and church choirs which were much loved. Walking Day Celebrations, a highlight of the year. Holidays taken during the wartime. Membership of the Boy Scouts and its enthusiasm for knots and British Bulldog. The annual Scout camp, a long remembered pleasure.

CHAPTER THREE: EARLY YOUTH

Grandparents and the Sunday ritual. Our gang and its regular activities. Building the truck and the boat, its launch and sinking in the valley. Playing football on the backfield stadium becomes a passion. Visits to local orchards and parents' reaction on my return home with a pocket full of fruit.

CHAPTER FOUR: LIFE AT A GRAMMAR SCHOOL

The Beveridge Report and the subsequent formation of the Welfare State and NHS. Ambitious parents and the Eleven Plus Examination. Reg Harris, the world class cyclist; one of my heroes. Enrolment at Boteler Grammar School. My school days at the Grammar School and looking forward to 4pm. The teaching staff and their characteristics and proclivities. Greatest pleasure at school was playing in the school football and cricket teams for each of the five years I was a pupil.

CHAPTER FIVE: MUSIC

School music policy. Brother learns to play the euphonium. I am allocated a violin which I am required to learn to play. Miss Pollitt, my violin teacher, both stern and strict. Miss Pollitt enters me for the Royal Schools of Music Grades 3 and 5 examinations with success. Join the school choir and take part in Gilbert and Sullivan operas. GCE O Levels, successful in seven subjects. Major triumph on the cricket field.

CHAPTER SIX: POSTWAR EVENTS

Discipline in schools and use of corporal punishment. Limited use of the cane at Boteler Grammar School. Statistics of children banned from school after corporal punishment abolished. My ambition to become a teacher lasts a few years. The war in Korea and the Conquest of Everest. Left school in 1954 with no job or career ambition.

PART TWO – A CAREER BEGINS

CHAPTER ONE: MY FIRST JOB

No career in mind. Applied for a job with L C Wakeman and Partners, Quantity Surveyors without knowing what service they provided. Accepted a position with them still without knowledge of what they did. Started work as a trainee in their Warrington office. In addition I undertook work in their office at Burtonwood Airbase. Commenced studying for the Royal Institution of Chartered Surveyors' Examinations on Day Release at Liverpool College of Building. Played football for Padgate St Oswalds and cricket for NALGO.

CHAPTER TWO: PINNACLE OF A FOOTBALL CAREER

Avoided national service by a whisker, due to age. Played semi-professional football in the Cheshire County League. Players were either professional or amateur, I was the latter. Became interested in girls. Local dance halls in Warrington the main pickup place. Wendy came to work at the office and we started courting. John Smith a neighbour and jazz enthusiast sold me an alto saxophone which I learned to play competently. 1956 Suez Canal Crisis.

CHAPTER THREE: OFF TO SWINDON

Office in Warrington was closed and work at Burtonwood Airbase dried up. I was transferred to a construction site in Swindon where my company was working for The Pressed Steel Company. Very good experience which proved of great benefit later in my career. My boss was Charles Medland, a first class person in all respects. Commenced Distance Learning Course which was right up my street and I passed the RICS Intermediate and Final examinations with ease.

CHAPTER FOUR: MARRIAGE

Engaged to Wendy at Christmas 1959, married 4th June 1960. Secured a small flat in Swindon just after Christmas 1959 and shared it with Dave Harvey and Mark Lane until I married, they then move out. 1962-63, coldest weather since 1814, average temperature in January 1963 of minus 2.1 degrees; the year of the Beeching Report. Applied successfully to move to head office in Birmingham, in order to gain more varied experience. Accommodation in Birmingham was very expensive. We rented a flat in Handsworth which was grotty but provided a roof over our heads.

CHAPTER FIVE: LIFE IN SHREWSBURY

Due to difficulties in recruiting staff at Head Office the company decided to open a branch office in Shrewsbury. Peter Martin and I were appointed as joint managers. We opened an office on Town Walls and became friendly with Mike Sandford, an Architect working in the same building who made many useful introductions. Purchased a bungalow in Great Ness in the heart of the country. The office did well and in addition to overspill work from the head office we secured significant work ourselves. Mike Sandford tragically killed in a boating accident.

CHAPTER SIX: LIVERPOOL, THE LAST OUTPOST

Ambition led me to apply to manage a new office in Liverpool which the company was planning to open. Had a spell in hospital due to malfunctioning kidney before moving to Liverpool. Started studying for the Bar Examinations employing a Distance Learning Course. Passed the three examinations necessary to qualify in four years. After five years in Liverpool I decided to start my own company as a one stop shop, offering a service relating to the settlement of disputes in the construction industry.

PART THREE
JAMES R KNOWLES - THE FIRM

CHAPTER ONE: UP AND RUNNING

One-stop shop for dispute resolution underway, a world first. Premises secured at Canada House, Manchester on a two year lease, rent £650 per annum. Need for a bank loan and secured overdraft of £2,000. Overdraft withdrawn and so changed bank and increased overdraft to £3,500. First client, Eric Parmley of Tysons in Liverpool, followed by Holland Hannen and Cubitts also from Liverpool. Work secured in Yorkshire for George Longden and Son and Pickles Brothers. Electronic calculators came onto the market and purchased one. Produced a claim document which became the industry standard.

CHAPTER TWO: TAKING ON STAFF

After six months I recruited Paul Cookson, a trainee, and Mike Wills, an experienced quantity surveyor. My wife Wendy undertook the role of secretary/receptionist but left after 6 months to become a full time mother. Appointed by Brian Hill of Holland Hannen and Cubitts to run a two day training course for the site staff. It was subject to a CITB grant. CITB appointed me to lecture at regular courses for them. Appointed by Shaws Linton to lecture all over the country at their training courses from 1974 to 1982. Began writing articles for the RICS' Chartered Quantity Surveyor magazine, which lasted for 18 years. All proved excellent marketing for the company.

CHAPTER THREE: EXPANSION

Undertook work for Worthy Thompson in Manchester. Moved from Manchester to premises in Knutsford. Opened new offices in Manchester and Liverpool; Bill Minnit, the

Manchester office manager, secured a commission for providing regular legal advice to members of the National Federation of Building Trades Employers. Appointed by Shrewsbury Building Contractors in relation to a dispute with Shropshire County Council. Appointed accountant Arthur Shaw to relieve me of accountancy duties. Declined the opportunity of introducing a staff pension scheme, which proved to be a good decision.

CHAPTER FOUR: THATCHER YEARS AND FALKLANDS WAR

Margaret Thatcher government came to power in 1979 and remained until 1990. Reduced state involvement in people's lives. Reformed Trade Unions, undertook deregulation and expanded privatisation and introduced tax cuts. Falkland Islands invaded and captured by Argentina on 2nd April 1979. Britain retaliated with its own invasion on 21st April 1979. General Belgrano sank on 2nd May 1979. Poll Tax introduced in Scotland and Wales in 1989 and England in 2000. Poll tax scrapped 1992.

CHAPTER FIVE: EXPANSION IN SHEFFIELD AND LONDON

Company policy was always to recruit the best, who were not usually the cheapest. No business plan, decisions based mainly on common sense. We billed monthly and produced monthly management accounts. Became the RICS representative on the Joint Contracts Tribunal and continued to lecture nationwide. This provided extensive publicity. Opened offices in London and Sheffield. Appointed by Sheffield Corporation to investigate the construction problems on a major project at Skye Edge. Moved office in Knutsford to Wardle House.

CHAPTER SIX: SCOTLAND AND THE IRISH DIMENSION

Recruited Paul Jensen, a major acquisition in 1981. Commenced in Scotland with Ian Strathdee appointed as manager of the Glasgow office. During the troubles in Northern Ireland I lectured for the RICS in Belfast and undertook training courses for the Northern Ireland Housing Executive. Opened an office in Belfast with Fergie Bell as manager. Troubles in Northern Ireland culminating in Bloody Sunday. Conciliation moves led to the Sunningdale Agreement and finally the Good Friday Agreement which ended the troubles.

CHAPTER SEVEN: CRAWLEY AND WINCHESTER OFFICES OPENED

Colin Archibald opened an office in Crawley and Mike Hall replaced him as manager in London office. Following a Shaws Linton Course in Southampton, I was approached by Richard Brazier concerning an arbitration with a subcontractor. The subcontractor was represented by solicitors and counsel and so Braziers did likewise. We lost the case. I liked Winchester and opened an office there with David Somerville as manager. When he retired Richard Hawkins replaced him.

CHAPTER EIGHT: RUNNING OUR OWN SEMINARS

Mike Milne of Eden Construction rang requesting that I run a seminar for them. Mike later joined our company and opened an office in Cheltenham. Mike suggested that in preference to me lecturing for Shaws Linton, we should run our own seminars which he and his secretary Penny would organise. First seminar at Cheltenham Racecourse entitled "Are You Up to Date" attracted 180 delegates followed the next day with 66 at Winchester. Shortly after we ran the seminar in Glasgow to a full house of 120 delegates and had to put on a repeat performance for those who could not secure a place. Opened in Morpeth but due to modest success relocated to Newcastle upon Tyne, with Andy Dunn as manager. We undertook fifteen disputes for Silkstone Construction of Barnsley against the local authorities in Barnsley, Leeds and Wakefield which were all settled to the satisfaction of Eric Rigby, the client's representative.

CHAPTER NINE: OPENING OVERSEAS

Mike Charlton returned to the UK from Singapore and successfully applied for a position with us. After about twelve months he informed me he would like to return to East Asia. We opened an office in Hong Kong with Mike as manager. Mr Morris visited my office concerning a dispute he had relating to the renovations of a cottage in the Lake District. Tragedy occurs when he is electrocuted by an electric blanket. We open an office in Leeds with Les Birkett as manager. Ann Glacki, a librarian, is recruited and produces a monthly bulletin of all matters of a legal nature that arose during the month. This was sold on subscription and styled BLISS Building Law Information Subscribers Service which was an industry first. It was intended to provide important information for our staff, but in addition we sold it to people from outside the company on a subscription basis.

CHAPTER TEN: EXPANDING THE MARKETING EFFORT

The marketing consisted of me writing articles and giving lectures and the company's nationwide seminars. I decided to expand the marketing by employing a full time marketing manager and appointed Ian Phoenix. This was later expanded to the recruitment of a marketing manager for each of the regions, being London and South East; South West; Midlands; North West; Yorkshire and North East and Scotland. Golf day arranged by George Goodchild which only lasted a few years as it was considered that it didn't provide value for money. Opened office in Sutton Coldfield with John Wood appointed as manager. A sub-office opened in Birmingham managed by Tony Phillips.

CHAPTER ELEVEN: EXPANSION INTO SOUTH WALES AND THE SOUTH WEST

Patrick Lineen appointed as Finance Director followed by improved cash collection. Cash flow forecasts and budgets now produced. Overdraft and invoice discount required to provide working capital. Car fleet sold and leased back. Computers introduced. Opened an office in Bristol with Simon Bayliss as manager; he left after two years and was replaced by Malcolm Roberts. Cardiff office opened on the back of major work for Cwmbran Council with Mark Entwistle as manager. I was involved in a major commission for Clive Hughes, Cardiff office's most colourful client.

CHAPTER TWELVE: MORE AND MORE SEMINARS

Opened an office in Colwyn Bay where Terry Williams and later Nick Gurney were managers. Suzanne Cash appointed as marketing assistant, later to take over the running of all the seminars nationwide. In contrast with other seminar organisers we produced fully comprehensive notes which could be used by delegates at some future date. In addition to Are You Up To Date, we developed seminars relating to the Preparation of Claims, the JCT and ICE contracts and Recent Legal Cases. Developed a seminar based on the questions regularly asked by delegates, entitled 50 Contractual Nightmares and Their Solutions which became a great hit over many years and attracted large numbers of delegates.

CHAPTER THIRTEEN: EXPANSION IN MIDDLE ENGLAND

From the beginning of the 2000s the numbers attending the seminars reduced considerably but we continued to run them as a publicity exercise. Quality Assurance became a must but it was left to managers to decide whether it should be adopted. Only seminars, marketing and the Sutton Coldfield office instigated Quality Assurance. The service offered by these three had always been excellent and Quality Assurance therefore had no effect on performance. Opened offices in Nottingham and Cambridge.

CHAPTER FOURTEEN: EXPANSION IN EAST ASIA

Derrick Morris who had experience of working in Singapore joined the company; he recruited Terry Cleary, a one-man band quantity surveyor who was based in Singapore. Office in Singapore officially opened. I made an annual visit to Hong Kong and Singapore to present seminars each autumn. Kuala Lumpur office opened with Leonard Kok appointed as manager. Rod Martin joined the company and succeeded Leonard Kok as manager when he left. Opened office in Brunei and held seminar at the Sultan's polo club, later closed. Undertook a commission in London for the Sultan's brother, Prince Jefri. Office established in Shanghai but closed after three years.

CHAPTER FIFTEEN: TECHNOLOGY ARRIVES

Terry Cleary left Singapore and was replaced by Chris Nunns. Chris takes a few of us on his yacht and David Price falls into the drink. Derrick Morris unexpectedly died and I attended his funeral on Dartmoor the day after Boxing Day and became snowed up. Word processors arrive on the scene and all offices, and eventually every fee earner had one. Patrick Lineen opts for a voice recognition system in preference to a word processor. Avoid making typists redundant. Computers came into use in the preparation of delay analysis as part of the production of claims. Glasgow office expands and we open in Edinburgh.

CHAPTER SIXTEEN: OPENED IN DUBAI AND KUWAIT WITHOUT SUCCESS

Further expanded in Scotland, with a new office in Stirling managed by David Carrick, which was successful. We opened an office in Aberdeen in the hope of securing work related to the oil industry but closed it after three years due to a lack of success. Opened an office in Cyprus as a stepping off point for the Middle East. Despite successful seminars in Dubai, Abu Dhabi and Oman we failed to secure work outside of Cyprus. Opened an office in Dubai with Nick Longworth as manager, but after three years it was closed down due to lack of success. Purchased a company in Kuwait from Alan McArthur who wished to return to the UK and the manager's position was passed to Bruce Parry. Iraq invaded Kuwait in 1998. Bruce refused to leave and remained during the occupation. Kuwait liberated seven months later with Bruce unharmed. Bruce was awarded the OBE for his bravery. The office in Kuwait never reopened.

CHAPTER SEVENTEEN: PROFITS IN THE MIDDLE EAST AT LAST

Recruited Gordon Moffat who reopened the Dubai office which was followed by offices opened in Abu Dhabi and Qatar. In all we had over 60 employees in the Middle East and making profits. An interesting trip to Cairo but considered it not suitable for an office. John Dobson appointed as manager of the London office. He soon organised a move to a building in Bedford Avenue. John returned to Gloucester after three years and Geoff Brewer was appointed as manager. We moved again this time to Bedford Square where the rent was £175,000 per annum on a 25 year lease with no break clause. We held big ticket marketing events and the office became very successful.

CHAPTER EIGHTEEN: DIVERSIFICATION AND OVERSEAS DEVELOPMENT

Opened offices in Brentwood and Weybridge to work in conjunction with the London office which worked successfully. Decided to diversify and appointed David Parker and Colin Dawson to establish Knowles Loss Adjusters which was very successful. Appointed Bert Hamilton to set up a Project Management company. It proved successful in securing work but struggled to make a profit and was closed. Started Staff Placements as a body shop which was successful at securing work at home and overseas, but the profits were modest. Provided free advice on the telephone and discounted fees to trade association members of The Federated Association of Specialist Subcontractors. This was very successful in securing clients but came to an end when the director John Huxtable left and his successor Ron Davies appointed a firm of solicitors to undertake the task. By the mid-1990s we had twenty offices in the UK and needed to concentrate on overseas development. Set up the International Division in view of the turndown in work in the construction industry in the late 80s and early 90s, run by David Price and Reg Thomas. After a slow start it became very successful.

CHAPTER NINETEEN: WORKING IN KOREA AND THE LATHAM REPORT

David Price and I attended a meeting in London with Mr Kong of Hyundai regarding the possibility of us providing services in relation to the Jamuna Bridge project in Bangladesh. Before making a decision Mr Kong suggested we visit the site and Hyundai's office in Korea at our financial risk, following which a decision would be made as to whether we would be appointed. Visited the site and Hyundai's office in Korea and were appointed. We delivered three one-day seminars in Seoul to the International Contractors Association of Korea. We set up an Engineering Division to try to secure more work in the engineering industry. One of the projects secured was for Zannen Dredging on the River Conway Crossing. Commission obtained on the Storebelt tunnelling project in Sweden. Following major problems in the construction industry Sir Michael Latham was appointed to produce a report referred to as The Latham Report.

CHAPTER TWENTY: THE CONSTRUCTION ACT

Following Sir Michael's recommendations, Parliament passed the Construction Act which came into force on 1st May 1998. The provisions of the Act introduced adjudication to settle disputes; also provisions regarding payment of contractors. Organised a roadshow of seminars at various locations around the country, which dealt with the Act and proved very successful. Mike Milne in Cheltenham set up the Academy of Construction Adjudicators to act as a nominating body. After four years we had represented parties in 1,000 adjudications. Latham Report recommended partnering to foster good relationships and avoid disputes. Nigel Barr in Sheffield recruited a few staff and set up a service for introducing partnering which was extensively used by Local Authorities. We became friendly with the Federation of Property Societies, a Local Authority organisation; produced a partnering contract entitled Public Sector Partnering Contract.

CHAPTER TWENTY-ONE: SOUTH AFRICAN TOUR AND NORTH AMERICAN EXPANSION

Met Chris Binnington of Binnington Copeland who attended one of our seminars in Reading, who asked if I was interested in undertaking with him a lecture tour of South Africa where his company was based. Together we presented seminars in Jo'burg twice, Durban, Capetown and Botswana which were very successful. Geoff Brewer, London office manager, handed in his notice to start his own company. Opened an office at Gadbrook Park, Northwich and transferred all head office functions from Wardle House, Knutsford. Secured a listing on the AIM market to provide funds for expansion. Sir

Michael Latham and Rod Sellers appointed as non-executive directors. Commenced expansion in Europe by opening an office in Munich. Opened an office in Toronto with Roger Bridges as manager. Purchased a company styled BBCG with offices in Toronto, Montreal and Vancouver. Gene Bennett appointed to open an office in Los Angeles.

CHAPTER TWENTY-TWO: EXPANSION IN EUROPE AND START-UP IN AUSTRALIA

With success in Munich we opened in Paris, which proved very disappointing and was eventually closed. In the meantime we had opened offices in Madrid and Milan which failed. I came to the conclusion that Europe wasn't for us. Mike Charlton offered to supervise an opening in Australia. John Donnelly and Charles Elliott had worked for us in the UK and emigrated to Australia and were contacted by Mike Charlton. As a result we opened offices in Melbourne and Sydney. Danny Atkinson started Knowles Law which was very successful and made very good profits.

CHAPTER TWENTY-THREE: NEW VENTURES

David Barker became a go anywhere man and was sent off to Taiwan with a team to prepare a claim for a client. Started up a magazine entitled Constructional Law, which after three years due to a down-turn in the industry we sold on. Wrote book entitled 100 Contractual Problems and Their Solutions. Later editions styled 150 Contractual Problems followed by 200 Contractual Problems. Established The Institute of Commercial Litigators, which was shot down in flames by Lord Stein. Brian Quinn instigated the setting up of Knowles Solicitors which was replicated by Mike Charlton in Australia. Set up Quantity Surveyors International (QSi) which was successful.

CHAPTER TWENTY-FOUR: MY LAST DAYS WITH THE COMPANY

Gave a lecture in Lagos, Nigeria and required to take out kidnap insurance. Seminar went well and returned the following year to lecture for ITB, a Nigerian company, following which we took on claims work. Stood down as Chairman and CEO but retained the post of Executive Chairman. Mike Charlton and Brian Quinn became Joint CEOs. As I approached 70 my interest began to wane. No longer being CEO I didn't have the day-to-day involvement in all matters relating to the company. I tendered my resignation and the company delisted and was sold to Hill International an American company. My last day was 31st August 2006.

CHAPTER TWENTY-FIVE: POSTSCRIPT

Patrick Lineen and I formed Baqus from three existing quantity surveying companies and in December 2007 secured an AIM flotation.

PART ONE

THE EARLY YEARS

Chapter One

The Second World War

1.1 I was born on 22nd October 1937 just short of two years before the Second World War was declared. At the time my parents Arthur and Beryl and elder brother Alan lived in Hillock Lane, Woolston which is located just outside Warrington. Unfortunately the builder who constructed the row of houses, of which ours was one, had difficulty in selling all but a few. He therefore opted to let the remainder to tenants. My parents considered that the type of people to whom the houses were let displayed antisocial behaviour of which they disapproved. Matters came to a head when our next door neighbour acquired a donkey which was kept in the front room. Enough being enough, we moved to Jubilee Avenue in Padgate, the next village to Woolston. Padgate was no different from many small villages at the time. A spine road, which runs from Warrington to Leigh, passes through the village and most parents spent time on a regular basis advising their children of its dangers, as it had in its past claimed a number of fatalities as well as its fair share of serious injuries. John and Rene Morris, who lived three doors away from us, had twin boys, Brian and Geoff. Disaster struck one day when Brian, at the tender age of six, was knocked down and killed whilst trying to cross the road. The family tragedy didn't end there as Geoff, having grown up, married and with two children, was killed in a road accident which occurred whilst he was taking his family on holiday. Ron

Pollard, who became a close friend, when a child, was involved in a serious accident on the same road, but fortunately survived. Padgate also has a railway station on the Liverpool to Manchester line. There is a recreation ground which was donated by a local farmer, Mr William Bennett, on which could be found children's swings, a war memorial listing those local men who had fallen during the First World War and three football pitches.

1.2 There are two schools in Padgate, both of which are faith based, one C of E, the other RC. The three churches C of E; RC and Methodist, all of which are still functioning, played a major part in village life. In addition to the regular Sunday services, which were well attended, and in the case of the RCs packed to the doors, the churches provided the core of village life. There was no TV at that time and an expensive night out was a visit to a cinema in Warrington, which most people could afford once per week at the most. Otherwise it was left to the churches to provide the necessary social life in the form of regular dances, whist drives and the like together with thriving church-affiliated organisations such as Young Wives, Mothers' Union, Boy Scouts and Girl Guides. One of the major football leagues in the Warrington area was the Warrington Sunday Schools League which was also organised by the churches.

1.3 Padgate's main claim to fame during my early years was its RAF camp. It was built at the outset of the war, which started in 1939 and both during and after the war had come to an end was used as a training camp for new recruits. During the war and for many years after it was over, young men were conscripted to serve in the armed forces and so there was a regular flow of young men into the village which greatly pleased the local ladies. This period proved something of a bonanza for the women of the area, as in addition to the RAF camp, there was a naval camp and an army barracks. The most prized catch as far as the females were concerned however, was the arrival of the American Air base, which was located at Burtonwood just to the west of Warrington. The American troops arrived, once the USA had entered the war in 1942, smartly dressed in their uniforms, equipped with charm, and arms full of chocolates, nylons and promises of a good time which, if rumour is a good guide they delivered, all of which proved irresistible to many of the local ladies.

1.4 We moved to Jubilee Avenue as tenants in 1938 when I was just over 12 months old. It was the year of the Munich Agreement entered into by Neville Chamberlain, our prime minister at the time. When he arrived back into the country on 30th September 1938, having signed the Agreement with Adolph Hitler, he spoke to the crowds who had gathered at Heston Airport, where he addressed them concerning the Agreement saying:

"This morning I had another talk with the German Chancellor, Herr Hitler and here is the paper which bears his name upon it as well as mine. Some of you, perhaps, have already heard what it contains, but I would just like to read it to you. We regard the agreement signed last night and the Anglo-German Naval Agreement as symbolic of the desire of two peoples never to go to war with one another again."

Later in the day, outside 10 Downing Street, the prime minister read to the crowd from the document and stated **"I believe it is peace for our time"** later to be regularly misquoted as "peace in our time".

This desire for peace was however short lived. Adolph Hitler went back on his word and Germany invaded Poland on 1st September 1939. On the morning of 3rd September 1939 the British Ambassador in Berlin handed the German Government a final note stating that unless we heard from them by 11 o'clock that they were prepared at once to withdraw their troops from Poland, a state of war would exist between us. As no such undertaking was received, the prime minister, in a broadcast to the nation, advised us all that we were at war with Germany.

1.5 We left Hillock Lane without selling our house, it was merely abandoned. My father, unable to meet the cost of paying off the mortgage as well as the rent, opted to cease paying the mortgage. The building society, after a short battle to recover the outstanding mortgage payments, abandoned this as a policy and took possession of the house. There was no house price inflation at the time and as a large slice of the repayments my father had made would have been interest, he seemed happy with the arrangement.

Jubilee Avenue comprised twenty small three up and two down semi-detached houses with modest gardens. The road was unmade and undulating, which meant that whenever it rained heavily, large areas of the road would fill up with rain water. Lighting was provided by a solitary gas lamp which gave off very little light and so on a dark wet night a short walk down the avenue could prove hazardous. Nobody in Jubilee Avenue or the surrounding roads owned a motor car and so all transport was by bus, bicycle or simply by walking. The people living in Jubilee Avenue consisted in the main of young couples with families. None could be classed as well-to-do but all the men in the avenue had jobs, or during the war served in the forces, with unemployment non-existent. Few of the women went out to work, their main role being to take care of the family. Social mobility was not an issue, all the people living in the Avenue when we arrived, with one exception, were still resident when I left twenty years later.

1.6 Life was by no means easy in those days. Nobody of my acquaintance had a telephone in their homes. The nearest one to where we lived was about a half mile from our house. As few people owned a telephone, the only calls one made were to the doctor, public authorities and utilities. The lot of the housewife, as they were known at the time, involved a great deal of hardship. There was no central heating and it was usually somebody's chore, often the lady of the house, to light the open fire first thing in the morning. This was a most unpopular task as it involved not only lighting the fire but cleaning out the previous day's ashes, a task which couldn't be undertaken until the ashes had gone cold, which was usually in the middle of the night. The open fire had more than one purpose; it kept the room in which it was located warm, but also heated the water. The house water system passed through a tank located at the back of the fire which heated up after the fire was lit; hence no fire, no hot water. There were no such things as toasters, the system for making toast involved impaling a piece of bread onto a purpose-made toasting fork and holding it as close to the fire as comfort would allow. As can be imagined with only one open fire in its main room, the house in winter was unbearably cold. The bathroom was an area in which nobody chose to loiter and going to bed during cold weather, even with the luxury of a hot water bottle, required an act of bravado.

1.7 Monday was washing day and Tuesday ironing day, or so the rhyme went. Washing machines hadn't been invented, the modus operandi being to put the washing into a large metal dolly tub with soap and hot water and beat the dirt out of the clothes using a specially shaped wooden dolly peg. Once this operation was completed the wet washing was transferred to the mangle which comprised two wooden rollers which could be rotated by means of turning a handle. The wet washing was passed between the rollers as they rotated to squeeze out the water. It was then time for drying the clothes outside the house, on the washing line in the garden. Whilst it was usually a Monday operation, the weather had to be right; sunny and windy was ideal; rain made the operation a non-starter. The area of the country in which we lived had more than its fair share of factories with chimneys which emitted large quantities of smoke, soot and other noxious matter. The daddy of them all in our area was Gorton's Glue Factory known locally as the bone works. The factory which rendered bones into glue was equipped with a very tall chimney, the object being to discharge the smoke, soot and fumes as far away from humanity as possible. Despite those best intentions, when there was no wind in the air, the despicable matter often fell from the sky and onto the freshly washed clothes which usually involved having to repeat the washing process.

Before the advent of the Welfare State and National Health Service in 1948, a visit to or by the doctor involved a payment. I can recall Dr Glenton, our GP arriving at our home to see my brother or me when one of us was suffering from a childhood illness, receiving a payment in cash from my mother before he left. A visit to the doctor's surgery was different from today as there was no appointment system. It was a matter of turning up and sitting in the waiting room until it was your turn. Watchful eyes among those waiting were always at work to ensure that nobody jumped the queue.

1.8 The days of the supermarket hadn't arrived in the years of my youth. In the village of Padgate there were two small grocers' shops and two small greengrocers' shops, one of which had a van which travelled around the villages selling fruit and vegetables. Milk and bread were delivered daily if required and we also had a newsagent. Just over the Padgate boundary and technically in Warrington there were a number of larger shops which included grocers, greengrocers, bakers and butchers. There was also a large Co-op which was popular at the time; most of its customers became members as it entitled them to be paid a dividend each year based upon the amount of goods purchased. However as people didn't have motor cars it was a case of filling up a shopping bag with the food for the family for the week and walking home. When one sees in supermarkets the shopping trolleys packed with food and often more than one trolley, it is amazing how in days past one woman could carry the family food shopping for a week in one bag whilst walking half a mile or further. It could be put down to unnecessary modern wrapping, but from the shape and sizes of many of those in the checkout queues it is obvious where a significant amount of the food is going.

1.9 Family life changed dramatically with the outbreak of the Second World War. Many of the men in our Avenue, including my father, were called up to fight in the armed forces, in his case it was the RAF. Some men were exempt from call up due to being too old, not physically fit, or in reserved occupations. Whilst there were a few in our Avenue who were too old, none of the remainder were found to be unfit or in reserved occupations. With many of the men no longer at home, the women were left to fend for themselves and their families. With the advent of the blitz, major cities near to us such as Liverpool and Manchester suffered badly from bombing raids by the Luftwaffe. We were fortunate in Warrington, as the Germans probably considered there was nothing there worth bombing; we escaped with little or no damage. The one exception was a bomb which was dropped on Kingsway, to the east of Warrington. It did little damage; however the blast from the bomb blew Mrs Cooper out of her bed. Mrs Cooper was a harridan of ample bodily proportions who lived quite close to where it fell. As somebody was heard to remark "To blow her out of bed, it must have been some bomb".

1.10 The German bombing campaign was referred to as the blitz which commenced on 7th September 1940 and went on continuously until 21st May 1941. London took the brunt of it and was attacked 71 times with more than one million houses damaged or destroyed and more than 40,000 civilians killed. Liverpool which was a major Atlantic sea port was heavily bombed causing 4,000 deaths. Hull turned out to be an easy target, being located on the home run for the pilots, which received bombs when the German bomber pilots were unable to find their primary targets. There were 86 raids with 95% of the housing stock destroyed or damaged. Other cities which took a hammering were Birmingham, Plymouth, Coventry, Bristol, Glasgow, Manchester, Southampton and Portsmouth. The objective of the bombing was to demoralise the British and damage their war economy, which failed, as British morale was maintained and the bombing never seriously hampered production of weapons. Hitler expected that the bombing would facilitate an invasion of Great Britain which the Germans referred to as Operation Sea Lion, but this never materialised. The threat of an invasion petered out in May 1941 when the blitz came to an end. By then Hitler was concentrating his war effort on Russia and the East.

1.11 The war in Europe ended with the surrender of Germany in May 1945. Some amazing statistics emerged at the end of the war. In April 1945, 1,500,000 German military personnel were taken prisoner by the Western Allies and 800,000 on the Eastern front. However the most well documented and remembered events of the war were the evacuation at Dunkirk between 27th May and 4th June 1949 and the Normandy landings on 6th June 1944. The British prime minister, Winston Churchill, described the events leading up to Dunkirk as "a colossal military disaster" but the transfer of troops back to England as a "miracle of deliverance". After Germany had invaded Poland in September 1939, the British Expeditionary Force was sent to aid in the defence of France. In the fighting which followed, the German forces trapped the British, Belgian and French forces in an area along the northern coast of France. The only route for evacuation was across the channel from Dunkirk. Unaccountably Hitler gave a halt order to the German forces which provided the Allies with an opportunity to assemble the troops and transfer them across the Channel. On the first day of the evacuation 7,669 men were evacuated and by the ninth day 338,226 soldiers had been rescued by a hastily assembled fleet of over 800 boats. Many of the troops were able to embark from the harbour's protection onto the 39 British destroyers and other large ships, while others had to wade out from the beaches waiting hours in the shoulder deep water before being ferried out to larger ships by the famous flotilla of hundreds of merchant marine boats, fishing boats, pleasure craft and lifeboats called into service for the emergency.

1.12 The Normandy landings were a different story. Early on the morning of 6th June 1944, 7000 ships of all sizes approached the coast of Normandy which was the largest flotilla the world had ever seen and has never been surpassed. The five beaches selected for the landings were known by their code names; the two American beaches Utah and Omaha; the two English beaches Sword and Gold and the Canadian beach Juno. Originally the landing was planned for 1st May 1944, but was postponed for a month to enable more troops and equipment to be gathered. A deception plan, Operation Fortitude, was mounted to give the Germans the impression that the main target was Pas de Calais. In addition to the 7000 ships, 11,000 aircraft were employed. In all 75,215 British and Canadian troops together with 57,500 US troops were landed by sea and another 23,400 by air. When the landings began there were only 14 of the 58 German divisions in France facing the Allies. Nonetheless the Allies encountered stiff resistance.

1.13 The greatest hardship from a family point of view during the war was the introduction of rationing. Food rationing created a huge problem for families. Rationing books were issued to each family and took account of the size of the family to be fed. It was necessary to register with a butcher and grocer from whom families could collect their food. Allowances were incredibly small and those with growing families suffered the most. Butchers and grocers regularly ran out of food, but when stocks were replenished the word was quickly on the street and queues formed outside the shops within minutes. The successful butchers, and there were quite a few, had clandestine arrangements with some of the less scrupulous Cheshire farmers and obtained meat off the record. This was sold "on the black market" to customers after closing time at enhanced prices. We were fortunate in that my grandfather owned a butcher and grocery shop and made sure we had enough to eat. Many other commodities were also rationed such as fuel, sweets and clothes. This caused us no hardship as our coal merchant, Len Barlow lived in our Avenue and was a friend of my parents. Sweet rations were sold by the more needy families and worn out clothes were the subject of repair and not renewal. We had, compared with many others, what could be classed as a good war. My father returned home in as good health as when he departed; we avoided the bombing and were largely unaffected by food rationing.

1.14 Modern life, so it is said, creates such pressure that people need, nay deserve regular holidays. Mothers often went to bed during the Second World War, worried about the possibility of a bomb being dropped on the house overnight, afraid of the chances of word arriving next day of their husband being wounded or killed and wondering when she would be able to top up the dwindling stocks of food; now that's pressure. Holidays were very much a luxury in the 1940s. Many of the men were away fighting the war and even when it was over, due to the large numbers stationed overseas and the chronic shortage of suitable transport to bring them home, it was often months and in some cases years before they were brought back.

CHAPTER TWO

Village Life

1.15 It has been said that our school days are the happiest days of our lives. Whilst I would never wish to assert that I was unhappy at school, 4pm when school ended usually came as a great relief to me. My brother is three years my senior and so I followed him to the schools he attended, Padgate Church of England School being the first. The alternative to Padgate Church of England School was Oakwood School located just inside the Warrington Borough boundary run by the local authority, and St Oswald's R C School which limited entrance to the children of RC members. Few parents accompanied their children to school, there being no school run. Up to the age of about seven most children went with a sibling or an older child who lived in the same road. As there were only two schools in the village this was usually easy to organise. In my case I was accompanied by my brother. After the age of seven children were considered old enough to walk to school alone. Our school, which admitted children from five years of age until eleven, comprised four buildings, the smallest being a single classroom, the next largest building comprising two classrooms. Three classrooms were provided in the largest building which was divided up by means of sliding partitions. The heating was primitive to say the least, being provided by coke burning stoves, one in each building. Water, heated by the stoves, circulated round the system through large diameter pipes and radiators. The problem was that the water cooled as it passed round the system leaving those nearest to the stoves roasting hot with pupils located farthest away extremely cold in winter. The system however met with the full approval of the pupils and probably the teachers during the very cold winter of 1948 when the stocks of coke ran out and we had to stay at home for a few days until stocks were replenished. A building repair budget seemed non-existent as in the larger building, when it rained, water came through the roof at such a rate that children seated below the leak had to be relocated into another area of the classroom until the weather became more clement; a situation which continued for years. Nowadays we would say the school was short of funding. There were no inside toilets or playing fields. Two small dirt-covered playgrounds were provided, with what could best be classed as toilet facilities, with no running water, located at the end of one of them.

1.16 The headmaster Mr R. R. Rice ran the school with a rod of iron; discipline was a high priority and the saying that children should be seen and not heard was very apt at Padgate C of E School. Having said that, I do not recall any physical punishment being administered to pupils, except for the occasional clip around the ear resulting from gross misbehaviour. Truancy was not permitted and I recall the occasion when one boy failed to arrive at school and there had been no note from his mother to explain his absence. Mr Rice summoned me and told me to go to the boy's house and bring him to school. "Drag him here if necessary" was the instruction. I went to the house where the boy lived and he accompanied me to school without any trouble whatsoever. Mr Rice lived in the school house located next door to the school, which no doubt came with the job. He was a short, stocky man with plastered back hair which he regularly smoothed over, using his hand, whilst addressing a class. He didn't have a study, merely a roll top desk located at the front of the top class at one end of the largest building. One of the tasks required of pupils was to feed Mr Rice's rabbits which he kept in a cage at the back of his house. This was a task I disliked being lumbered with, as the food the rabbits ate was the leftovers from school dinners, a most disgusting sight. Each of the six classes had its own teacher with Miss Grounds for starters and finishing with Mrs (Gert) Walker teaching the final year. The teachers were responsible for teaching all subjects. Miss Grounds was a lovely grandmotherly type whose job it was to make the children feel at home and relaxed. The first year was very much organised playing for the children, to get them used to being away from home. Mrs Heathcote, who taught the second year, was a different kettle of fish. It was her job to teach the children that they were at school to learn, beginning with reading and simple arithmetic. These two classes were referred to as the infants, whilst the remaining four comprised the junior school. By the time children left the school they could all read to a reasonable standard, were familiar with basic English history and world geography, and could carry out basic arithmetic. Many of the brighter pupils proved to be very able at all subjects. Being a C of E school we were also all taught the bible. There were a few slow learners who found it difficult to read. In these cases the more able students were detailed off to teach the slow learners during lunch breaks, or playtime, to ensure they reached the acceptable standard. The children from a local children's home invariably struggled with their studies and more often than not were the ones to receive extra reading tuition. It was obvious that these children, deprived of a settled home life, were at a great disadvantage.

Padgate was a rural area with a number of farms. During the 1940s they were still very labour intensive. Tractors were very expensive and so the primitive equipment used for ploughing and reaping was horse drawn. Planting, harvesting and fruit picking still relied upon large numbers of people and the milking machine had still to arrive. In an effort to generate interest in husbandry, the school had a vegetable garden of about half an acre in which all children had to work for two or three hours a week as part of the school curriculum. We grew potatoes, beans, peas, shallots and asparagus which we were allowed to take home when they were ripe. There was also a shed and chicken run in which hens and a cock were located. A member of the top class was detailed off to take care of the fowl which included feeding them. In return for these efforts all eggs which were laid became the property of the carer. The most successful by far at this job was Malcolm Hewitt, who clearly loved the job to such an extent that he became known to his school colleagues as Hens. Even the teachers referred to him as Hens. If I met Malcolm in the street, not having seen him for 60 years, I am sure I would address him as Hens.

1.17 Singing was very popular at Padgate School. Mr Hughes, who had his own class to teach, also organised the school choir. All pupils with anything like a decent voice were encouraged to join. Many of us developed a love of music from those early days of singing in the choir which lasted a lifetime. The church choir master, Mr Rubin Knight, recruited from the school choir and my brother and I found ourselves joining its ranks. This involved church attendance at the Sunday 10.30 am and 6.30 pm services and choir practice on Wednesday evenings. The first half hour of choir practice was for the boys alone, later to be joined by the tenors and basses; there were no women in the choir in those days. Mr Knight had a music language of his own when dealing with the choir boys. For example if he considered the singing was flat, which occurred regularly, he would exclaim that we were not on top of the note but were guilty of strap hanging. There was often a role for a solo singer at some of the special services such as the annual Christmas Carol service. This was a task which most of us dislike intensely. Fortunately we had one boy in the choir, Brian Dean, who had a great voice and was always available which spared the rest of us. Whether he liked singing solos or not remains unknown as he never expressed a view on the subject. My six years in the church choir I look back on with great affection. It was not just the singing but the camaraderie and fun occasioned from being with boys of my own age and outlook. It also introduced me to church attendance which has stayed with me all my life.

1.18 For a child growing up in Padgate in the 1940s, the most looked forward to event was Christmas; Walking Day followed a close second. The annual walk which took place in some of the towns in South Lancashire such as Warrington, Wigan and St Helens and also many of their surrounding villages, started in the early to mid- part of the 19th century and is essentially an act of Christian witness whereby members of the congregation of the various churches walked the streets of their district in the form of a procession. Warrington had their walk on the first Friday in July and at its peak some 15,000 to 20,000 took part in the procession with in excess of 100,000 standing on the pavement watching. Some of the surrounding villages such as Padgate, Stockton Heath, Grappenhall, Winwick, Penketh, Stretton and Orford had their own walks. Padgate's walk was fixed for the last Saturday in June and included Woolston and Fearnhead, both adjoining villages. There were usually six churches represented in the Padgate walk, C of E and Catholic from both Padgate and Woolston, and Methodist from Padgate and Fearnhead. Each church has its own banner which is held aloft followed by the members of its own congregation. It was a matter of each church taking its turn to lead the procession, which was the pride of place. Behind each banner, but before the members of the congregation, came the band and as schoolboys we liked to consider that the band which played with our church was the best. It is the custom for those who stand on the kerbside to give money to persons walking in the procession. Once the walk was over, the children in the procession retired to their own church hall where a bumper tea was provided. Despite food shortages the tables were groaning with food. Once the tables were empty, with the exception of a few crumbs, it was off to the fairground. It was traditional in Padgate for a travelling fair, usually Silcocks, to be erected in farmer Jeff's field especially for the walk, which was open on the Friday evening, all day Saturday and Monday evening. There was money in everybody's pocket due to the generosity of those watching the procession.

1.19 Despite the shortage of money, food and other essentials, I recall two holidays we spent during the war. Almost without exception the majority of people from Lancashire have experienced a holiday at a Blackpool boarding house. Most of the holiday accommodation had originally been built for large families, which was the norm in the early 1900s and consequently the houses had plenty of bedrooms. The more enterprising families let some of the bedrooms to holidaymakers during the summer season. Usually the man of the house went out to work leaving his wife to organise the guests which often numbered between six and ten. The Blackpool landladies had, with some justification, a reputation for standing no nonsense. It was to such a place as this that my mother, maternal grandmother, brother and I spent a week during the summer of 1943. Due to it being war time, there was little going on and my brother and I found it rivetingly boring. The next year followed a similar pattern, but this time the resort was Prestatyn and the accommodation was an old single decker bus which had been converted into a caravan. There was a little more to do on this holiday as we found a disused fairground which held plenty of attractions for my brother and me. On my father's return from the war we had a couple of holidays prior to my eleventh birthday in Anglesey and the Isle of Man. Once I reached the age of eleven family holidays were a thing of the past as Boy Scout camps took their place and presented me with an exciting prospect.

1.20 From the age of about eight I was desperate to join the boy scouts, but was held back as the minimum age for joining was eleven. My brother and his pal, Stan Houghton, who lived across the road from us, had joined and recounted to me the great things that went on in the scouts; in particular the annual camp which was looked forward to by them all from one year to the next. I was however allowed to join the working party which assembled before the annual camp to check all the kit to ensure it was in good working order. The most important items were the tents. In those days money was in extremely short supply and so all the tents had been acquired second hand. We had to make sure the supporting ropes were in order and that any holes were repaired. It was also necessary to apply waterproofing which involved erecting the tents and applying the necessary liquid waterproofing with paint brushes. All cooking utensils also had to be checked before the all-clear could be given that the kit was ready for the forthcoming camping holiday. The scout troop my brother and I joined was the 26th Warrington, 2nd Padgate troop. Peter Leach was the scout master with Norman "Norky" Fryer his assistant. They were joined some years after I became a member by Major Cliff Green who was known as Rajah after he appeared at a scout camp fire evening dressed as an Indian potentate. The troop met on Friday evening at Padgate C of E school. Being in the scouts provided us with a great deal of fun but also discipline, self-reliance and respect for others. It was necessary to learn the Scout Law which required loyalty to God and also the King, who at the time was George Vl. Each new member went through an induction ceremony when he was required to recite the Scout Law. Scouts worked in groups known as patrols, each of which had a distinctive name, in my case I was in the Eagle patrol. Each patrol had a leader and in these groups we were taught skills on which we were tested individually, usually by a scout master from another troop and if successful awarded proficiency badges. The best publicised of the skills we were taught was how to make knots of various types. I can recall the sheepshank and bowline but after that my mind is a blank. We were also taught skills which could be used on a more regular basis such as first aid. The Friday evening always finished off in the same manner with a game of British Bulldog. To play this game required a large room in which at the outset one boy, usual somebody physically strong for his age, was required to stand in the middle of the room with the remainder of the troop congregated at one end. The idea was that on a given signal the whole troop would dash across the room past the boy stationed in the middle. His job was to grab a passer-by, usually one of the smaller boys, and lift him off his feet which resulted in there then being two boys in the middle. The process was repeated until all bar one boy had been grabbed and lifted off his feet in the dash past. This one remaining person was declared the winner; a sort of last man standing result. The game was madly popular even with the less robust boys.

1.21 The annual scout camp couldn't come soon enough for most of us. The working party met a month or so before the off to check the kit, which was almost without exception given the all-clear. None of us boy scouts had any particular preference as to where the camp would be located. There may have been fixed camp sites in those days but our scout masters preferred renting a field off a farmer probably on the basis of cost. Llangollen was a regular location for the camp, but I recall one year going to Conway. We were not too concerned as boys where the camp site was located. There were usually 25 or 30 of us and the normal mode of transport to the camp site was by one or more lorries. On arrival the first task was to unload the kit and erect the tents hoping that it wasn't raining at the time. Each boy was expected to bring a waterproof ground sheet and blanket together with a tin cup and plate, knife, fork and spoon. Most boys were able to secure a kit bag, usually one which had seen military service and served for carrying the necessities, together with washing kit and a change of clothes. By modern standards, to say the least, the camping methods were primitive. One of the first tasks was to construct a latrine which comprised a hole which was dug out of sight of the camp. Cooking was over an open fire using billy cans. We all had to take turns in doing the cooking and the first lesson learned was always to have plenty of wood for the fire, as to run out with the food half cooked was a disaster; and also when carrying out any cooking operations, to stand upwind, as otherwise there is a distinct chance of getting smoke in one's eyes which could be dangerous when standing close to an open fire. We were required to stay in camp in the mornings and given various tasks to undertake including a daily kit inspection. This comprised laying out on our groundsheets everything we had brought with us, to be inspected by the scout master. In the afternoon we were free to leave the camp and go wherever the fancy took us, subject to returning not later than a fixed time. This was regarded by all as the best part of the camping holiday. The great attraction was the freedom these camping holidays provided. The scout master ruled with a light hand and provided we acted in a sensible manner, we were free to do as we wished in the company of our pals.

CHAPTER THREE

EARLY YOUTH

1.22 My paternal grandfather James Knowles was born in 1849; he married Mary Jane Morris, who bore him ten children, including twins, who died when a few months old. Mary died in 1900 and shortly after, my grandfather married my grandmother Elizabeth Kelsall and she gave birth to another three children including my father in 1907; grandfather died in 1936 the year before I was born. It was the norm in those days to have large families; with no welfare state the families were expected to look after the older generation when they reached old age. It was taken for granted that at least one of the girls in the family wouldn't marry leaving her available to look after the parents when they became old. My grandfather had two daughters who didn't marry, Lily and Doris who cared for grandmother after grandfather had passed away. The three of them lived in a house in Great Sankey, opposite the church and next door to Mary, another of my aunts, where she ran a grocer's shop. My grandmother and aunts were therefore well catered for both physically and spiritually. It was the norm after Sunday lunch for certain members of the family who didn't see grandmother during the week to meet at grandmother's house, ostensibly to see how she was faring and exchange any family news. The hidden agenda however was to discuss politics, religion and rugby league. After Sunday lunch my parents, brother and I would catch a bus from Padgate to Warrington and then another for the onward journey to Great Sankey. After the niceties had been exchanged, somebody would raise a matter on which firm views were held and then the arguments would start to flow in earnest. Nothing personal was intended and none taken. Anybody viewing what was transpiring however would have understandably considered that they had inadvertently stumbled into a family row of major proportions. To those partaking in the row it was just part of the usual Sunday afternoon pastime. My brother and I used to slip away at the earliest opportunity to visit cousin Peter who lived a few hundred yards away. He usually had a few interesting matters on the go and one or two friends to make the encounter more enjoyable. Perhaps the greatest attraction to visiting Peter was the magnificent tea of cakes and sandwiches produced by his mother, my Aunt Annie who was a great cook. There was another ritual associated with a visit to grandma's house on a Sunday afternoon and that related to her dog Jock, a little dark-haired Scottish Terrier. Any newcomer to the house was greeted by Jock with a great deal of tail wagging. When it came time to leave however Jock was not a happy dog and needed to be distracted whilst the person wanting to leave slipped out of the door. This however often proved difficult for the last person to leave. Tales were told of an uncle who on one occasion when wishing to leave and finding himself alone in the room with Jock had to make his exit via the window.

1.23 Young girls seemed to have a best friend whilst young boys go round in groups, sometimes referred to as gangs. This is an unfortunate use of the word as it often denotes groups of young men up to no good. In my early youth the boys in the 6 to 12 years of age bracket who lived in our avenue and the three adjacent avenues Lawn Avenue, Bruche Drive and Bruche Avenue congregated together with no particular purpose in prospect, but it didn't take long before we found one. The young lads who regularly made up our gang comprised Warren (Crowe) Kerr and his kid brother

Doug; John Kenwright and his kid brother Norman; John (Bogs) Naughton and his kid brother Kenny, Peter Dunbill, Geoff (Mongoose) Morris, Kenny Dalton, Arthur Mercer, Derek Knox, Alf Seed, Tony Smith, Billy Bragg, Tony Ham, my brother Alan and me his kid brother, often referred to as big nogger and little nogger. The houses in which we lived were built in the early 1930s when house builders had not developed the skills of building the maximum number of houses on any given area of land. Thus Jubilee Avenue, Lawn Avenue, Bruche Avenue and Bruche Drive were laid out in a square with all the back gardens facing onto a vacant area of land which the builder had used as his on-site storage area, and referred to as Cooper's Pit. We used to congregate in this area which had the chassis of an old wagon, a lime pit and a few heaps of builder's rubbish. It was the custom, once a few had arrived, to light a fire and plot the activities of the day. We had nothing apart from the odd bicycle which required attention and a few tools such as a hammer and screw driver. What we did have were ambitions to make something; a long term project was to make a truck. To enable the project to get underway we required wood, wheels, axles, nails, hammer and saw. It was then a matter of putting heads together, talking to parents and shopkeepers and any other person who may have access to the necessary equipment. With persistence, imagination but no skill, we managed to produce something which was mobile and could carry four boys, although it had to be said that the steering mechanism left much to be desired. We were however madly proud of the results of our efforts but it would not have appeared on any prize list, in fact any passer-by would probably have thought it ready for the scrap heap. We were more successful at making kites. The only equipment required was paper, string, canes, glue and a sharp knife. Most of the kites we made managed to fly, but the time in the air was usually limited with the kite often finishing up on somebody's roof.

1.24 Just outside Padgate station there was a branch line the purpose of which was to allow good trains to bypass Warrington station. Where the two lines met was an area of waste ground which contained a large pond. It was referred to by us all as the valley. One of our long term projects was to build a boat and sail it on the pond in the valley. Once completion of the truck was out of the way, we started work on the boat in earnest. After many months all was ready and a day fixed for the launch. Word of the date soon got around, which guaranteed a big turnout, as everybody wanted to be in on the action. When the big day arrived the truck came into its own acting as the mode for transporting the boat to the valley. Getting the boat up the railway embankment across the railway lines and down the other side into the pond proved a tricky problem, but as we were all fired up, with the adrenalin running high, nothing was allowed to get in the way. The boat would only hold three and those selected as crew were the ones who had worked hardest to get the boat completed. The boat was duly launched onto the pond and the three intrepid sailors climbed aboard. Almost immediately the vessel began to sink. Panic struck and the three abandoned ship making a leap for safety onto the railway embankment. Our much loved boat slowly sank despite our efforts at a rescue and was never seen again.

1.25 Football was a passion with most of us. We all had football heroes and teams we supported. My team was Preston North End and Tom Finney, the flying plumber, my hero. He was called the flying plumber by the press as his father insisted on him retaining his job as a plumber even though he was a professional footballer. My brother's team was Blackpool with Stanley Matthews, the wizard of dribble, his hero. The press referred to Stanley as the wizard of dribble due to his ability to beat fullbacks on a sixpence, or so it was said. We had our own football stadium, the back field, being a patch of waste ground which ran at the back of the houses in Bruche Drive. It was about 60 yards long and 30 yards wide with little or no grass, the surface being mainly hard trodden-in soil. Along one side ran a brook and wingers needed to tread carefully to avoid finishing up in the drink. The summer holiday was our football season when on most fine days our stadium was in full use. The footballs were of a mixed quality. In those days footballs had an inner tube a bit like a bicycle tyre which was where the puncture repair kit came in handy. The casing was often subject to damage which required the loan of a mother's needle and thread and a boy with dexterous fingers, of whom there were a few in our midst, to carry out a repair. The early part of the day was devoted to making sure the ball was in a fit condition for the game. Immediately after lunch, or dinner as it was styled in our part of the world, just after 1pm all was ready for the kick-off. First of all it was necessary for a set of jackets to be placed on the ground at each end of the field to act as goals. The kick-off started when four boys arrived, enough for two a side. As more appeared they were allocated to one side or the other until on some occasions the numbers grew to as many as 15 a side. Word spread round the district and boys came from far and near to play. The game started to tail off about 5 pm as boys started to drift home, but the game only came to an end when four boys remained, often the same four who arrived first. A problem relating to using the back field as a football stadium was the presence of a number of allotments located behind one of the goals. A player anxious to retrieve the ball took little care in ensuring that the potatoes, cabbages, shallots, peas and the like came to no harm, which left the allotment owners in a state of high dudgeon. One allotment owner in a state of severe agitation stuck his gardening fork through the ball when it entered his allotment, which ended football for the day.

1.26 If it should be thought that we were all little angels making kites, boats and trucks, or playing football all day, nothing could be further from the truth. The language of some of the boys was foul enough to make even a Liverpool docker blush. Being a rural area there were plenty of orchards which we considered needed relieving of the fruit. Ease of access and exit were prime requirements for an orchard to receive our attention together with the absence of an owner's dog of any size. On one occasion my brother and I arrived home with a few apples which caught my mother's eye. On enquiry as to the source of the supply we felt obliged to tell the truth having learned the hard way not to lie, as parents have a knack of finding out the truth. We admitted how the apples came into our possession, but expecting to be in for it, were amazed at the response which was for us to return to the orchard to secure a few more apples, as there were not enough for mother to make a pie.

CHAPTER FOUR

LIFE AT A GRAMMAR SCHOOL

1.27 It was 1948 when I left Padgate School, the year the NHS was born. The idea of a Welfare State had been developed during the war, based upon a report entitled Social Insurance and Allied Services written by Sir William Beveridge, a highly respected economist and expert on unemployment problems. The Beveridge Report became the blueprint for the Welfare State. Opinion polls reported that the majority of the British public welcomed the report's findings and wished to see them implemented as quickly as possible. The report and its findings were supported by the Labour Party who as a result won a landslide victory over the Tories in the post-war election held in June 1945. It was the intention of the report to provide a comprehensive system of social insurance "from cradle to grave". It proposed that all working people should pay a weekly contribution to the state and in return benefits would be paid to the unemployed, the sick, the retired and the widowed. The NHS was established to comply with the idea that good healthcare should be available to all regardless of wealth, free at the point of delivery. Prior to healthcare being provided by the NHS, there were many hospitals in the country run by different organisations such as charities and local authorities, but to varying standards and the general consensus of opinion was that the system was in a mess. There were an adequate number of GPs, but patients had to pay for their services. Various schemes had been suggested for the introduction of a national health system, but it was not until 1945 with the Labour Party in power, after Aneurin Bevan presented the Cabinet with a submission which included the nationalisation of all hospitals, that a proper plan was formulated and the NHS got underway. It commenced on 5th July 1948 and despite opposition from the medical professions, was a momentous achievement. On 5th July 1948 the NHS took control of 480,000 hospital beds in England and Wales and an estimated 125,000 nurses and 5,000 consultants to take care of patients. In its first year the NHS cost £248m to run, £140m more than originally estimated. The NHS has grown to become the world's largest publicly funded health service, being egalitarian and comprehensive and has as its core principle that good healthcare should be available to all regardless of wealth.

1.28 When, in my youth, boys reached the age of 11, the world for them began to change, as for many of us the onset of puberty arrived. In those days all boys up to the age of about 11 wore short trousers, accompanied by long stockings which finished just below the knee. Once we had gravitated to secondary school at the age of 11, most of our parents decided that it was time for change and so long trousers were purchased. Almost without exception this was met with a great deal of joy as in our minds we were now grown up, or at least well on the way.

1.29 Padgate became a recognised parish in 1838; for most of its history up to the outbreak of the Second World War in 1939, it was devoted solely to farming and housing agricultural workers. Expansion occurred in the 1930s when it became an overspill of Warrington. Houses in a ribbon development were constructed along both sides of the spine road, and cul-de-sacs built off which included our road. Nearly all the houses built during this period were small semi-detached of a similar design and with three bedrooms suited families with up to four children. Most of the adults had received a rudimentary education, leaving school at 14 years of age with no qualifications. With the changes that had taken place in education following the end of the war, most parents held high hopes for their children that they would receive a better education and as a result secure better paid jobs and with it a higher standard of living than they had experienced. It was considered that education at a grammar school was the route to success and was the basis for many parents' ambitions for their children. To gain entry to a grammar school required the applicants to pass the Eleven Plus Examination. Our parents, without being too pushy on the matter, made it clear that the passport to success lay in passing this examination. My brother being three years my senior was the first to jump the hurdle which he achieved successfully, then it was my turn. There was no private tuition available and examination papers from earlier years were unobtainable. However the schools were very keen for their pupils to pass the examination as it was common knowledge in the village how many pupils had been successful and from which schools, and this acted as a magnet or a deterrent to attracting pupils in future years. Our school proved as helpful as it could possibly be in preparing pupils for the examination. I always considered my brother to be brainier than me and therefore his success provided me with no comfort. However all's well that ends well and I continued to follow in his footsteps in gaining access to a grammar school. It was the custom at the time for parents to purchase a bicycle for their children who had been successful in the Eleven Plus Examination. My brother chose a Raleigh and I a BSA. One of the sporting heroes at the time was the international cyclist Reg Harris. Reg won the world amateur sprint title in 1947, two silver medals at the 1948 Olympics and professional sprint titles in 1949, 1950, 1951 and 1954. Reg retired from competitive cycling in his mid-thirties. However some twenty years later he was so disgusted at the poor quality of British track cyclists that he made a comeback and immediately won the British Championship in 1974. The following year he came second and retired for good. For many years after retiring Reg could be seen riding his bicycle around the country lanes of Cheshire where he lived and carried on cycling right until the end when he passed away in 1992. Many of the young boys with bicycles liked to emulate Reg. With this in mind I chose a BSA bicycle with dropped handle bars and raced around the roads like a boy possessed.

1.30 There were four grammar schools in the area; Wade Deacon Grammar School located in Widnes, Urmston Grammar School in Urmston near Manchester, Boteler Grammar School in Latchford and Warrington Girls High School, the latter two being located within the Borough of Warrington. My brother attended Boteler Grammar School and as the policy was, where possible, for siblings to attend the same school, this was the one which accepted me. The school had been founded in 1526 from the will of Sir Thomas Boteler. My parents, from their earlier experience of kitting out my brother, were familiar with the requirement for pupils to have a standard school uniform and the name of the stockist. I was therefore provided with a blazer, emblazoned with the school badge, cap and tie. The colours were black and yellow and once school started I learned from the other boys that the blazer was generally accepted, tie to be avoided if possible and cap to be hidden or preferably lost.

1.31 My first day at Boteler Grammar School occurred during the first week in September 1948. Latchford was not one of the most attractive parts of Warrington, not that there are many, but the school looked magnificent as it was approached. A pair of impressive wrought iron gates guarded the drive which was lined on both sides with flowering cherry trees, a truly wonderful sight when in flower during April. There were well manicured lawns on either side of the drive immaculately kept by Jim Boyle, the full time school gardener. The present school had been constructed in 1940 and to my eyes looked an architectural gem. An imposing front door to the school was located at the end of the drive and once through the door, one entered a large entrance hall from which access could be gained to the school assembly hall, headmaster's study and the school office. We congregated in the assembly hall which was huge, with an elevated stage at one end and were addressed by the headmaster who cut an imposing figure. This was followed by us being advised of the forms to which we had been allocated. There were three first year classes 1A, 1B and 1C. The brightest, based on the Eleven Plus examination results, went into 1A, the next in order of brightness into 1B and the also ran into 1C. I found myself in 1C which caused me no concern as I felt myself lucky to have made the grade at all. My brother being brighter than me started off in 1B.

1.32 The classrooms were something of a let-down. When planning the school they didn't seem to have taken into account the likely number of children to be accommodated, or there had been some miscalculation along the way, as there were insufficient classrooms to house all the boys attending the school. As a result three temporary single storey classrooms which housed forms 1A, 1B, and 1C were built on the edge of the playground. We assembled in our respective classrooms and were addressed by the form master. Boys like to give their school master nicknames. The form master for 1C, when I first arrived, was Mr Glover, who at some stage had been given the sobriquet of Betsy. These names often resulted from some physical characteristic or mannerism. Mr Glover, who taught physical education and English, had a somewhat feminine manner in his deportment. He believed in the boys bettering themselves and in the case of Brian Davidson, an improvement in his diction was called for. Brian, like many born and bred in Lancashire, had a tendency to drop his h's, which Mr Glover considered in need of correction. During an English lesson, Mr Glover decided to demonstrate before the class his skill by correcting Davidson's diction. "Now Davidson say after me: houses" Davidson promptly replied "ouses" "No Davidson, houses" Davidson replied "ooooouses" "Davidson, take a deep breath and then slowly say houses" responded Mr Glover. Davidson duly took the deep breath and out came "ooooouses" This line of interrogation continued for a short while before Mr Glover realised he was licked and moved on to other matters. The whole episode went down well with the other boys in the class as Davidison, being a good footballer, was popular and the event was regarded by the boys as a member of the class getting one over a master. We had at various times a Conk, who was well blessed in the nasal region and taught us geography, and Bucket Head who had a well-developed cranium and taught us history. There was also a clergyman who came to instruct us on the bible, fondly referred to as Hank. Boys being boys, we liked to acquire, read and pass round novels with a heavy sexual content. The best known writer of such novels at the time was an American, Hank Jansen. The clergyman used to adopt something of a salacious leer when addressing us, hence his nickname.

1.33 The subjects we were taught in the first two years gave us a good basic knowledge, leaving us more able to select subjects for specialisation in the third year onwards. The lessons in the first two years were Maths, English Language, English Literature, French, Geography, History, Physics, Chemistry, Music, Woodwork, Art and Religious Education. At the end of the second year we were given choices as to the subjects we were taught. Maths, English Language, English Literature, and French however were compulsory but other subjects were introduced such as Biology, German, Spanish, Latin, Economic History and Metalwork. There was no advice provided by the school as to which subjects we were best suited to be taught, but left to our own devices with perhaps input from our parents. In my case I chose Physics, Chemistry, Metalwork and Economic History. The school operated a streaming system for the compulsory subjects with the best pupils in set 1, the not so good in set 2 and those who struggled with the subject in set 3. We were also all given one lesson of PE per week, except those who were excused on health grounds.

1.34 There were two headmasters who filled the post during my stay at the school. Mr Nat Clapton, followed two years after I arrived by Mr P M Jackson. If it was the policy of Mr Clapton to put the fear of god into the boys, he succeeded with plenty to spare. He was a man of large squat stature and it was the rumour in the school, no doubt started by him, that he was a former Scottish champion wrestler. His prowess with the cane was legendary. If one found oneself passing the headmaster when walking down the corridor, it was not unusual to receive a clip round the ear with a gruff "get your shoes cleaned", "comb your hair", "smarten yourself up" or other such instruction intended to ensure you improved your appearance. If I saw him coming towards me it was my strategy to do an about turn as quickly as possible and return in the direction from which I had arrived. My brother on one occasion, whilst ascending the main staircase, found himself in the beady glare of Mr Clapton coming in the opposite direction, but it was for my brother too late to take any evasive action. Mr Clapton growled as he came alongside my brother "Are you Knowles?", "Yes sir" came the reply, "Well pull yourself together" was the response. My brother was relieved not to receive the anticipated clip around the ear. Possibly Mr Clapton, due to his girth, was more concerned to ensure he didn't lose his balance when descending the stairs and was holding tightly onto the stair rail with the hand he normally used for clipping boys around the ear. In retrospect I felt that Nat Clapton's bark was worse than his bite, others may argue that as I had never experienced his bite, I was in no position to judge.

Mr Jackson was almost the complete opposite to Nat Clapton, being a kindly, caring sort of chap, tall and slim. Unfortunately he wasn't on the same wavelength as the pupils. He had been educated at Oxford and his career before arriving as headmaster at Boteler Grammar School was probably limited to teaching at a public school. On one occasion there had been a theft at the school and the culprit identified by the school authorities. The theft had been of a wheel from a bicycle parked in the bike sheds, probably more of a prank than a theft. However Mr Jackson decided to make an announcement to the whole school of the incident at the morning assembly. He started his announcement by advising us that we had a miscreant in our midst. At this stage he had lost more or less the whole of his audience as few understood the meaning of the word miscreant. There were a number of boys at the school with foreign names, probably their parents were immigrants who arrived during the 1930s, and one of them was identified as the culprit. However when making his announcement, the headmaster pronounced the name as it would be in the foreign tongue and hence none of the assembled could identify to whom he was referring. His attempt therefore at name and shame, to act as a warning, fell completely to the ground.

1.35 When I first arrived I was allocated into 1C, the classroom for which backed onto the sports field, and with me being keen on sports, it caught my eye immediately. The school was very proud of its successes at football and cricket and was always on the lookout for fresh talent. Each class period lasted for 40 minutes and once per week for two periods in the afternoon, we played football during the autumn and winter terms and cricket in the summer. Eagle eyed sports masters, from our displays on these afternoons, were able to spot boys who they considered met the standard required to represent the school. This was by far the best part of my school days. The worst part of my school days was detention which was a well-used disciplinary method favoured by most of the masters. Nat Clapton liked to have a hands-on approach to any problems which arose in the school and never more so than in the infamous desk top drama. Harry Benson, one of the members of Form 1C was a burgeoning talent at wood carving, who liked to practise his art on the desk tops of the other boys in the form. When about half the desks had been the subject of his attentions word must have been passed to

Nat of the disfigurement of many of the desks in Form 1C. He decided to see with his own eyes and so made an unexpected visit to the classroom. He inspected every desk and took the names of those boys whose desks had been the subject of Harry's handiwork. Having finished his task Nat, obviously not an art lover, announced to the class that those boys whose desks had been disfigured would not be permitted to take part in the games periods for the remainder of the term, but would be required to stay in class and write out continuously "I must not disfigure my desk" whilst the remainder of the class took part in the usual football sessions. Unfortunately I was one of the boys subjected to the punishment, whilst Harry had been too busy attending to the desks of others to bother with his own and so escaped. Nobody grassed Harry up, as it would have been strictly against the school boy ethics of the time. However the game of football in which we took part during the games period in the autumn and winter terms was the highlight of the school week for many of us, made worse by the ban coming into operation in the early part of the autumn term. There was talk of stringing Harry up from a tall tree by his bootlaces, but nothing came of it.

My talents, whilst limited, were of a standard which guaranteed selection to the school football and cricket teams for the full five years I spent at Boteler Grammar School. However if I am honest, I would have to admit that my energy and enthusiasm for sports well outweighed my talents, and representing the school at football and cricket was by far the happiest part of my schooling. A number of us who played football for the school team also played on the Saturday afternoon in a local football league. Whilst it was met with disapproval by the school authorities, there was no outright ban. From the age of 13 until I left Boteler Grammar School at 16, I played on Saturday afternoon for Grappenhall Boys Club. Brian Litton, who kept goal for the school team and Grappenhall Boys Club, suggested I might like to play for them. He was very friendly with the manager Jack Kermode, and in keeping with the norm there was a trial match held just prior to the football season commencing, when existing players turned out together with any other players wishing to be considered. I must have created a good impression on Jack Kermode as I was signed on and selected to play in the first game of the season. Playing two games on a Saturday could present its problems. The school matches usually kicked off at 10 am finishing about 11.45. This gave me plenty of time to have a shower, cycle home, have something to eat and then cycle to the sports field in Grappenhall where the afternoon matches were played. This could become a bit more tricky if the school team played away at places such as Wigan, Manchester and Liverpool when it could be after 1pm before the coach used for the away fixtures returned to the school, where we were dropped off. It was then a matter of skipping lunch and going straight to the location of the afternoon fixture. Fortunately the afternoon games were all played, if not at Grappenhall Boys Club home ground, in or around Warrington involving little pedalling time from the school.

1.36 Sports day was held each year at the end of the summer term on the school sports field and taking part gave me a great deal of pleasure. The events were either for juniors being years one, two and three, or seniors from years four, five and six which gave the older boys a distinct advantage. This however never failed to deter me and it was the norm for me to enter every event. On no occasion during my appearance at each of the five school sports days in which I took part did I ever finish in the first three in any event; fourth in the 880 yards was the best I ever managed. I was a little more successful in the annual cross country race, of which there were two, one for juniors and the other for seniors. All pupils in the school, except those with health problems, were required to take part and I usually managed to finish in the first half dozen which resulted in selection for the school cross country team on one occasion, due to illness of a regular. For me it was all about taking part; we all like to win but if not then it is still enjoyable. We had drilled into us that it is not the winning that is important but the taking part. How the modern education theory that it is bad for children to lose at sport and therefore there should be no competitive sports in schools came to be accepted at some schools, beggars belief. It is probably based on the old maxim that if you tell a lie often enough it becomes the truth.

CHAPTER FIVE

MUSIC

1.37 Music played a significant part in my school days at Boteler Grammar School. My mother played the piano to a good standard and was anxious for her sons to learn to play a musical instrument. I commenced piano lessons when I was about six years old but had no interest and the lessons were abandoned. My mother however didn't give up. The school as one of its out of school activities arranged lessons for any boys wishing to learn to play a musical instrument. A note of this activity was sent to our parents who instructed my brother and me to take advantage of the offer. An announcement was made during the first week of the term for any boy wishing to learn a musical instrument to go to the assembly hall immediately after school on an allotted day. My brother went through the process before me and was allotted a euphonium. He seemed quite pleased as it was a masculine type of instrument and whilst a bit bulky to carry on the bus seemed to suit the image he wished to portray. The band master in charge of tuition of the wind instruments and conductor of the school brass band was Billy Rutter, a man of military bearing, albeit a little on the short side, with a toothbrush moustache. My brother developed some aptitude at playing his instrument but at one of the band practices matters took a turn for the worse. It seems the tune under rehearsal had a short part which featured the euphonium unaccompanied. However as the melody progressed and reached the part for the euphonium solo there was a deathly silence where my brother's playing should have featured. It would not have been in his nature to bottle out and therefore there must have been another explanation. However the truth never came out and I assume either my brother had allowed his attention to wander or perhaps he was operating a couple of bars behind everybody else and got his entrance wrong. Whatever the reason, his enthusiasm for the instrument seemed to wane after this incident.

1.38 When it came to my turn I arrived at the assembly hall on the allotted day and noted there were a substantial number of musical instruments laid out on the stage. Mr Sidney Dell, the music master, duly arrived to allocate them. He was a lovely man, much liked and admired by all and in addition to being the music master, he was the organist at Warrington Parish Church. We were given no choice of the instrument we were to learn to play, but told to collect a given instrument and be on our way. Of all the instruments on display, the one I would have avoided at all cost was the violin, but this was to be my lot. Playing a violin was definitely regarded among most young boys as un-masculine, fit only for girls and cissies. Violins when played by untutored hands emitted a noise which resembled a cat who had recently suffered an injury, which was another reason for reluctance on my part. As I had no choice in the matter I took the instrument home where it was greeted with much enthusiasm by my mother who had immediate visions of piano and violin duets. Having enrolled to learn to play a musical instrument, been allocated a violin by the music master and anxious not to disappoint my mother I was stuck with it. However in a fairly short time I grew to enjoy playing it and looked forward to the piano/violin duets. There was however a further downside to playing the violin and that was the attitude of the local toughs, who resided in Padgate and the surrounding districts. There were a few of them, who like birds of a feather were often seen congregating together in the lanes and avenues with their eyes open looking for a bit of trouble. Boys carrying violins were usually fair game. It started with cat calls and often developed into something more aggressive. Having seen them in action, I knew what to expect and so when walking on my way to and from school with my violin under my arm, the sound of catcalls was the signal for me to run. Fortunately I was quicker than the toughs even with a violin under my arm and was able to avoid the worst aspects of the encounters.

1.39 The day arrived for my first lesson which took place in one of the classrooms. When we arrived Miss Pollitt, the violin teacher, was waiting for us with her violin at the ready. She was an unsmiling person with a voice like a sergeant major, totally impersonal, who referred to us all by our surnames. The set-up was a beginners' class, a junior orchestra and a senior orchestra. There were six of us, five who had just arrived at the school and one from the previous year who hadn't been able fully to master the basics of playing the instrument and therefore required a repeat of the beginners' tuition. Miss Pollitt got matters underway by explaining the importance of the bow and how good bowing was the secret to successful violin playing. She showed us how to tighten the horse hair on the bow and to apply rosin to keep the hair in peak condition. The strings which were G, D, A and E needed to be tightened up to their right tautness to enable notes to be emitted when addressed by the bow. Fortunately we could all read music and so it was a matter of beginning the slow process of learning how to play. It all started with scales and progressed onto simple tunes. It was instilled into us all that there would be little in the way of progress if we didn't practise at home. I dutifully practised at home and made good progress. After about six months I was instructed to go and see Mr Dell the music master. I had no idea what was the purpose of the meeting as I had done nothing wrong as far as I could recall. To my surprise Mr Dell advised me that I was Miss Pollitt's star pupil and suggested that if I were to make good progress I should take private tuition lessons from Miss Pollitt and to advise my parents accordingly, which I duly did. My parents were fully supportive and as a result I was off to Miss Pollitt's house once per week after school for private lessons.

1.40 Miss Pollitt lived in a house located at the foot of the cantilever bridge which spans the Manchester Ship Canal between Latchford and Grappenhall. After school on one day per week my violin and I made our way to Miss Pollitt's house for my lesson. At no time during our five years of teaching and learning did she ever address me other than Knowles. There were never any pleasantries between us, the only topic of conversation was music. After having been a pupil for about 18 months Miss Pollitt announced that she was entering me for the Royal School of Music Examination Grade 3, as she considered that I had reached the level of skill necessary to pass the examination. In those days children were not consulted about key opportunities which may emerge in their lives, merely advised as to what direction they were required to take. In my case having decided I would like to learn to play a musical instrument under pressure from my mother, I was presented with a violin, sent off to have private lessons and advised that I was to be entered for an examination, for which a great deal of practice would be necessary if I was to be successful, without as much as a by your leave. It was considered, probably correctly, that most children would do the minimum if left to their own devices and achieve very little. To prepare for the examination I had to learn the set pieces and scales and practise sight reading, as all these skills would be tested as part of the examination. It was necessary to have a piano accompaniment and Miss Pollitt's sister undertook the task. She turned out to be very similar in character to Miss Pollitt. We had one practice together, following which Miss Pollitt expressed her satisfaction and we were ready for the off. On the big day I had to present myself at Miss Pollitt's house, at the set hour, from which we were transported by Miss Pollitt's sister in her car to Altrincham where the examination was due to take place. There were a couple of sour faced examiners awaiting us, who said very little throughout the whole performance. As we took our leave Miss Pollitt indicated that she thought my performance was good enough to secure a pass which turned out to be the case. Miss Pollitt, with the bit firmly between her teeth, shortly thereafter announced that she was entering me for the Grade 5 examination. I wondered what had happened to the Grade 4 examination but felt it better not to ask. The procedure was the same as the last time, however on this occasion Miss Pollitt's sister and I got out of synchronisation part way through one of the set pieces. Fortunately I didn't panic but carried on playing. What it sounded like I shudder to think. However I passed the examination and the examiners without laying blame, mere noted in their report what had occurred indicating that it was unfortunate. Miss Pollitt clearly with the bit between her teeth decided I should start immediately preparing for the 6th Higher Grade examination, but unfortunately there was a snag. This examination involved both playing the instrument and also undertaking a written test on the theory of music. This was a brick wall for me as I had no interest in or understanding of the theory of music. They say that you can take a horse to water etc. By this stage I was coming up to the GCE "O" levels and my concentration was firmly fixed in that direction. Miss Pollitt was perhaps happy that on her CV it indicates that she had successfully coached another pupil to Grades 3 and 5 at the Royal School of Music and so turned her attention elsewhere. Had I been given a choice at the outset I would not under any circumstances have chosen to learn to play the violin. However from time to time I pull out a drawer at home where the two Royal School of Music certificates are kept and look at them with great pride and feel pleased that events turned out the way they did.

1.41 Singing in the choirs at Padgate school and church had given me great pleasure and so when Mr Dell asked for volunteers from the new arrivals to join the school choir, without any pre-thought, my hand went up automatically. Before officially becoming a member it was necessary to undergo an audition conducted by Mr Dell. The new applicants were ordered to stand in a row and individually instructed to sing up and down the scale. Having been given the starting note on the piano by Mr Dell, we individually sang up and down the scale and few failed the test. The highlight of the year for the choir was Founder's Day. In the morning all the school pupils and most of the masters attended a service at Warrington Parish Church. The choir sang an anthem, selected by Mr Dell, which usually gave pleasure to rehearse and sing. A military band also took part in the service which I thought produced a wonderful sound. Perhaps it was the line-up of the band, or the acoustics in the church, or the music they played but it was well worth waiting for. We were all then given the afternoon off, which for most of us made it a perfect day.

1.42 It was announced at one of the morning assemblies that the school intended to put on a production of HMS Pinafore by Gilbert and Sullivan. My music knowledge at the time was limited in the main to music played on the piano by my mother, music normally sung in church, popular classics and pop tunes played on the radio, but Gilbert and Sullivan were outside my knowledge bank. The choir was informed by Mr Dell that they would be performing in the production and when rehearsals would be starting. Being an all-boys school and many of the parts and half of the chorus being for females, it was necessary for some of us trebles to take the part of the females. Rehearsals got underway and from the off HMS Pinafore was a hit with me. I thought Sullivan's music enchanting, the storyline pleasingly bizarre and Gilbert's libretto clever and amusing. We often fail to realise the effect on us throughout our lives of experiences and knowledge gained at school, other than the basic education. In my case I have had the pleasure of attending many Gilbert and Sullivan productions throughout my life, many of which were given by the sadly now defunct D'Oyly Carte Opera Company, named after Richard D'Oyly Carte who first produced Gilbert and Sullivan's operas in the late 1800s. This company toured Britain and America for over 100 years performing exclusively Gilbert and Sullivan's operas. Their annual two weeks in Manchester was guaranteed to involve a visit by me to at least one of its performances. Unfortunately due to shortage of funds it closed in 1982. Bridget D'Oyly Carte, Richard's grand- daughter, left a legacy to the company which enabled it to run from 1988 to 2003, but lack of funds did for it in the end. The English Arts Council, which each year pumps millions of pounds of taxpayers' money into Covent Garden and English National Opera, refused to provide as much as one pound to help support the D'Oyly Carte Opera Company, which is a national disgrace and probably reflects the snobbish values of the Arts Council. The school production was a great success with the school hall filled to capacity with pupils, parents, relatives and passers-by, on the four nights it ran. The next year the school performed The Yeomen of the Guard to equal success. By then my voice had broken and as a consequence I was no longer able to fulfil the role of a treble. There was no system at the time in either the church choir, or school choir, for boys to automatically move up to tenor or bass, it was left to the individual to make the first move. In my case my voice seemed to be unable to reach the top notes, or go down to the bottom ones and so I decided that I would be unable to secure a place in a choir as either a tenor or a bass; this being the case I left my singing activities behind me for good. This meant that I had no involvement in The Yeomen of the Guard as a singer, However I was approached by Miss Pollitt, who enquired if I would like to play the violin in the orchestra. I jumped at the chance and was duly appointed. There were seven of us in the orchestra, Miss Pollitt and myself, plus two others from the school orchestra and three professional musicians who were hired in for the occasion. Due to the continued success of these Gilbert and Sullivan operas, the next year they produced The Pirates of Penzance, when I was again a member of the orchestra.

1.43 I found the basic education side of school difficult; perhaps I could have been described as a slow learner. Examinations came round all too quickly in January and June each year. My redeeming feature was that for some deep seated reason I was terrified of failure. I don't think this came from my parents, who encouraged my brother and me to do well, but they didn't spent time looking over our shoulders to ensure we had completed our homework. As a result, I spent disproportionate amounts of time studying prior to the arrival of the examinations and hence I always seemed to do well. It was probably a mixture of learning things parrot fashion and hard graft that helped. When it came to the GCE examinations I applied the same policy but added some. As a result I achieved 7 "O" levels out of the 9 subjects we were all required to sit, my two failures being French and Metalwork. In those days there were no grades, it was either a pass, or a fail. However I did excel at one subject, being Economic History, which I found easy to understand and retain. As a result I was awarded the school History prize for the highest mark in the GEC examination for both History disciplines. I chose as the prize a book entitled "A Textbook of Light" for no apparent reason and it remains to this day unread on my bookshelf.

1.44 They say that everybody in a lifetime has a moment of fame and every dog has its day, I certainly had mine. I was an average footballer and cricketer at school, good enough for the school team, but by no measure what could be classed as a star. There was one occasion however when we were playing Helsby Grammar School at cricket on their ground when everything went my way. Helsby batted first and were all out for 11 runs and I took eight wickets for no runs; unbelievable. It was the norm for the headmaster to make an announcement at the Monday assembly of the names of any of the school representatives who had excelled themselves on the sports field on the previous Saturday. Following my triumph at Helsby, Mr Jackson's announcement at the Monday assembly featured my performance. At the time the Sunday Chronicle, a long since defunct newspaper, offered a cricket bat for the best performance by any schoolboy in the country during the previous week. The headmaster sent off the details of my success and I was awarded the cricket bat which was much treasured for years to come.

CHAPTER SIX

POST WAR EVENTS

1.45 Discipline at school was never an issue. The teachers were in full control and it was a matter of "don't speak until you are spoken to." I don't recall any corporal punishment being handed out at Padgate School except the odd clip around the ear; the teachers all had loud voices when enforcing discipline, which they used to full effect when children were misbehaving. Parents were very supportive of teachers and we were all therefore reluctant to step out of line. By the time boys reached the age of 11, some of them had developed unacceptable standards of behaviour. The likes of Nat Clapton at Boteler Grammar School had his policy for dealing with such boys, where the threat of the administration of the cane played a large part in his strategy. There was no log which was available to demonstrate how often the cane was administered, but there is no doubt that it was in fairly regular employment during Nat's time at the school. The system was for a teacher who considered that the boy's level of behaviour was unacceptable, such as stealing, or starting a fight, to be sent by the master to the headmaster for punishment. Mr Clapton was liberal with the use of the cane, whereas PM Jackson was more inclined to give the boy in question a good talking to. Word soon got round the school that PM Jackson was an easy touch and there was a resultant marked increase in the level of bad behaviour. In addition to being able to send boys who had severely misbehaved to the headmaster, teachers could instead opt to order boys to be detained after school. There was a points system whereby, dependent upon the severity of the misdemeanour, boys were given points which were logged in the form book until they reached the level which qualified for detention, being a two hours' extension of the school day. The master had power to circumvent the points system and send boys who misbehaved straight to detention. Some of the masters had a reputation for this type of action and generally achieved better behaviour in their classes.

1.46 A movement began to have corporal punishment in schools banned. To achieve this end the liberal thinkers changed the title from corporal punishment to child beating and there are few if any who would support child beating. As a result the use of the cane in state schools was banned in 1987 and private schools in 1999. In these days of enlightenment few would advocate going back to the days of caning boys who misbehaved. However, surprisingly in 2008 a poll of 1,162 school teachers found that 20% were in favour of the cane being used in "extreme cases". There is no doubt that the standard of behaviour in most schools in recent years has plummeted. The murder of Philip Lawrence at the school gate in 1995, when he tried to break up a fight taking place and the murder in Leeds in 2014 of Ann Maguire in front of a classroom of children shocked the nation. Other statistics make dismal reading; 12,550 pupils were banned from English state schools for assaulting an adult in 2011 and in the same year 16,970 suspensions from school orders were handed out. The current thinking is to blame the teachers for bad behaviour of the pupils and as a result many incidents do not get reported as they go down on the teacher's record which could affect future job prospects. Teachers are now in the invidious position of having all the responsibility for misbehaviour, without much authority. As a relative of mine stated recently after leaving school and starting work "the difference between work and school is that we have to do as we are told at work whereas we did as we liked at school" Another example of a name change with the intention of altering attitudes is "being true to oneself" which by many is recommended. In earlier days this was referred to as being selfish which we were taught was wrong as we should think of others before ourselves.

1.47 From the age of about 10 until 14 or 15 I had a burning ambition to be a school teacher. However as I got a little older, for no particular reason that I can recall this ambition wore off. Once I had completed the "O" levels I was at a loss to decide what I should do. There were no careers advisers at the time and my parents took the view that it was up to me to make up my own mind. In the absence of any other alternative I decided to stay on at school and as a result entered into the sixth form. There were about 90 boys in each year and of these about 25 to 30 stayed on into the sixth form. Of those who stayed on about half at some stage left school to start work or to attend a College of Further Education to train for a particular career. Usually it was only a dozen or so who went to university. We were required to study three subjects in the sixth form and I chose Geography, Maths and Economics. I soon realised that it was a mistake, as I struggled in the extreme with Maths and Economics. It was clear to me that at best I would finish up with one A level, namely Geography, which led me to conclude that my best course of action was to leave school, which I did just before my seventeenth birthday in October 1954.

1.48 During my early years, the country had been engaged in World War II which came to an end in 1945. One would have thought that the powers that be would not engage in any more conflicts of this nature for many years to come, but this proved not to be the case as in 1950 we entered the Korean War. At the end of World War II Korea was a colony of

Japan. As the war drew to a close in August 1945 two US colonels proposed that the Soviet Union take responsibility for accepting the surrender of the Japanese in the part of Korea north of the 38th parallel, with the US troops accepting surrender to its south. This decision was to have catastrophic consequences in later years. It was the intention that the division between north and south would be temporary and that elections would take place leading to the unification of Korea. However the Soviet Union blocked the idea of elections. A leader was appointed for each separate part of Korea, Kim Il Sung in the north, which became the Democratic People's Republic of Korea and Syngam Rhee in the south, which became the Republic of Korea. Both were committed to unification, but they supported different ideologies. The Soviet Union and the US, by agreement withdrew their military forces, but left many advisers in place. The two sides were in continuous talks concerning reunification but this never came about. There were however regular skirmishes across the border, but the war formally began when forces from the north, 75,000 in number, crossed the 38th parallel on 25th June 1950 and launched an attack on the south. By September the armies of the north had occupied most of the south with the southern army pushed into a small area around Pusan. The United Nations Security Council prompted by the US demanded that the northern armies withdraw from the south. To ensure that the withdrawal took place the United Nations sent troops from fifteen nations including the US which sent the greatest number together with the UK, Australia, Belgium, Canada, Columbia, Ethiopia, France, Greece, Luxembourg, the Netherlands, New Zealand, the Philippines, South Africa, Thailand and Turkey. As the international forces began to succeed in pushing back the forces of the north toward the border between Korea and China, the Chinese became concerned and sent troops to support the north. The objective of the US was to ensure that the northern troops didn't become established south of the 38th parallel. Finally it was agreed on a demarcation line near the 38th parallel and the authorities in the north and south together with the United Nations signed an armistice on 27th July 1953. Both the south and north agreed to a demilitarised zone two miles wide which both sides would patrol. In all some five million soldiers and civilians lost their lives during the war. Publicity for the war continued long after the armistice through the media of the TV programme M*A*S*H which was set in a field hospital in South Korea and ran from 1972 to 1983.

1.49 1953 was an eventful year on the international front, as it was the year that Mount Everest was conquered for the first time, or was it? In June 1924 George Mallory and Andrew Irvine attempted to climb Everest, but they never returned to recount whether or not they had succeeded. There had been sketchy reports of sightings of what were thought to be the remains of the two, but nothing concrete had ever resulted and so the question did they or did they not reach the top was never answered. In 1999 the Mallory and Irvine Research Expedition set out to try and find evidence as to whether or not they had reached the summit. A body was discovered which was thought to be that of Irvine, but it turned out to be Mallory. It was hoped that a camera would be found, which would have contained a picture of the summit. No camera was found but many items were found on the body which left unanswered the question of whether they had made it to the top. A pair of goggles was found in Mallory's pocket, which suggested he was descending at night when he fell.

An envelope was discovered on which Mallory had noted the amount of oxygen in each of their cylinders, which the expedition thought may have indicated that they took three cylinders on the final ascent and were now on their way down. Mallory had taken a photograph of his wife, which he intended to place at the summit when they arrived, but no such photograph was found on his body.

1.50 Other expeditions have taken place in 2001, 2004 and 2007 to try and find Irvine's body and hopefully to solve the mystery, but to no avail.

There have been several other attempts at reaching the summit, the nearest to success being a Swiss expedition in 1952, but the climbers had to turn back due to bad weather and exhaustion, when 240 metres from the top. It was left to Edmund Hillary and Sherpa Tenzing, as part of the British expedition to make it all the way, which they achieved on 29th May 1953. The expedition totalled 400 people, which included 362 porters, twenty Sherpa guides and 10,000 lbs of baggage; the success of the expedition was the result of a team effort. The base camp was set up in March 1953 with the final camp being located on the South Col at a height of 25,900 feet. Two teams were selected for the assault, Tom Bourdillon and Charles Evans and Hillary and Tenzing. Bourdillon and Evans were given first go at climbing to the summit, but had to turn back when Evans' oxygen system failed. At the time they were only 91 metres from the summit. Hillary and Tenzing then had their opportunity, but were held up for two days due to snow and wind. On the morning of the final climb, Hillary found his boots were frozen solid outside the tent and it took two hours warming them before they could be used. They reached the summit, which is 29,028 and the highest point on earth, at 11.30 on 29th May 1953. There was at the outset the question as to which climber was first to reach the summit. On their return from the summit neither climber was prepared to give an answer, however Tenzing in his narration entitled "The Dream Comes True" indicated that it was Hillary who was the first to step onto the summit. They spent fifteen minutes on the summit; Tenzing left chocolates and Hillary left a cross which had been given to him by John Hunt, the expedition leader. When they were descending George Lowe came to meet them bringing with him hot soup. Hillary was heard to remark "Well George we knocked the bastard off".

PART TWO

A CAREER BEGINS

CHAPTER ONE

MY FIRST JOB

2.1 1954, the year that Roger Bannister broke the world record for the four minute mile, was the year I left school. Roger had represented Great Britain in the 1952 Olympics at 1,500 metres and expected to be among the medals, but unfortunately only managed fourth place; however in doing so he broke the British record. Perhaps spurred on by the disappointment he aimed to break the world record for the mile. By today's standards his training routine was not too onerous, as he regularly ran only 35 miles per week. On 6th May at Iffley Road Track in Oxford, Roger Bannister set a new world record of 3 minutes and 59.4 seconds for the mile. He was aided by two pacemakers Chris Chataway and Chris Brasher. John Landy, the famous Australian runner and great rival of Bannister, refused to recognise the record as he claimed that the use of pacemakers, whilst not contravening the rules, was against the spirit of athletics. Bannister's record only lasted six weeks when it was broken by John Landy, who lowered the record by more than a second.

2.2 With no school, no job and no prospects, the future didn't look too inviting. There were no careers advisers in those days, you were on your own. My father, after being demobbed from the RAF, took up a job with the Air Ministry which was open to ex-RAF personnel. In one of our chats about my prospects, or lack of them, he mentioned that there were a number of people where he worked, styling themselves as Quantity Surveyors. He didn't know what they did, but considered they seemed to do very well for themselves and would I like him to find out a little more of their operations; I gladly agreed. He talked to me a few days later about the matter and advised me that there was a firm of Quantity Surveyors operating in Warrington looking to recruit a trainee and was I interested. Neither my father nor I knew what services were provided by Quantity Surveyors but in the absence of any form of alternative whatsoever I readily agreed. In anticipation of this response my father had secured the address of the firm concerned to which I duly wrote enquiring about the position. I received a reply inviting me to attend an interview. The name of the company was L C Wakeman and Partners and their office was in Palmyra Square in the centre of Warrington. I had no idea what to expect would happen at the interview and made no preparations, not even undertaking any research as to what services Quantity Surveyors performed. In fact it never crossed my mind to undertake such enquiries. In any event where would I start to look for the information as there was no internet in those days?

2.3 The building which housed the offices was located in a long terrace of similar buildings which had obviously been dwelling houses sometime in the past. I was greeted by a lady whom I assumed was the receptionist or secretary and ushered into a room in which two gentlemen sat. One was in his late twenties, thin, not very tall, with mousey hair, wearing spectacles, who introduced himself as Mr Richardson, the local manager. The other was a man by the name of Chandler, one of the partners from the head office in Birmingham, about the same age, with straight back hair, a bit chubby and a little taller. Mr Chandler did all the talking and spoke with a very posh accent, but he seemed to have a sense of humour. After they had spent about fifteen minutes mainly asking about myself, they declared the interview over and said that they would contact me in the near future. When later in the day I discussed the events that took place at the interview with my parents, I couldn't offer any opinion as to how well or otherwise I had done and still didn't know what services Quantity Surveyors performed. All I could recount was that I had been asked a lot of questions about myself and I had provided answers. However a couple of weeks later I received a letter offering me the job of Trainee Quantity Surveyor working in the offices of L C Wakeman and Partners at 15 Palmyra Square, Warrington at a salary of one pound and ten shillings per week, with two weeks holiday per year. I was delighted to receive the offer, as were my parents and immediately wrote off an acceptance letter.

2.4 L C Wakeman and Partners had only a small set-up in its Palmyra Square office; John Richardson, Angela his secretary and finally me. We had four rooms, two on the first floor occupied by John and Angela and two downstairs, one in which I worked, the other was never used. There were two other firms occupying the building: the London and Manchester Insurance Company on the ground floor and Cheetham, a firm of Architects on the first and second floors. From the outset I considered that the name Cheetham was inappropriate for a commercial organisation, but understandable as the owner's name was Cheetham. London and Manchester Insurance Company was managed by Mr Wooding a very cheerful man in his 50s who was assisted by Sylvia. Cheetham employed four Architects Brian Giles, Mike Mannion, Ian McKrell, Sid Clarke and a secretary, Mrs Monk. Brian had been a pupil at Boteler Grammar School, but as he was a few years older than me I knew him only vaguely. Unfortunately he contracted TB and spent a considerable amount of time in hospital, but I am pleased to say he made a full recovery. Mike and I played football together, but he was unsettled in the job and about a year after I arrived he left to join a specialist roofing organisation. Ian was an old class mate of mine and we got on well, whilst Sid was a small cheeky chap, liked by everybody. These five were something of a blessing for me as I worked in a room alone with nobody else in the firm with whom I could communicate on an equal level. This was the complete opposite to school and took a bit of getting used to. The five who worked for Cheetham, whilst seeming to work from time to time, were usually available on most occasions during the working day for a chat and a laugh.

2.5 Quantity Surveying involves the management of the financial matters relating to construction projects. Those who are contemplating engaging in the construction of a building scheme will often engage a firm of Quantity Surveyors to manage the financial side of the scheme as between the building owner and the building contractor. Building contractors usually employ their own in-house Quantity Surveyors, or sometimes employ a firm of Quantity Surveyors to undertake the work. There was a great deal of distrust between those representing building owners and building contractors which resulted in a significant amount of checking of figures and calculations submitted on behalf of one side or the other. Attitudes have changed over the years and an element of trust has developed which wasn't present when I became a trainee Quantity Surveyor.

2.6 I found the work to be extremely boring, however I had little option but to put up with it. As luck would have it L C Wakeman and Partners had another unit which operated from the USA airbase at Burtonwood, where they employed a few Quantity Surveyors. Burtonwood was the maintenance and supply base for the US Air Force throughout Europe during the Second World War and was responsible for supplying another 30 US bases located in Britain, where in total there were 70,000 personnel employed. Originally the site was occupied by the RAF, but the US Air force moved in after the USA entered into the war in 1942, following Pearl Harbour. It provided bombers and fighters to US squadrons and undertook modifications and repairs. At the end of the war there were over 18,000 personnel stationed on the base. Burtonwood remained a military camp for the USA forces after the war due to the onset of the Cold War. It started to run down in 1959 and finally closed in 1965. When de Gaulle took France out of NATO in 1967, the US stores located in France were all moved to Burtonwood, which was reopened to house the stores. They were located in a large warehouse, referred to as the Header House, the biggest in Europe, occupying 47 acres under one roof. When the Cold War came to an end, a decision was taken to close down Burtonwood, however it took 18 months to complete the task and closure finally took place in 1993.

2.7 Part of the arrangements with the Americans was that the maintenance of the airbase and airfield was to be undertaken by the British Government, represented by the Air Ministry. The management of the financial aspects of the maintenance work was placed into the hands of L C Wakeman and Partners. The system involved maintenance work which was identified by the occupiers, such as a leaking roof. One of the maintenance supervisors employed by the Air Ministry would inspect the problem and then write out a works order sheet. This was passed to the resident contractors with instructions to carry out the work. L C Wakeman and Partners' task was then to value the work after it had been completed and arrange for payment. It seems that they were short-handed and John Richardson, who was probably glad to get shut of me, volunteered my services. My skill at the time in valuing maintenance work undertaken by the contractor was nil, but they needed somebody to hold the end of the measuring tape and undertake other necessary menial jobs of which there was usually a ready supply.

2.8 When I arrived on the scene, there were three others involved in valuing the maintenance work. Rex Snowling, who was in charge and in his mid-twenties and Geoff Hunt who was in his mid-thirties, were the two experienced surveyors. The most friendly and helpful was Brian Donley who was about my age and a little more experienced than me, but not by much. Brian had been the dogsbody until I arrived, following which the role was passed on to me. Brian and I became great friends and remain so sixty years later. He was keen on playing cricket and football which immediately gave us a common bond. Jim Battersby, another experienced surveyor, arrived after I had been at Burtonwood for about eighteen months and proved to be a good friend to Brian and myself. The office occupied by L C Wakeman and Partners, provided by the Air Ministry, was a little basic. It comprised a Nissen hut heated by a coke burning stove, which required lighting each morning. There was no coke provided and it was necessary for the dogsbody, whose job it was to light the stove, to sneak round to the contractor's office and by one means or another acquire some of theirs. The contractors who undertook the maintenance work, A Monk and Co when I first arrived and later Sir Alfred McAlpine, employed their own Quantity Surveyors, among them Bernard Higgins, Doug Williams, Cliff Rowe and Bob Adlard who were of a similar age to Brian and me and therefore we generally enjoyed working with them and ensured that work became fun, whatever the work comprised.

2.9 Shortly after starting work at L C Wakeman and Partners I was advised that it was the policy for Trainee Quantity Surveyors to sit the Royal Institution of Chartered Surveyors examinations. Tuition for these examinations was either by Correspondence Course, as Distance Learning Courses were then known, or alternatively I could attend the Liverpool College of Building Day Release Course, which comprised one day and one evening per week. I opted for the Day Release Course. There were three examinations, the First, Intermediate and Final Examinations. Normally the course for each one was two years making it six years as a minimum before achieving qualification. The examinations to say the least were tough to pass. They lasted a full week with two examinations per day except for the Final Examination where on the last day there were three examinations. Each examination lasted between one and a half hours and two and a half hours. There were no re-sits of individual subjects, you either passed the lot or failed. The failure rate was high and rarely did any more than 30% of the candidates who sat the examinations secure a pass. When sitting down in the examination hall with about 100 other candidates, which was the norm, you were very conscious that only 30 of those present were likely to pass. One other difficulty with these examinations was that you were allowed to fail the examinations only twice and then you were barred; a sort of three strikes and you are out approach. I struggled with the course at Liverpool College of Building and being a slow learner didn't think the talk and chalk method of teaching suited me. It came as no surprise therefore to learn when I had taken the First Examination that I had failed. Realising that I had to do something different if I were to avoid the three strikes and you are out syndrome, I decided to supplement the teaching I received at Liverpool College of Building with additional evening classes in building construction and book-keeping at Warrington Technical College on two evenings per week. The one day and three evenings approach seemed to do the trick as I passed at the second attempt. Matters however took a dip as I failed the Intermediate Examination at my first attempt. There were many Quantity Surveyors who commenced work as trainees but failed to qualify, but none-the-less held down good jobs with attractive salaries. Quantity Surveying firms were more interested in what you could achieve in your job, when converted into fees earned, rather than paper qualifications. However paper qualifications came into their own, when applying for a new job.

2.10 There was no degree entry into the surveying profession or any other profession at that time. The governing bodies for Architects, Solicitors, Accountants, Surveyors and other like organisations, set the entry examinations in respect of the professions for which they were responsible. Those wishing to enter one of these professions usually left school at the age of sixteen and would be engaged by a firm practising the profession. Some offered positions as trainees on a very small salary, whilst others offered articles which required a commitment for five of six years usually with no salary. However those who entered the profession at the age of sixteen were very competent by the time they reached twenty two, were usually qualified, in demand and able to command a good salary. When degree entry became acceptable, the professional governing bodies were pleased to be relieved of the task of setting and marking examination papers. However it soon became obvious that the knowledge and skill necessary to secure a degree was not good enough for the professional bodies to grant candidates full membership of their institutions. It became necessary to undergo a period of usually two years after university, working in the profession and keeping a diary to demonstrate the necessary experience and in some cases more examinations to pass before being accepted as a full member of the institution. Those emerging from universities, now that education is no longer free and fees have to be paid, can find themselves with massive debts and in many cases no job. There is no turning the clock back to the days when entry into the professions occurred at the age of sixteen, working for little or no salary for the next six years, but a good well paid job at the end of the period. Any suggestion of going back would be met with howls of "slave labour" from those who disapprove of the system and so tar the system with a name which is abhorrent.

2.11 I left school approaching my 17th birthday and was therefore no longer eligible to play football for Grappenhall Boys Club as they operated in the Warrington Sunday Schools under 16 league, where players had to be under sixteen at the start of the season. I was therefore on the lookout for a new club. Bogs Naughton, who lived across the road from me, was a good footballer and played for Padgate St Oswalds in the Warrington Sunday Schools under 18 league. On hearing that I was looking for a club, Bogs suggested that I meet the manager Jack Buchanan. As luck would have it, despite the season having started, they were currently a bit short of players. At Boteler Grammar School I had been classed as a winger and being labelled as such couldn't get myself selected as a central defender which was my best position and the one I had occupied for Grappenhall Boys Club. The footballing style was very much either a long ball in the air down the middle, or out to the wing and a cross into the centre. What all good defences required was somebody tall who was a fearless header of ball, which were my main attributes. The balls were leather and in wet weather they became extremely heavy hence the need for a fearless header of the ball. Jack responded favourably to my request to play at centre half where I was selected for their next match. After the first few matches where we had achieved indifferent results, it was obvious that more than a few of our players were unfit; as some of them were heavy smokers this was hardly surprising. As I was probably the most vocal concerning this matter, Jack decided that I should make it my job to improve the fitness of the team and was therefore appointed as trainer. I had no idea of what I would do to improve fitness levels and so decided to take them all on a five mile run. It was not too difficult to produce a route through Padgate and Woolston, which covered about five miles without crossing a road of any consequence. Rather surprisingly, despite a few grumbles, this became the main weekly activity designed to get the team fitter. I am not sure whether it worked, but the levels of fitness seemed to improve as did the results. In my own case I became so enthusiastic about the run that I was still doing it sixty years later.

CHAPTER TWO

PINNACLE OF A FOOTBALL CAREER

2.12 At the end of my first season playing football for Padgate St Oswalds, Bogs together with Peter Dunbill and Bill Monk two other players were called up into the armed forces to do their National Service. At the outbreak of the Second World War all men of 18 to 41 years of age were called into the armed forces to fight the war. Some of the men were rejected on medical grounds whilst others were not called up as they were engaged in vital industries or reserved occupations. This was extended in 1942 to include all men up to 51 years of age and women between the ages of 20 and 30. Some of those conscripted were sent to work down coal mines and became known as Bevin Boys named after Ernest Bevin, the government minister responsible for the system. This continued after the war was over, but only applied to men between the ages of 17 and 21 who had to undertake two years' military training. Bogs, Peter and Bill had reached the age of call-up and off they went to undertake their training. This started with what was referred to as square-bashing which lasted six weeks, the purpose being to get the new entrants fit for battle. After this initial period was over they were given jobs to carry out. There were plenty of positions for chefs, cleaners, drivers, mechanics, clerks and the like which were necessary to keep the units functioning. After two years had expired they were released back into civvies, however for a further period of four years they could be called back into service, should a military emergency arise. Anybody who was at university, or studying for examinations, could request that the call-up be delayed until the age of 21 had arrived. My brother did his national service and referred to the six weeks' square-bashing as hell and the remainder of the two years as rivetingly boring. Influenced by his experiences I applied successfully to have my call-up deferred and by the time I was 21 the whole system had been scrapped; I was lucky.

2.13 Whilst playing football for Padgate St Oswalds, at the end of one of our matches, I was approached by a spectator, and there weren't many of those, enquiring whether I would like to go for a trial with Winsford United. This was a big boost to my ego as Winsford were a semi-professional team who played in the Cheshire County League. I thought it could be a wind-up but answered in the affirmative. The season was coming to an end and the trial would be held prior to the beginning of the next season. When I spoke to Jack Buchannan about the conversation he was very supportive and expressed the view that I should go for it. The trial took the form of a pre-season practice match and I must have performed reasonably well as they signed me on after the match. In those days there was a distinct division between professional sportsmen who received pay for playing and amateurs who played purely for the love of the game. Some football teams were made up solely of amateur players whilst others had a mixture of amateur players and professionals. The FA organised a cup which catered for amateur teams only. This began in 1893 and ended in 1974 when the distinction between amateur and professional sportsmen and women was abolished. During the heyday of the competition the amateur cup final was held at Wembley Stadium and regularly attracted crowds of 100,000. Bishop Auckland of the Northern League won it on ten occasions, more than any other team, the last winner being Bishop Stortford. Winsford United's financial situation was governed by its ability to sell its professional players on to teams who played in the Football League. For them it was a balancing act in ensuring that professional forms were signed by any really talented player who was clearly going to become a full time footballer, or for whom enquiries had been made from teams playing in the Football League. The remainder of the players who had little or no prospects of being snapped up by a league club made up the numbers. I fell into the latter category, but managed to make a little money as they paid generous expenses to the amateurs. I played at Winsford for two seasons which I thoroughly enjoyed. This represented the pinnacle of my football career and came to an end when I moved south with my job.

2.14 Playing football and cricket were my great passions, for me Saturday couldn't come round quickly enough. Having left school in the autumn of 1954 and sorted myself out with a football club, as the spring of 1955 approached my thoughts moved to finding a suitable cricket club for the coming season. There was only one league which operated in the area, being The Manchester Association and I didn't think I was good enough to secure a place in any side which played to this standard. The alternative was to find a village team or works team to which I could attach myself. By chance in the early spring I met Elvin Meechin, a school friend who left school at the same time as me and who went to work for Warrington Borough Council. He was a good cricketer and as we chatted he mentioned that he intended to play for the NALGO local government cricket team in the coming summer. He soon ascertained that I hadn't become fixed up with a club and suggested that I may like to consider playing for his new team as he was aware they were short of bowlers. Elvin invited me to attend a preseason net practice. I must have created a reasonable impression as I was selected to play in the first match of the season. With the football and cricket seasons overlapping by a couple of Saturdays it was my policy always to be available for selection for the first game of the season, whether football or cricket, which involved missing the last two games of the season for my other sport. As the teams I played for were rarely in contention for any trophies, my absence didn't create too much of a problem. However, missing two games at the start of the season could have jeopardised a regular place in the team.

2.15 NALGO's fixture list comprised some of the local works teams and a number of village sides, about eighteen fixtures in all, often playing teams both at home and away. The players were without exception likeable and quite a few were very good cricketers. Jack White was the captain, a slow bowler and something of a character. Jack's stock in trade bowling included a good smattering of full tosses and long hops; he could also turn the ball well. He was regularly ribbed by other members of the team concerning his full tosses and long hops but his response was always the same that it was part of his master plan. After playing with NALGO for some time and seeing the number of occasions Jack would send down a full toss for the batsman to be caught out by the only fielder on the leg side, I began to believe in Jack's master plan theory. Unlike today where these types of games involved each side being allowed the same maximum number of overs to bowl, in our matches time dictated how long a side could continue to bat. The match usually started at 2.00pm with a tea interval from 4.30pm to 5.00pm, the finish being scheduled for 7.30pm. The side which batted first had to declare at the tea interval, if not already all out. When sorting out a fixture list and contacting sides we wished to play against, desire for a repeat fixture wasn't based upon the quality of the opposition players, or the state of the ground, pavilion or location, but the quality of the teas they provided. If an opposition side produced a poor tea they were scratched off the list for next season. I played for NALGO for four seasons with some excellent cricketers; we rarely lost a game. The teas were nearly always excellent.

2.16 By the time I left school, girls had come very much into my focus. Until this stage in my life my involvement with them had been relatively small. Whilst at Padgate School I showed little interest in girls. At Boteler Grammar School there were no girls, neither were there any in the church choir, or boy scouts, and even in the Avenue in which I lived there were only a few girls and they were not in my age bracket. I had however gathered around me a few male friends, having met them through the boy scouts, and included Ron Pollard, John Mountfield, Derek Warburton, Dave Lancashire, Henry Purcell and Alan Howard, who was always referred to by my mother as Yorkshire due to his propensity to "hear all, see all and say nowt". All of them had developed a keen interest in girls, but with little to demonstrate that the interest had developed into something more positive. There was no internet dating and none of us had been to universities which could provide an opportunity for fraternising with the opposite sex. In the 1950s boys looking to meet girls would gravitate to one of the many dance halls there were at that time. In Warrington the most popular ones were the Parr Hall, the Baths Hall, where a temporary suspended dance floor was placed over the swimming baths, Fletchers and the Liberal Club. When my friends and I first started going dancing the best looking girls we considered were those who frequented St Thomas's Church Hall, located in Stockton Heath, just outside Warrington, commonly referred to as the Vicarage Hop and this was the venue where my friends and I could be found on most Saturday evenings. Nearly all who attended the dance halls were unattached, the girls going in pairs and the boys in groups. Every dance hall worth the name had a live band. The line-up differed from one dance hall to another, but comprised in the main a rhythm section, made up of piano, bass and drums, two saxophones and a trumpet or trombone, plus a vocalist and in some cases two. The band struck up at 7.30pm and finished at 11.00pm with a half hour interval somewhere in the middle. The boys in general congregated on one side of the hall with the girls on the other. When the music started the boys would walk across the room and request the girls they had selected to join them in a dance. Occasionally the invitation was declined but by and large it was accepted. Before requesting a girl to dance it was the unwritten rule that the boy before going the dance hall had learned to dance. None of us attended any dance lessons but some instruction was necessary to enable us to become familiar with the steps of the usual dances which were the quick step, waltz, slow foxtrot and occasionally a tango. The teaching was normally provided by an elder sibling or friend. One of the objectives of the evening was to identify a girl you fancied, dance with her a couple of times and then request to see her home. If successful in securing a girl, it would involve a bus journey to her home and as it was usually the last bus, it could result in a long walk home. If the relationship developed, a few trips together to the cinema would normally follow and then it would either go on from there, or fizzle out. In my case they fizzled out.

2.17 Angela, the secretary in the office left and was replaced by Wendy. By this time I was spending about half my working days in the Palmyra Square office and the remainder at Burtonwood. I took rather a fancy to Wendy and I must have had a similar effect on her as, when I asked her out, she accepted, a process which was regularly repeated. On leaving school I had become interested in jazz and bought an alto saxophone from John Smith, a neighbour of ours. John experienced difficulty in holding down a job and seemed to change employers every few weeks, to such an extent that my father always referred to him as the Heinz man. Heinz claimed to produce 57 different varieties of food which according to my father equated to John's job experiences. John was crazy about jazz and played a trombone with a significant level of skill. His claim to fame was that he once had an audition to join Freddy Randle's jazz band, which was well known nationally at the time. The audition involved John playing his instrument into the telephone, which was held by a friend, with Freddy listening at the other end, but it came to nothing. John could play the saxophone moderately well, but wishing to concentrate on playing the trombone, sold it to me and gave me one lesson. With the benefit of the lesson and a tutor book, which came with the instrument, I learned to play to a fairly good standard. One of the very few regrets I have in life is that I didn't get to play in a band. With this interest in jazz, I and a few of my friends began to visit the Bodega, a jazz club located in Manchester and it was here that I took Wendy on our first date.

2.18 1956 wasn't a vintage year for the UK as far as international relationships were concerned, due to the Suez Crisis. Surprisingly, it all goes back to 1854 when Ferdinand de Lesseps, a French former diplomat, persuaded the Viceroy of Egypt, Mohamed Said, to permit the construction of a shipping canal through the 106 miles of desert which runs between Africa and Asia. Great Britain had regarded the increased influence of France in the region with great suspicion and organised a boycott, resulting in a shortage of investors. Egypt therefore acquired 44% of the shares. Construction began on 25th April 1859 and the canal was opened in November 1869. In its first year, three-quarters of the vessels using the canal were British. In the mid-1870s Viceroy Ismael, who had become Viceroy on the death of Mohamed Said, had set out to modernise Egypt, but incurred massive debts and offered his country's shares in the canal for sale. They were bought by Benjamin Disraeli on behalf of the British government for £4 million, thus establishing Britain's influence in the running of this extremely important waterway. It provided Britain with a shorter sea route to its empire and as the use of oil grew in importance, produced a shorter route to the oilfields.

2.19 It was on 26th July of 1956 that the President of Egypt Gamal Abdel Nassar announced his intention to nationalise the Suez Canal. It resulted from the withdrawal of an offer made by Great Britain and the USA to fund the construction of the Aswan Dam, in response to Egypt's new ties with the Soviet Union and its recognition of the People's Republic of China. Relationships between Egypt and Britain became further strained when Egypt purchased Soviet made aircraft and tanks and arms from Czechoslovakia for use against Israel. Guy Mollet, prime minister of France, Anthony Eden, Britain's prime minister and David Ben-Gurion, prime minister of Israel agreed to make a joint attack on Egypt. On 29th October 1956 the Israeli Army led by General Moshe Dayan invaded Egypt; two days later British and French bombed Egyptian airfields and destroyed the Egyptian Air Force. On 5th November 1956, the British and French forces landed in Egypt, soon overcame the Egyptian resistance and reached El Cap just south of Port Said at the northern end of the Suez Canal, by which time the Israelis had captured the Sinai Peninsula. President Eisenhower became very alarmed at the events and announced that he was going to suspend aid to Israel in protest at the invasion of Egypt. In the House of Commons the government was accused of being involved in an international conspiracy. The General Assembly of the United Nations passed a cease-fire resolution by 65 votes to 5 and faced by a united international community the governments of the United Kingdom and France agreed to a cease-fire and to the withdrawal of their troops, who were replaced by those of the United Nations. General Nasser then blocked the Suez Canal which meant shipping had to take the much longer route round the Cape of Good Hope at the Southern end of Africa. Nasser also urged Arab nations to reduce oil exports which led to petrol rationing in the United Kingdom and some other countries.

CHAPTER THREE

OFF TO SWINDON

2.20 I had arrived at the age of 21 and my career had hardly caught fire. The work I was doing in the Palmyra Square office was fairly routine, although I worked on a large public sector housing project in Leeds and the Norwich Union northern headquarters, also in Leeds, which was good experience. Regarding my work at Burtonwood, the best I can say is it wasn't too taxing. Overall I consider that my experience and hence knowledge gained was modest. My examination success provided little better reading, having entered myself for the Royal Institution of Chartered Surveyors First Examination and passed at the second attempt and failed my initial effort at the Intermediate Examination. However, life for me was about to change. John Richardson advised me during late 1958 that the firm had decided to close the Palmyra Square office, and Mr Chandler would be having a word with me concerning the matter when he next paid a visit to Warrington. A couple of weeks later we met and he repeated what John had already indicated, but went on to say that they couldn't justify employing me full time at Burtonwood. I thought I was for the chop, however he advised me that the firm were in a position to offer me a post as site surveyor on one of its projects in Swindon. I didn't know where Swindon was located but as they had a football team,

Swindon Town, who played in the then Third Division South, I assumed it was in the South of England. I was advised of the salary which was a little more than my current stipend. Mr Chandler then went on to say that in addition to the salary I would be paid subsistence which at £5 per week was generous. The clincher for me was when he indicated that the job carried with it a car. I had learned to drive in my brother's car; he having secured a job in a bank with a decent salary could afford to run one. The state my brother's car was in when purchased gave me the impression that the purchase price was to say the least likely to have been modest. I failed the driving test twice and was left scratching my head wondering what to do to make sure it didn't run to three in a row. Fortunately it was whispered in my ear that I would never pass the driving test if I turned up in an old banger accompanied by my brother. I was advised to seek driving lessons from a recognised driving school where I would be taught how to pass the test. In addition, as most driving examiners had started their careers as driving instructors, they were all brothers under the same skin. Good advice as it turned out; I then went on to pass the test with ease having arrived in a British School of Motoring car, accompanied by one of its instructors.

2.21 The great day arrived and following a train journey I collected the car from the offices of LC Wakeman and Partners in Edgbaston, just outside Birmingham, on my way to Swindon. Edgbaston was very much the better side of Birmingham and Highfield Road comprised upmarket offices one of which belonged to L C Wakeman and Partners. There were no sat navs in those days and even road maps were not easy to come by and so I had to acquire directions to Swindon from members of the staff. One knowledgeable chap by the name of Alan Cross pointed me in the direction of the road to Stratford and advised me to travel along it until I arrived at a signpost which indicated the way to Cheltenham. Follow that road until you arrive at the turnoff to Swindon, he advised, and when in Swindon ask for directions to Highworth, a village on the outskirts of Swindon, which was my destination. The car was an Austin A 30 with 35,500 miles on the clock, not in its first flush of youth. There was no heater, which meant that during the winter I had to travel dressed in a duffle coast with sea boots and long socks. In the absence of a heater the windscreen was constantly frozen up in cold weather. In the summer the windows were open on most journeys to cool it down inside. The registration number was OOP 957, the only number I can still remember out of the significant number of cars I have driven over a period of fifty plus years. The journey went without a hitch and I arrived at the Saracen's Head hotel in Highworth, which was run by Herman and Dolly Hacker, where a room had been booked for me by my predecessor in the job, Richard Birch. There were about eight other guests who stayed during the week and returned home at the weekend. We were all booked in for dinner, bed and breakfast and all I can remember about the hotel is that the food was good, but being late autumn the bedrooms, having no heating, were cold. En-suite was for the Ritz and the like and therefore in the mornings it was first up got first use of the bathroom. I didn't stay long at the Saracen's Head but moved to the Salutation in the village of Farringdon on the Swindon to Oxford road which proved to be better with regard to accommodation and price. Villages such as Farringdon were full of public houses usually run by the wife, with the man of the house going out to work all day and serving in the pub in the evening. The Salutation was no exception where mein hosts were Mr and Mrs Bill Bailey.

2.22 The site where I was sent to work was located at Stratton St Margaret, which is about two miles from the centre of Swindon. Work was ongoing when I arrived for The Pressed Steel Company which was a large manufacturer of motor car bodies who had purchased the site in Swindon in 1953 to facilitate an expansion of its activities. The Pressed Steel Company already had plants in Cowley in Oxfordshire, Theale in Berkshire and Linwood in Scotland. They were acquired by The British Motor Corporation in 1965 and were at that time the largest manufacturers of motor car bodies in the world, employing 26,000 people and producing bodies for Austin, Daimler, Hillman, Humber, Jaguar, Lancaster, Morris, M.G, Riley, Singer, Rover and Wolseley in addition to many overseas car manufacturers. The British Motor Corporation took over Jaguar Cars in 1966 and merged with Leyland Motors in 1968 to form British Leyland Motors Corporation which wasn't a great success and was ultimately sold off to BMW in 1994. By the end of the 1990s the factory at Swindon was redundant and consequently razed to the ground; the site now has other uses including a cinema complex. I recall passing the site whilst on a train journey from Bristol to Oxford and witnessing, with some sadness, the demolition in progress.

2.23 My immediate boss at Pressed Steel was Charles Medland, a man in his early forties, fairly short in stature, spectacles and a moustache. He was a most delightful man, full of good humour who visited the site about once per week to keep an eye on me and undertake tasks beyond my capabilities. One of his most endearing qualities was that he treated everybody in the same manner. It was common at the time for people to look up the ladder with deference and down the ladder with disdain which was well illustrated in The Frost Report Class Sketch with John Cleese at the top of the ladder and Ronnie Corbett at the bottom. Ronnie Barker was in the middle looking up at John with deference and down at the other Ronnie with disdain. Charles lived in Bristol and was a keen follower of Bristol City football club, who were in the old Second Division, but none-the-less had on its books an England player, John Atyeo, a prolific goal scorer. He represented Bristol City 654 times scoring 351 goals and his goal scoring record for England was just as good. In the six games for which he was selected he scored five goals. Why was he not chosen to play more often? John's other claim to fame was that in later life, after his football career came to an end, he became a quantity surveyor. Unfortunately he died at the fairly young age of 61 in 1993.

2.24 Pressed Steel had taken over a large area which had been fields on which they were building the factory complex comprising an office block and a number of massive car body pressing shops. Two of the pressing shops had been constructed when I arrived and the project on which I worked was the third. The construction company was Holland Hannen and Cubitts, a London firm. Some of their management staff came from London and travelled down each week whilst others were local. I became very friendly with two of the locals. Charles Amour, a portly jolly man whose laughter could be heard well down the corridor of the site office and outside when the wind was in the right direction. Charles was the onsite quantity surveyor and so we worked together on matters of a financial nature relating to the project. I had a great deal of respect for Charles following a tragedy which occurred in his family. Charles had two young children, a son and daughter. One morning they awoke to find the son dead in bed with no apparent cause; Charles bore his grief with great dignity. The other employee of Holland Hannen and Cubitts with whom I became friends was Percy Lawson, the plant manager. Percy had been a great goal keeper in his day, or so he claimed. He had a cutting taken from the local newspaper showing him in action which he had pinned on his office wall, proof enough, Percy would say.

2.25 It was well into the football season by the time I arrived at Swindon and therefore finding a football team soon became a priority. I played one game as a guest for Highworth, courtesy of Percy Lawson who had some influence in that direction. My interest however was focused on Vickers Armstrong who had a factory just outside Swindon. They were a massive organisation who at the time manufactured aircraft, ships, military vehicles and armaments. Like many large companies at the time they had their own sports ground which was by far the best in the area. The only sports ground to run it close was owned by British Rail who had massive works in Swindon but insisted on all members of the football team being employees. One of the other guests staying at the Salutation Hotel worked for Vickers and introduced me to the football team manager. With my recent experience of playing in non-league football to boast about, they selected me to play in one of their matches as a trial. They seemed to like my style as I continued to play for them for the whole of my stay in Swindon. I learnt one sporting lesson whilst playing for Vickers and that arose from a five-a-side tournament which was held on Marlborough's ground on a very wet Easter Monday. There was little in the way of shelter, no change of strip, only one pitch and long periods of time between each round. The start of the tournament was 10.00am and it finished about 6.30 pm. We were soaked through by the end of our first round game and were like half-drowned rats by the time we had progressed to the final. We lost in the final and I was convinced, taking into consideration the conditions, it would have been preferable to have been knocked out in the first round and we could then have all gone home.

2.26 The work in which I was engaged proved to be interesting and being a project where the construction work was ongoing, I learned a great deal. My examination successes to date, comprising one successful strike out of three attempts, weren't impressive and in real need of improvement. When working in Warrington I had attended a Day Release Course at the Liverpool College of Building. There was no similar course available in Swindon or anywhere near and so reluctantly I enrolled on a Correspondence Course now styled Distance Learning. The course was designed and delivered by the College of Estate Management which is based in Reading. For each subject, a course study book was produced which was divided into somewhere between eight and twelve sections dependent upon the complexity of the subject. At the beginning of each study book a reading list was provided and at the end of each section a test paper, which had to be completed and submitted for marking before proceeding to the next. This method of study didn't suit all students as it involved attendance at work each day and then progressing with the Correspondence Course in the evening, or alternatively getting up early and studying before going to work. The whole idea sounds most unattractive and so it did with me at the outset. However being a slow learner, I could go at my own pace and if uncertain, go over the ground a second or even third time. I had never been afraid of hard work and so this method of study suited me down to the ground to such an extent that I passed the Royal Institution of Chartered Surveyors Intermediate and Final examinations in two years. Under Tony Blair's government attendance at universities rocketed up and the professional governing bodies began to accept degree entry, hence studying employing a Correspondence Course took a downturn. Since the advent of students having to pay tuition fees to attend universities, entrance applications have fallen and studying employing Distance Learning Courses has started to increase. Some universities are obviously uncertain about the future and see Distance Learning Courses as serious competition. Their reaction has been to become vocal in claiming that Distance Learning Courses can never compete with universities as they lack the necessary interaction between student and tutor. I remain to be convinced.

2.27 With the cricket season on the horizon, whilst still playing football for Vickers Armstrong, my thoughts were turning to finding a cricket club. Nobody at the site or the Salutation Hotel had any interest in cricket and therefore I had to scratch my head as to what to do to find a club. There were only two top teams in the area of which I was aware and which caught my fancy, British Rail Cricket Club and Swindon Cricket Club. As British Rail Cricket Club limited its players to employees, this left Swindon Cricket Club. Never being short on a bit of brass neck, I decided to pay Swindon Cricket Club a visit. I called in at the clubhouse one evening to find a few people leaning on the bar with drinks in hand who advised me of the evenings when net practice took place. I turned up with my kit to one of the net practices the following week and sought out the captain, explained who I was and of my interest in finding a club in the area. To cut a long story short I attended a couple of net practices and was selected to play for the Sunday eleven on the first weekend of the season. Thereafter I played regularly for Swindon Cricket Club, the opposition being small towns in Wiltshire and Oxfordshire, which I found thoroughly enjoyable.

2.28 Even though based in Swindon I was still courting Wendy. I got home fairly regularly and was able to keep the relationship going. The trusty Austin A30 managed to hold itself together without giving me too much trouble on my trips from Swindon to Warrington. In those days there were no motorways and so it was a matter of following a route through various towns and villages such as Tarporley, Whitchurch, Wellington, Bridgenorth, Evesham, Broadway and Lechlade before arriving at Swindon, all very picturesque, but after a number of trips covering the same journey I seemed to travel on autopilot. The trip covered 150 miles and the journey time about three and a half hours. Most of the journeys proceeded without incident however when I think back on those trips one occurrence comes back to haunt me. Travelling from Warrington to Swindon, a couple of miles before arriving at Tarporley, I ran out of petrol. In my defence at the time the gauge showed the tank still to have a little left and so I had felt safe that I could get to the next garage where I intended to fill up. Even had I been a member of the RAC or AA there were no mobile phones, nor a handy public phone box and so a walk to the nearest garage a mile or more away to secure a can of petrol was inevitable. Despite the car now having petrol, it still failed to start. The only option was to push the car to the garage which was no easy task on a fairly busy road. Fortunately there were no hills and the A30 was reasonably light. Having arrived at the garage and explained the situation, a mechanic lifted the bonnet, primed the pump, at the same time diverting his eyes skyward in a pitying manner and I was on my way.

CHAPTER FOUR

MARRIAGE

2.29 They say that absence makes the heart grow fonder and this must have been the case with Wendy and me as we became engaged to be married at Christmas 1959 and set the wedding day for 4th June 1960. It was before the arrival of the Swinging Sixties and its accompanying sexual revolution. It was the norm in those days for couples to marry in their early twenties as all nice girls were taught that there should be no sex before marriage, I was twenty-two and Wendy twenty-one. Unmarried couples who lived together were said to be living in sin. Any man who reached twenty-five without having become engaged was the subject of rumours as to his sexual proclivity and if he reached thirty and was still unmarried the rumour developed into it being a racing certainty. This was always kept closely under wraps as gay relationships were illegal in those days. Had anybody suggested that gay marriage would be recognised at some time in the future they would have been considered to have arrived from a different planet. It was the bride's family's responsibility to arrange the wedding which left me with little or no input. It was my responsibility to find us somewhere to live. I started my search in early January and within a few days I had found a flat which seemed to fit the bill. Wendy came to view the accommodation, gave it her approval and by the end of January I had moved in. The flat occupied the ground floor of a two storey terraced house owned by Mr and Mrs Varney, located in York Road near to Swindon Town Football Club. It comprised a bedroom, living room and kitchen on the ground floor with a shared bathroom on the first floor. I had by then acquired a couple of close friends, Dave Harvey, a likeable Irishman, who was the setting out engineer on the site and Mark Lane, a trainee solicitor. They were unhappy with the digs in which they were currently living and so volunteered to share the flat in York Road with me until my wedding, by which time they expected to have found themselves suitable alternative accommodation. After leaving Swindon Dave Harvey emigrated to Australia to work on a project in the Snowy Mountains, and Mark Lane set up in practice as a solicitor in Cheltenham and was my solicitor for over thirty years until he upped sticks and went to live in Africa.

2.30 Our wedding took place on a glorious summer's day at St Benedict's church in Orford, just outside Warrington, with a large number of friends and relations present. We held the reception at Walton Hall and spent our first night in the Blossoms Hotel in Chester. The trusty Austin A30 was up to the job of taking us on honeymoon to London for a few days and then to Bournemouth. When that was over we started our married life in the flat in Swindon. Wendy took a job as a secretary at Gerrard's, who were the contractors on Saint Margaret's Hospital site and married life began.

2.31 It was 1962 and I was still working in Swindon. The winter of 1962-63 was one of the coldest on record in the United Kingdom. A blizzard swept across the South West of England in late December and I got caught out in it when travelling between Highworth and Swindon. I passed a bus stop where there stood a lady on her own, no doubt hoping against hope that a bus would arrive. I stopped and offered her a lift which she readily accepted as we were both heading for Swindon. I hadn't gone very far when the car skidded off the road and into a ditch which ran parallel to the road. Both the lady and I scrambled out unhurt. As luck would have it we had come off the road a few hundred yards from Lucknow Garage where I had my car serviced and usually purchased my petrol. I explained to the owner my dilemma and he offered to help. His rescue vehicle was an old Morris saloon car which I didn't think was up to the job. The lady and I however piled in and the owner drove his car the few hundred yards to where my car was stuck in the ditch. We all got out and I wondered what his modus operandi was going to be. I was surprised when after a few minutes a large tanker appeared through the snow, which the garage owner flagged down. With some confidence he asked the driver if he would be prepared to use his tanker to pull my car out from the ditch. The driver agreed, the garage owner produced a tow rope and within minutes the job was done. The garage owner slipped the tanker driver some beer money and I paid the garage owner there and then in cash and the lady and I continued our journey to Swindon.

2.32 During that winter the snow lasted for over two months in some areas. Snow lay 6 inches deep in Manchester, 18 inches deep at Keele University in Staffordshire, 8 feet deep in Kent and 15 feet deep in some areas of the West of England. January 1963 was the coldest since January 1814 with an average temperature of minus 2.1 degrees and in some places it got as low as minus 19.4 degrees. The sea froze for one mile from the shore of Herne Bay and four miles out from Dunkirk. The most noticeable consequences of the Big Freeze, as it was called, was its effect on the sporting calendar. For many weeks most football matches in England, Wales and Scotland were postponed. Several ties in the FA Cup had to be rescheduled as many as ten times. The same story occurred in rugby league and rugby union. National Horse racing was also badly affected with 94 race meetings being cancelled; no racing taking place between 23rd December 1962 and 7th March 1963. One of the consequences of the big freeze was that the water pipes in the kitchen at our flat froze up most nights. To ensure we could make a cup of tea for breakfast, wash up and perform other functions requiring water, it was essential to fill the kettle before retiring to bed. In the morning we would light the gas stove and set the kettle to boil. The boiling water was then poured on the frozen pipes which then allowed us to have a supply of water.

2.33 Work on the two body pressing shops on which I had been engaged since my arrival in Swindon in 1958 had come to an end, however it was confidently expected that an instruction would be given by Pressed Steel to get on with the next one. However the weeks went by and there was no news. We were all turning up for work, some played card whist others filled in the time the best way they could. I became bored and frustrated and decided that it was time to move on. I had passed the Final Examination of the Royal Institution of Chartered Surveyors and sitting on a site in Swindon was doing nothing for my career. Both Wendy and I liked Swindon and the surrounding Cotswold Area and so I applied for a couple of jobs locally but they came to nothing. I had a feeling that Pressed Steel would decide not to proceed with the next pressing shop or the decision would be so long in coming that some of us would be given our marching orders. My experience so far in my career had been limited to the post contract services of quantity surveyors and was in need of the necessary pre-contract work to provide me with an all-round experience. I knew I could gain this type of experience in the head office of LC Wakeman and Partners in Birmingham and so decided to take the bull by the horns and rang Mr Chandler to enquire if there was any chance of me being transferred to the Birmingham office as the work had ground to a halt in Swindon. He rang me back a few days later offering me a job in Birmingham to start a couple of weeks later. Wendy and I would have preferred to stay living in Swindon, however the situation was too uncertain. The longer the delay continued the more likely I would be out of a job. The alternatives in the area were few. There were four firms of quantity surveyors in the region and the two I had been interested in joining came to nothing and the other two I didn't find appealing. I could work as a quantity surveyor for a construction firm and obtaining a job with one of them would not have been too difficult, however the Royal Institution of Chartered Surveyors' Contractor Rule stood in the way. The rule stipulated that any quantity surveyor who went to work for a construction company had to resign from membership. This represented the Institution's view that any surveyor working for a construction company would not be providing independent advice. To compound the problem, if a quantity surveyor went to work for a construction company and later switched back to employment by a firm of quantity surveyors, before being re-admitted to the membership of the Institution, it was a requirement that the applicant had to pay all the subscriptions for the intervening years. Having worked hard to qualify I wasn't prepared to lose my qualification. Taking all into consideration, Wendy and I decided to try our luck in Birmingham where I started work in early 1963.

2.34 1963 was also the year of the Beeching Report entitled "The Reshaping of British Railways" which recommended a significant reduction in the route network, closure of stations and restructuring of the railways in the country. They became known as the Beeching Cuts and in some quarters the Beeching Axe. With the introduction of mass car production and the resultant greater use of the car as a mode of transport, it was anticipated that the use of the rail network would reduce. The use of the railways over the past few years had remained constant, but the costs of running them had escalated. By 1961 the losses were running at a rate of £300,000 per day before the publication of the Beeching Report, which resulted in a reduction in the rail network. Since 1948, when the railways were nationalised, 3,000 miles of track had been closed and the numbers of railway staff had fallen by 26% from 648,000 to 474,000. Beeching carried out a survey of traffic flows and income. It transpired that the least used 1,762 stations out of a total of 4,300 had annual passenger receipts of less than £2,500 the equivalent of £48,700 in 2014. The least used 50% of stations contributed only 2% of the total passenger revenue and one third of the route miles carried only 1% of the passengers. Beeching's recommendation was for 6,000 miles of track out of a total of 18,000 miles to be closed entirely and some of the remainder to stay open for freight only. A total of 2,128 stations were to close approaching one half of the total number. He made other recommendations such as freight services to be used for minerals and coal and the introduction of containerised handling systems which was eventually adopted by Freightliner. There was a great deal of public protest at the proposed cuts and as a result some of the stations and lines were saved. The effect on jobs was significant with the loss of 67,000 positions on the railway network. A number of routes have since been reopened, some were incorporated into the National Cycle Network or used for road schemes; others were used for building land or converted back to farmland.

2.35 It was essential that we found somewhere to live in Birmingham as quickly as possible. Unfortunately accommodation was expensive and whilst my salary had increased significantly over the four year period we spent in Swindon, the perks of working out on a site had ceased. This resulted in the subsistence payment coming to an end and having to return the car. Sadly we lost the trusty old A30 and had to purchase a car of our own. It was a matter of finding a place which matched our financial resources. We decided that I would start my new job and for the time being Wendy would remain in Swindon with me travelling home at the weekend. This was not an ideal situation for a couple married for less than three years. Fortunately Wendy doesn't complain when the situation is not to her liking, she just gets on with life. Until we found a place in Birmingham I needed a roof over my head during the week. It was suggested by one of my new colleagues that cheap accommodation could be found at the Toc H hostel, located not far from the office. I called in and was advised that there was a bed available. Toc H was founded as a Christian organisation during the First World War by two clergymen, the Reverend Neville Talbot and the Reverend "Tubby" Clayton. It was started in Poperinge in Belgium where a hostel, Talbot House, which was named after one of its founders, was built to provide rest and recreation for soldiers passing through. Toc H was the shortened version of Talbot House and became the name of the organisation. A hostel had been set up in Birmingham just after the First World War for soldiers returning from the front who had nowhere to live and it seems there were a great many of them. The sleeping arrangements were in dormitories and I found myself in one with two other men about my own age. It turned out to be a laugh a minute and I enjoyed my stay. Eventually I found a flat to rent within our price range in Handsworth, which is on the outskirts of Birmingham, the sort of place where one doesn't venture out late at night. The accommodation and location of the flat were such that one would wish to stay for only the minimum period and even that would be too long.

2.36 The immediate task was to try to buy a house, as we felt that paying rent was dead money. I joined a self-build group but didn't stay long as the likely date for moving into a house we might jointly build, would probably coincide with my retirement date. The price of houses in Birmingham was extortionate and outside our price range and so we looked further afield. We managed to find a decent new build on an estate in Litchfield, which is about an hour's drive from Birmingham, on which we put a deposit. At that time work hadn't started on constructing the houses and so there was going to be something of a wait before we could move in. We vacated the flat in Swindon and moved to Handsworth after about two months. Wendy managed to secure a job almost immediately with James Roberts, a well-known Architect located in the centre of Birmingham and so the family finances were again running smoothly.

2.37 LC Wakeman and Partners was owned and run by four partners, Sidney Plaister, very much the boss who personally looked after all the firm's financial matters; Eric Lees who headed up post contract services; John Warren in charge of pre-contract services and Roy Chandler who was something of a floater and dealt with matters which fell outside the ambit of the others. They liked to create an image, which involved always coming to work wearing a bowler hat. As I was employed in the pre-contract department John Warren or EJW as he was always called, being his initials was my immediate boss. They were firm but usually fair, however they liked everything done in a manner which was correct in their view. All letters and reports were signed by one of the partners and before signing documents they read them through and if a document wasn't up to their standard it would be sent back for redrafting. The typewriters were all manual, as electric, if on the market by then, would have been considered too expensive by our partners. If typing errors could be seen to have been corrected using some form of obliterator, the offending document would be returned for retyping. The company wasn't a hire and fire organisation, although I do recall one employee being fired. He decided to go out for a haircut in mid-afternoon only to find Eric Lees, one of the partners, sitting in the next barber's chair to him. It may have been more appropriate for a warning to be given but perhaps there were other undisclosed reasons for his dismissal. I shared a room with three others, Richard Birch, who was my predecessor at Swindon, Neil Poutney and Alan Cross. Neil, Richard and I were about the same age, Alan being about ten years our senior, knew a great deal more about the job than us three and didn't hesitate to let us know. We had a good relationship but with four men sharing a room a certain amount of ribbing and ribaldry was inevitable. The work was mainly for the motor car industry and local authorities such as Birmingham City Council and there was usually more than we could reasonably cope with. This resulted in ample opportunities for overtime, which was paid for at time and a quarter, making it very attractive to the likes of Neil and me. Mrs Dalby, one of the cleaners who had what must have been the broadest Brummy accent on the planet, seemed to take a liking to us. After arriving at the office in the late afternoon she would nip out to a local shop and purchase a pie or two which she would then warm up in the oven for Neil and me, thus keeping the hunger at bay, allowing us to get in a couple of hours overtime. Mrs Dalby, who had a large brood, seeing us in our early twenties and obviously in need of some sexual enlightenment, advised us on several occasions that "it's not them as 'as the most, as 'as it the most". Still she was a real dear and well liked.

2.38 Playing football and cricket was never very far from my thoughts and so it was quite convenient that the company had a football team which played in the Birmingham and District league and a cricket team which played in a 20/20 league, although it wasn't called that at the time. It was customary to bring in a few outside players to enhance the standard of play. It seemed to have worked as we won the cup at football and the league championship at cricket, both being a first for me. In life tragedy is never far away. One of the oldest employees was Johnathan White known to us all as Chalky. He was a hail fellow well met type, the life and soul of any party, well liked and respected. He had recently married for the second time to a lady much younger than himself and they had a baby, much to the delight of Chalky. A period of three days elapsed when Chalky failed to arrive at work and as phone calls to his home were unanswered the powers that be became concerned. EJW therefore decided to visit Chalky's home to find out if there was a problem. After arriving at Chalky's home, EJW found him dead, he had committed suicide. It seems that he was experiencing matrimonial problems and his wife had left him taking the baby with her. Chalky in a state of depression had taken his own life. This caused great sadness throughout the office.

CHAPTER FIVE

LIFE IN SHREWSBURY

2.39 The office internal phones had the normal 'ring ring' but there was also a facility for producing just one single ring which signified that Mr Plaister the senior partner was on the line; it was referred to as the long ring. I had been working in Birmingham for about two years when the long ring occurred and it was for me; the boss asked me to go down and see him. He explained that the company continued to receive large numbers of commissions but experienced difficulty in recruiting sufficient numbers of staff to cope. The company had a successful office in Caernarvon and they thought as Shrewsbury was about midpoint between the two offices it would be in a good location to set up a new office to deal with any oversupply of work. The partners also considered it would be fairly easy to recruit staff in Shrewsbury. I couldn't understand why he should bother to explain all this to me until he then dropped the bomb-shell by saying that he would like Peter Martin, a colleague, and me to become joint managers of the Shrewsbury office. I didn't consider myself by any means a rising star; since arriving from Swindon I had kept my head down and just got on with the work. It could be that the partners wanted to have the new office managed by qualified staff of which there were few working for the firm. The four main senior members of staff, which included John

Richardson, my old boss from Warrington, had recently been promoted to the positions of Associate Partners which ruled them out as they were given specific responsibilities in the Birmingham office. The job came with a pay rise and a car which added to the excitement. Peter Martin was a good man, about my age, very competent and confident and if I had to share a responsibility with anybody, there would be no better person than Peter.

2.40 It is said that where a really momentous event occurs you always recall when and where it first came to your knowledge. On the morning of Saturday, 23rd November 1963 I received a knock on our flat door and opened it to find Norman standing outside. Norman and his wife Mil lived in the flat across the corridor from us. Norman worked at a local hospital and both were originally from Liverpool with accents to match. "Have you heard the news" asked Norman. "What news" I responded," President Kennedy has been assassinated" was Norman's reply. It had happened on the previous day in Dallas. The president and first lady had spent the previous night in Fort Worth and following breakfast went by motorcade to Carswell Air Force Base for a thirteen minute flight to Dallas. A crowd was awaiting their arrival and the first lady was given a bouquet of red roses which she took with her to the awaiting limousine. The governor John Connolly and his wife Nellie were already seated at the front of the car and the president and first lady got into the back. The journey involved a ten mile route through Dallas to the Trade Mart where the president was due to give a speech at a luncheon. As the car passed the Texas School Book Depository at about 12.30pm there was the sound of gunfire. The president was hit in the neck and head and the governor in the chest. The president was rushed to a nearby hospital where he was given the last rites and died at about 1.00pm. Within an hour the police had arrested Lee Harvey Oswald, a recently hired employee of the Texas Book Depository. On 24th November, Lee Harvey Oswald was being transferred from the police headquarters to the county jail, when he was shot at point blank range by Jack Ruby a local night club owner.

Oswald died two hours later at Parkland Hospital and Jack Ruby was charged with murder. He denied the allegation on the grounds that his grief over the assassination of the president had caused him to suffer "psychomotor epilepsy" and as a result he shot Harvey Oswald unconsciously. The jury found him guilty but the Texas Court of Appeal reversed the decision on the grounds of improper testimony and the fact that Ruby could not have received a fair trial in Dallas. Jack Ruby died of cancer in January 1967 while awaiting a retrial. In 1963 President Lyndon Johnson appointed a commission to investigate the assassination of John F Kennedy, known as the Warren Commission, which concluded that neither Oswald nor Ruby were part of a large conspiracy either domestic or international to assassinate the president. However in 1978 the House Select Committee on Assassinations concluded in a preliminary report that President Kennedy was probably assassinated as a result of a conspiracy that involved multiple shooters and organised crime.

2.41 The office the firm rented in Shrewsbury was located on Town Walls which overlooked the river Severn. The river swept round the town in the shape of a horseshoe over which there were two bridges known as the Welsh Bridge and the English Bridge. The Welsh Bridge carried the road used to travel to Oswestry and on into Wales and the English Bridge to Wellington and the English Midlands. The office was in a three storey building with offices on the ground floor, ours on the first floor and a flat at the top of the building. The building was owned by Graham Goatley who practised as an Architect and occupied the ground floor. He employed a senior assistant by the name of Mike Sandford and in life one never meets more than one Mike Sandford, or Sandy to his friends. He knew everybody and was everywhere. He bounded up the stairs on our first day and offered his assistance in any way which would help us. He turned out to be a really good friend who introduced us to people who became clients and also assisted us to integrate into the social side of the town. Peter and I had brought work with us so there was little time for bedding in. We had decided that we did not wish to be solely reliant on surplus work from the Birmingham and Caernarvon offices as this would leave us a bit vulnerable and not masters of our own destiny if those offices ceased to have surplus work. Securing our own work, however, was never going to be easy, due to the strict rules laid down by the Royal Institution of Chartered Surveyors, which banned advertising and touting for business. It was necessary therefore to have a very active social life to meet as many people as possible and to ignore the rules of the Institution as far as we were able. It would only become a problem if one was caught out contravening the rules. Producing a company brochure and writing letters of introduction was therefore out of the question.

2.42 Wendy's mother had been taken seriously ill and so she was needed at home to nurse mother-in-law back to full health. This coincided with our move to Shrewsbury and so we left the flat in Handsworth for the last time with great relief, Wendy moving temporarily back to Warrington with me staying in a hotel during the week and travelling to stay in Warrington at the weekends. Peter was in a similar position travelling home to Birmingham at weekends and so we stayed at the same hotel, The Prince Rupert, which had a fine reputation for producing good food which we discovered, at a cost to our waistlines, wasn't exaggerated. We needed to find a house in the Shrewsbury area and I visited estate agents and house builders to ascertain what was on offer. Eventually I encountered a small house builder, Onions and Rowley, which was run by Fred Onions and his son John. They had acquired a small plot of land in the village of Great Ness on which they had planning permission to build four bungalows. Great Ness is way out in the countryside, about eight miles from Shrewsbury, having a small number of houses, a large old house which had been converted into flats, three farms and a church at the end of a cul-de-sac, opposite which was located the plot of land. Property in Shrewsbury was cheap and the further into the country, the cheaper it became. At £3,750 the bungalow, which had three bedrooms, lounge, large kitchen, garage and good sized garden, was very inexpensive. We advised Fred Onions that we would like to purchase the bungalow, paid the deposit, appointed a solicitor and asked him to arrange for contracts to be signed and exchanged as soon as possible. Work hadn't started on construction but we were advised that as we had agreed the purchase an immediate start would be made. Regular visits were made by me to the site to check on progress, which I reported back to Wendy. Work got underway almost immediately and they were soon up to damp proof course level at the base of the external walls. Work then ground to a halt leading to a great deal of frustration on my part. Regular phone calls and visits were made to Fred Onions, which were met with conciliatory responses that a restart would be made any day. It got to August and when I demanded to know when the bungalow would be finished Fred was sufficiently evasive to advise me it would be sometime in Oct-ember. What Fred had omitted to tell me was that the brick manufacturer had ceased to make the colour of facing bricks for which Fred had receive planning consent and he had to make a new planning application for the revised colour. It was awaiting this revised planning consent which was holding up construction. He probably thought that if he told me the truth we would go off and find an alternative. Eventually the consent was received and Fred put his best foot forward and construction completed fairly quickly thereafter. Mother-in-law made a full recovery and we moved in with a combination of relief and excitement just before Christmas in 1965, our first house, having been married for over five years.

2.43 The office got off to a good start with work flowing in from Birmingham. We were advised that it was expected that we would build up the office into a good profitable unit. As two of us with a secretary in a fairly large office wasn't a formula for making profits, we needed to build up the fee earning staff. We had no guidance as to how to run an office profitably but I consider that Peter and I between us had an ample level of common sense. John Tancock was the first to join us having previously worked for Shropshire County Council. John was followed by Brian Watt, Derek Kent, Richard Davies, Chris Metcalfe and Barney Peagum. Barney was something of a character who ran a pre-war Austin 8 in which I accepted a lift on one occasion. However on seeing the road passing underneath us through a hole in the floor as we sped along, I decided that it would be the first and last lift I would accept from Barney. In our first year, in addition to the work passed to us from Birmingham we secured work from Shropshire County Council and Wrexham Borough Council together with some industrial work in Staffordshire. Sandy introduced us to a couple of organisations of which he was a member with the object of putting ourselves around. He was a keen oarsman being a member of the Pengwern Boat Club which both Peter and I joined and took up the oars; in my case not very successfully. Sandy was also a member of the Round Table which is for young men under 40 years of age. It has an objective of raising money for charity and in modern parlance is good for networking. We were also keen to meet Architects as they were a first class introduction to work sources. Sandy's great pal was David Morris of Catterall and Morris, a firm of Architects, whom we got to know well through Sandy. Both of them made introductions which brought us work. By way of a coincidence David had been a colleague of Wendy's at James Roberts when they both worked for the firm in Birmingham.

2.44 I missed the football season due to the move but was determined not to do likewise with the cricket season and was therefore anxiously looking for a local club to which I could attach myself. I heard of a club located in the village of Knockin which was about five miles from Great Ness and went through my usual procedure of getting to know the name of the captain and securing an invitation to join the members of the team at a net practice and subsequently a place in the team. It was 1966, the year when the World Cup was scheduled to take place in England. On the day of the final when England was due to play West Germany we had a match arranged. There was no suggestion of cancelling the match to allow the players to watch the game on television. The idea of watching any sport in preference to playing was tantamount to heresy, even if it was the World Cup Final featuring England. There were however some concessions made in allowing transistor radios to be brought to the match and players on the field of play being kept abreast of events as they were unfolding at Wembley. It was unanimously agreed that the tea interval be extended by fifteen minutes to allow the players to listen to the last few minutes of extra time. When the 1966 World Cup is discussed, Geoff Hurst's controversial second goal is usually the main topic of conversation. The Swiss referee however didn't signal the goal until he had discussed the matter with the Soviet linesman. Photographic technology has been unable to offer decisive evidence as to whether or not the ball had crossed the goal line. This is just as well for if technology had subsequently indicated no goal, it could have been the cause of an international incident. There is also the matter of the German equaliser immediately after a blatant handball in the penalty area by one of the German players which went unnoticed by the referee. It may have been forgotten that England were one of the favourites and didn't concede a goal until they played Portugal in the semi-final. Geoff Hurst's goal in the final minute, it is strongly rumoured, came from an attempt on Geoff's part to boot the ball into the crowd to take up the final minute of the game, but probably due to tiredness Geoff miskicked and the ball finished up in the net just as the TV commentator Kenneth Wolstenholme entered into English folklore with "Some people are on the pitch! They think it's all over! It is now." The other hero of the day was Pickles, the dog who found the cup on the afternoon of the 20th March 1966, after it had been stolen during a public exhibition of rare stamps which also featured the World Cup. Pickles, whilst taking a walk with his owner, found the World Cup which was wrapped in a newspaper, at the bottom of a suburban garden in South Norwood, London, seven days after it was stolen. The thief was never found. I managed to keep up my footballing whilst living in Shrewsbury playing for Nesscliffe followed by Baschurch, both village teams playing in the Shrewsbury and District League.

CHAPTER SIX

LIVERPOOL THE LAST OUTPOST

2.45 Ambition, so it is said, is a sin. Many decisions made in my life followed my ambitious desires. Ambitious people often become self-obsessed with ensuring that the object of their ambition becomes a reality, in many instances to the exclusion of the interests of others. It was the procedure for the four partners in the company to hold a monthly meeting in Birmingham to which the Associate Partners, together with Peter and me, were invited to attend. We presented a report of the progress of the Shrewsbury office whilst others in attendance produced reports in respect of their own areas of responsibility. Whilst attending one of these meetings Mr Plaister announced that the firm intended to open a new office in Liverpool and that they were looking for a manager. We had worked hard at Shrewsbury to build up the practice but had reached a plateau and bearing in mind the location and limited opportunities for securing work we were unlikely to grow much bigger. The office was making a profit and undertaking overspill work, and so from the partner's prospective, mission accomplished. However ambition was gnawing at my insides. Where would I be in ten years' time and would I be happy to remain a branch manager of a small office? The sole manager of an office in a place like Liverpool held much more attraction and the more I thought about the prospect the more attractive it became. I talked to Wendy about the possibility of moving to Liverpool which was met, to say the least, with a total lack of enthusiasm. Why would she be interested in moving to Liverpool? We had a lovely home in a glorious part of the country, I had a good, well paid job which meant she didn't have to go out to work; the work was enjoyable and didn't involve a great deal of travelling; who but a fool would wish to change this situation for a move to Liverpool? It would seem only a person who is absorbed by ambition. I promised Wendy that we wouldn't live in Liverpool but would find a nice place in Cheshire and that a move would involve better pay and prospects. In the end I probably wore her down and she reluctantly agreed to me applying for the job. Mr Plaister, when I approached him about me taking on the job as manager of the Liverpool office, readily agreed. No doubt he took into consideration the fact that Peter Martin would remain, who was more than capable of running the office on his own. However, shortly after I left to go to Liverpool, Peter, who must also have been bitten by the ambition bug, resigned to take up a position in London with Grosvenor Estates, one of the firm's clients. He was replaced as manager by John Tancock, our first recruit.

2.46 For some time I had been experiencing a dull ache, at the right side of my back, which came and went. I visited a local GP who examined me, prodded the offending part of my back and declared that there was no problem with my kidney. He prescribed some medication and suggested it would all pass off in time. The situation got worse and I revisited the GP who this time suggested it could be my car that was causing the problem and suggested a replacement might do the trick. A couple of weeks later I returned and demanded that the GP take some positive action to identify the problem and so he sent me to the local hospital for an X ray. When the results came through I was advised to pack a bag immediately and check myself into hospital. It seems the problem was being caused by a malfunctioning kidney. As kidney transplants and dialysis were for the future, a failure of the other kidney would have meant the end for me. The surgeon who carried out the operation must have attended the same school of thought as the character played by James Robertson Justice in the film Doctor in the House. When operating he liked the patent to be well and truly opened up to allow him to see what he was doing. I still have a scar, which runs from my midpoint front right round to my midpoint back, to show for my experience in the hospital. In modern times keyhole surgery would be the answer. My stay in hospital lasted two weeks and I was off work for a further four weeks. On my last day of working in the Shrewsbury office I went downstairs to say goodbye to Sandy, who wished me the best of everything and insisted we keep in touch. Tragedy usually strikes without warning, which it did in Sandy's case some years after I had left Shrewsbury. Sandy had worked for a few years in Bermuda and being a keen sailor had joined the Royal Bermuda Yacht Club, one of the oldest and most venerated in the world. Being Sandy he never lost an opportunity of advising people of his past connection. This being the case, one of his friends who owned a yacht which was moored in Southampton and needed to be transferred to a port in Northern France, knowing of Sandy's yachting prowess, asked him if he would like to undertake the task. Sandy readily agreed and recruited two of his friends, one being his stepdaughter's husband, to help crew the vessel. Sandy and his crew left Southampton during bad weather. Under normal circumstances he would probably have waited for the weather to improve but he was in a hurry to return to Shrewsbury to attend an important business meeting. Having left Southampton in bad weather Sandy and his two friends were never seen or heard from again. The English Channel is said to be the busiest stretch of waterway in the world and it was thought that due to poor visibility the yacht may have been hit by a large ship unknown to the ship's crew. For three young men to lose their lives in such circumstances was a tragedy of major proportions.

2.47 It was now 1968 and we sold the bungalow to the second person who came for a viewing and bought a house in Kingsley which is a village located in mid-Cheshire. It is a small village with at the time a pub, shop, garage, school and two churches, Anglican and Methodist. It is an hour's drive to Liverpool; alternatively there are regular trains from the nearby Acton Bridge station. We had taken the lease on an office in Rumford Place near to the Pierhead and I recruited my first members of staff, Mrs Maidmont the secretary, John Smith and Noel Blundell all of whom turned out to be first class in every respect. I followed the same process in securing work and building up the staff as we had carried out in Shrewsbury, which turned out to be successful. I ran the office profitably for five years.

2.48 Whilst working in Shrewsbury I had kept in contact with my old roommate from the Birmingham office days, Richard Birch. One day he announced that he had decided to enhance his qualifications by sitting for the Bar Examinations. This was the gateway to becoming a barrister and representing clients in a Court of Law. The Bar Council set the examinations and, provided one possessed the minimum entry qualifications, it was open to anybody to enter and if successful become qualified as a barrister. However before a start could be made it was a requirement that those aspiring to qualify as barristers should join an Inn of Court. It was also necessary to keep four Terms which involved eating dinner at your chosen Inn three times during a Term of which there were four per annum. This appealed to my ever growing sense of ambition and so, having checked the rules and found that I was eligible to sit the examinations, I decided to give it a go. I joined Lincoln's Inn and commenced attending the Inn and eating my dinners. I discovered that the Metropolitan College of Law provided a Correspondence Course, which suited me down to the ground, having been through the process with the College of Estate Management. The normal method of entry to the bar was by undertaking a course of study at the Inns of

Court School of Law. There were three examinations The First Examination, The Second Examination and the Final Examination. Candidates who possessed a law degree awarded by a recognised university were exempt from the First and Second Examinations but were obliged to sit the Final Examination. The Royal Institution of Chartered Surveyors' examinations included papers on legal subjects such as Contract Law, Property Law and the Law of Torts which I found interesting and fairly easy to understand. Getting to grips with the legal subjects necessary for qualification to the bar I found straight forward. The amount of time which I had to devote to studying was quite extensive and involved a couple of hours most mornings before setting out for work, not to mention evenings and weekends, but the pangs of ambition take some satisfying. From a standing start in early 1968 I managed to complete all the examinations by the autumn of 1971. There followed the formal Call to the Bar ceremony which was attended by all who had been successful in the examinations. It was a great occasion attended by friends and relatives in my case Wendy and my boss John Warren. Would I like to change professions and become a barrister? It certainly had its attractions.

2.49 Entry into the closeted world of working as a practising barrister isn't by any means easy. The rules are strict and the hurdles high. Barristers only operated from chambers in those days of which there were a fixed number, most of them being in London, each with a set number of places or seats as they were called. To practise as a barrister it was necessary to secure one of those seats and to do so it was important that you knew somebody with influence. Before being offered a seat one had to undertake a pupillage, which involved working in chambers for a pupil master, who was a practising barrister, and paying him or her a pupillage fee. This lasted for one year and it would then be a scramble to try to find a vacant seat. I didn't know anybody who practised at the bar and so I resorted to door knocking. It was the chamber's clerk one went to see to discuss these matters, if you could find one who would bother to give you the time.

The clerk's role is to deal with all business matters relating to the chambers leaving the barristers to provide the professional service. With my background and experience I was interested in practising construction law. There were two main chambers in the country which specialised in construction law, on the doors of which I knocked. It seems that securing a pupillage was a possibility as pupil masters liked to have a pupil as it created an income and a spare pair of hands to assist with the work. Even when a pupillage had been completed at the end of the year, there was no guarantee of being offered a seat as there were usually half a dozen good quality contenders. When a seat became available it was put to a vote of all the barristers in the chambers as to who should be offered the vacancy. I was advised by one of the chamber's clerks that in the scramble for work, with my background in construction, I would be seen as a threat to many of them and as such it would be unlikely for them to vote for me. I did have one success from my door knocking in that a Mr Roddis, who practised planning law from chambers in Southampton, offered me a pupillage. By this time I had decided that practising at the bar was not for me. However I had two qualifications, which was at the time I think unique, although many have since trodden the same path as me, and I wished to make use of them to my advantage, which wouldn't happen if I continued to work for LC Wakeman and Partners. I had been working for them for nineteen years and considered that I had gone as far as I was likely to go. It was 1972, I was thirty-four years of age and needed to move on. I applied for several situations vacant and was offered none and so I concluded if I were to get on I would have to work for myself. It was a little difficult to make definite plans as I was obliged to give the firm six months' notice of my leaving, which I submitted and started to make my plans during this period.

2.50 The hospital operation took place at the end of the summer of 1968 which left me in no shape to play football and so I decided to abandon any idea of playing during the coming season. When the next football season arrived, whilst having recovered from the operation, I didn't feel, at the age of thirty-two and having missed a season, sufficiently fit and confident to present myself for a trial at some local club and reluctantly decided that my days of playing football every Saturday during the season were over. I was a member of the Round Table, an organisation for men up to forty years of age, whose main objective was to raise money for charity and generally have an enjoyable time. I had joined the Shrewsbury Table and transferred to Northwich when we moved to live in Kingsley. There were over twenty Tables in Cheshire and North Staffordshire and, men being men, football matches were arranged including a cup and five-a-side competitions. The standard of play wasn't high as most of the players were over thirty years of age and had ceased playing regularly for a recognised football team. I played for the Northwich Round Table team until I was forty during which time we won both the cup and five-a-side competitions. Cricket was a different matter, as through being in the Round Table, I got to know John Pickup and Geoff Clarke, who were both members of Northwich Cricket Club and I played for them for four seasons, but like all good things it comes to an end. The time when I realised my abilities had faded fast came to a head when playing Bramhall Cricket Club at their ground. With my first ball I hit the batsman's middle stump but thereafter it was all bad news. The batsmen finished up hitting my bowling onto the roofs of the houses which ran alongside the ground. Enough being enough I knew it was time to finish playing cricket. For over twenty-five years I had experienced wonderful times playing football and cricket, never to be forgotten.

2.51 1969 was a momentous year internationally, as it was the year that man first landed on the moon. The Soviet Union had already launched the first man, Yuri Gagarin, into space and the US were developing a moon exploration programme which had originated during the Eisenhower administration. President Kennedy had been anxious to have a man on the moon before the Soviet Union and diverted money from other projects to finance the necessary expenditure on the moon exploration programme, which was referred to as the Apollo Project. Vice President Lyndon Johnson was very supportive of the President and the Apollo Project, as they saw it as a method of bridging the "missile gap" which was thought to exist between the Soviet Union and the US. The invention of the Saturn B booster, which had a perfect record of zero failures in thirteen launches, was the key to a moon landing. To satisfy the general public, Vice President Johnson advised that a moon landing would result in a medical breakthrough and produce interesting pictures of earth from space. This propaganda was required to defeat criticism from politicians on the left, who wanted more money spent on social programmes and those on the right, who favoured the money being spent on the military. However public opinion was swung in favour of the Apollo Project with 58% in favour. On 20th July 1968, Neil Armstrong became the first man to set foot on the moon on the Sea of Tranquillity. He had earlier reported the lunar module's safe landing with the words "Houston, Tranquillity Base here, the Eagle has landed" As he set his foot on the moon's surface he declared "That's one small step for man, one giant leap for mankind" He was joined shortly after by Edwin "Buzz" Aldrin and the two collected data and performed various exercises including jumping across the landscape and then planting the stars and stripes. They also unveiled a plaque bearing President Nixon's signature and an inscription which read "Here men from the planet Earth first set foot upon the Moon July 1969 AD" There have been further trips to the moon and in total twenty four US astronauts have travelled there but only twelve have walked on its surface.

2.52 My period of notice came to an end in early 1973 which became an important year in my life. It was also an important year for Britain as in January of that year we joined the EEC. We had made two applications for membership in 1961 and 1969 which were blocked by General De Gaulle of

France. In view of the great help we gave France in World War Two in providing a base for General De Gaulle and his Free French and the sacrifices of human life in liberating France following the Normandy landings, the action of the General was reprehensible. Various reasons have been suggested as to why the General blocked our entry, including a feeling that the UK lacked the political will; British membership would weaken the French voice in Europe; Anglo-American relations would lead to the USA increasing its influence in Europe and a fear that English would become the common language of the community. However the General resigned in 1969 leaving the way clear for the UK to join the EEC. The entry of the UK into the EEC brought the number of members up to nine. Under the Labour Government there was a referendum in 1975 on continued membership of the EEC. The electorate voted yes to staying in by 67.2% to 32.8%. In 1984, under the leadership of Margaret Thatcher, after threatening to halt payments to the EU budget, Britain negotiated an EU budget rebate. At the time the UK was set to become the largest net contributor to the budget. This was due to farming subsidies for which Britain was eligible to very little. It was agreed that this was unfair and Britain was granted a rebate. At the time 80% of the EEC expenditure was on the Common Agricultural Policy although that percentage has fallen in recent years. In 2005, under pressure from other EEC member states, Tony Blair agreed to reduce the rebate by 20%. A common currency, the Euro, came into existence in 2002, by which time the number of members had increased. The euro was adopted by twelve of the member states and some non-members such as Monaco and Andorra. Fortunately, as it would transpire, the UK decided to stay out of the Euro.

PART THREE

JAMES R KNOWLES THE FIRM

CHAPTER ONE

UP AND RUNNING

3.1. I was well into my six months' period of notice with no definite plans as to the services I intended to provide. Most barristers have a speciality such as insurance law, company law or medical law; my speciality was construction law. At the time, disputes in the construction industry were rife. A great deal of the construction work was being undertaken by medium size construction companies for public authorities. Overruns in terms of cost and time occurred on many projects. Contractors often underpriced projects where the design hadn't been properly completed by the Architect prior to tenders being received, which resulted in disputes when the final issue of drawings arrived at the contractor's office, often well after work had commenced, which showed differences from the tender issue drawings. The cost of additional work ordered by the Architect during the construction phase was also often the subject of disagreements and liability for time overruns was commonplace. Contractors seeking redress would normally refer the dispute to their solicitor. As there was often a legal issue involved, a barrister's opinion would be sought. There were frequently cost, time and quality issues, in which case expert reports were required from an experienced quantity surveyor and architect, or engineer. Solicitors were rarely prepared to give any clue as to the cost or time involvement at the outset, it could be many months later, after the case had been developed, before any indication would be given, by which time a substantial fee obligation had been incurred. If the matter wasn't resolved, it would be referred to a technical arbitrator for a decision, in accordance with the requirements of most standard construction contracts used in the industry. This could be very off-putting to those without deep pockets.

3.2 The idea slowly developed in my mind that I could undertake all the tasks relating to the resolution of a construction dispute. I had practised as a quantity surveyor for 19 years and, having been an expert witness in a number of cases, was familiar with the disputes resolution procedure. The solicitor's task was to gather together the information and condense it into a report form, which a barrister could easily digest, to enable a legal opinion to be sought. This was well within my capabilities. The barrister's opinion should be no trouble, nor the quantity surveyor's expert opinion. With regard to architects' and engineers' expert opinions, as I knew plenty of them, securing opinions would present no difficulty. I hadn't represented any organisation in an arbitration but was familiar with its workings. It soon became obvious that the service I ought to be offering was a one stop shop for the resolution of construction disputes. As far as I was aware there was no other organisation providing this type of service.

3.3 To enable me to set up a successful business I needed premises, working from home was never a consideration. I intended to start a business, not a one man band and therefore I needed an office I could rent. At the time I was friendly with Neville Deakin and Tony Callard who were both engineers. They ran a company Deakin Callard from offices in Canada House, Chepstow Street in Manchester. When hearing of my intentions, Tony mentioned that there were vacant offices in Canada House. I had a look at them; they comprised three rooms on the ground floor which were linked, car parking outside the window and a rent at £650 per annum, which was easily affordable. They were offering a two year lease period which suited me as it limited my exposure if things didn't turn out the way I hoped. A name for the company would be required and I chose James R Knowles as James is my first name and a frequently used family name, whilst Roger sounded a bit like a ladies' hairdresser. I needed letter headings and visiting cards which my pal Dave Lancashire, who ran a printing business in Warrington, produced in quick time and I was ready for the off. I had a little money saved but didn't want to fail as a result of running out of funds. I therefore decided to seek an overdraft from the bank. Had I been experienced at running a business I would have tried to calculate the amount of working capital required. In my first year my expenditure was £12,000 which is on average £1,000 per month. If I billed my clients monthly and they took two months on average to pay I would require working capital of £3,000. I didn't go into this type of detail but considered that if I could acquire an overdraft facility of £2,000, with the money I had it would be possible to exist for six months without receiving any fees. After the six months had elapsed without any income I would be in serious financial trouble. I arranged to see the manager of the National Westminster Bank who was very friendly and agreed to the £2,000 overdraft facility, subject to me taking a second mortgage on my house, to which I agreed. Some two years later, like many businesses in the early stages with things going well, there was a need for an increase in the overdraft facility. A visit to the bank found a new manager in post who informed me that the policy of the bank had changed and it was no longer providing overdraft facilities to small businesses and as a result he had intended to contact me to advise me that the £2,000 overdraft was to be withdrawn. This was indeed bad news; however I quickly made an appointment to see the manager of Barclays Bank in an attempt to remedy the situation. The manager's name happened to be Knowles, no relation, and he was very anxious to talk about qualifying as a barrister, as he was about to retire and considered it would be an ideal pastime for him. Having explained to Mr Knowles how the system works he offered me an overdraft facility of £5,500, despite me requesting one for £3,500; I declined the offer, being happy with the £3,500.

3.4 I was coming to the end of my six months' period of notice with L C Wakeman and Partners, which was due to expire at the end of January 1973 and had developed a service which I could offer to prospective clients, premises, letter headings, visiting cards, enthusiasm, but no clients. It would have been unethical to have been touting for business during my period of notice and in any event the rules of the Royal Institution of Chartered Surveyors prevented touting for business. However with a couple of weeks to go, I decided to ring a few contacts in the industry to let them know what I was planning. My first call was to Eric Parmley, the surveying director of Tysons, a well-established Liverpool construction company, whom I arranged to meet during my first week as a sole practitioner. I had dealt with Eric on many occasions during my five years in Liverpool whilst working for L C Wakeman and Partners and found him to be a very likeable and amiable man. He had served in the war and for a time had been imprisoned in a German prisoner of war camp. He never talked about his war time experiences, except on one occasion, when he mentioned being liberated. It seems when they awoke one morning, all the German guards had disappeared and the gates had been left open. Naturally all the prisoners made for the gates, however word spread that the Russian army was on its way. Due to the reputation of the Russian army, the British soldiers made off as quickly as possible in the opposite direction to that from which the Russians were expected to arrive.

3.5 It was one of those days when you are convinced that God is in his heaven and all is well with the world. I explained to Eric that I was now operating my own company and looking for commissions. Much to my surprise Eric produced a huge roll of drawings and said "In that case you can get on with these". At the time, for most contractors, undertaking construction work in Liverpool was difficult, due to problems with the unions in particular, and construction workers in general. Strikes which lasted for years, such as the Inland Revenue offices in Bootle and the Liverpool Teaching Hospital, were commonplace. There were however very few companies, Tysons being the main one, who could successfully work in Liverpool. This was due mainly to Tysons' policy of only employing Liverpool labour and Liverpool-based subcontractors and keeping on good terms with the union secretary. It seems that IDC, a Stratford upon Avon-based construction company, had been approached by the Post Office to construct a new Head Post Office on Copperas Hill in Liverpool. Being aware of the difficulties of working in Liverpool, they had decided to sublet all of the construction work to Tysons. It was on the very day of my meeting with Eric that all the drawings had arrived from IDC with a request for Tysons to provide a price for undertaking the work. Before Eric's estimators could get started they required all the quantities to be scheduled, which was a formidable task, bearing in mind the size of the project. This was the task Eric had in mind for me. His only instruction was for me to attend a meeting at his office at 8 am each Monday morning to report progress to himself and Mr Leslie Tyson and to ensure I sent him a fee account each month. It seems that Tysons had experience of working with solicitors, who often delayed for months before sending in their fee accounts, the size of which were often breathtaking. Eric didn't enquire as to the basis on which my fees would be charged, he obviously trusted me. IDC had been given three months to submit a price for the work and so we were all under pressure to get on with it. I needed help to fulfil my role and so engaged the services of a few old colleagues to undertake work for me on a freelance basis. I realised that the three months would soon come to an end and more work would be needed. Ken Hall, the MD of Holland Hannen and Cubitts Ltd, and I had been friendly for years and so a visit to Ken was called for. I came to the conclusion that in starting a new business there are often people who like to provide a helping hand, Ken being one of them. Cubitts had acquired a company, Lowton Construction Ltd, who produced factory manufactured houses, which was the aspect of the company which appealed to Cubitts, as they saw it as a possible growth area. Ken asked me to produce a standard Bill of Quantities for the factory manufactured house which I was happy to undertake, but doubted what use it would be to him. Perhaps Ken was manufacturing a job for me. My third early success was with George Longden and Sons Ltd, an old established Sheffield company. They had constructed new Physics and Chemistry Blocks on which they had disputes with Sheffield University and required my help in getting them resolved and were happy to engage my services.

3.6. Eric Parmley, having produced my first commission, when it was completed, asked me to keep the project under review and examine every drawing they received from IDC on the Head Post Office project as work progressed and to identify any design changes which would have the effect of increasing the price. There were about two hundred drawings issued by IDC from which I prepared the schedules of quantities; the drawings issued as the work progressed which illustrated the work which was to be built, ran into thousands. It was therefore essential to check carefully the construction issue drawings with the tender issue drawings and identify any changes. This commission lasted over two years. Ken Hall introduced me to his chief quantity surveyor, Brian Hill, whom I got on with famously. Holland Hannen and Cubitts had a major dispute in relation to the construction of a school for Rochdale Borough Council on which my services were required. The Chief Quantity Surveyor at Rochdale Borough Council was Brian Kitson. Brian and I both served on the Royal Institution of Chartered Surveyors Quantity Surveyors committee, I was the chairman and Brian the vice chairman. We therefore had little difficulty in reaching an agreement in respect of Cubitt's claim. Pickles Brothers Ltd, based in Halifax, was a company in the same group as George

Longden and Sons Ltd and managed by an old friend, Ray Walker. They were experiencing disputes with local authorities in the Yorkshire area and Ray, having heard I had started up on my own, got in touch. I provided dispute resolution services for Ray for many years thereafter.

3.7 Technology was slow to arrive, unlike the twenty-first century when there is something new almost each month. There were no calculators when I commenced my firm in 1973, all calculations had to be completed manually. However in the early part of 1974 I noticed in a stationer's shop window in Manchester a calculator which was for sale at a price of £75, which is over £1000 in 2014 money. However I realised if I purchased one it would save a vast amount of time in respect of the quantity surveying work I was still undertaking, and so took the plunge. Typing was mainly undertaken on manual typewriters, but electric versions were starting to become available. It wasn't however until the 1990s that word processors came into common use. As I was the only person operating a one stop shop relating to dispute resolution in the construction industry, there was no existing system for me to follow, it was necessary therefore for me to develop my own. I decided that my client's entitlements, whether in respect of time and/or money, should be encapsulated in one fully comprehensive document headed "Construction Claim". The Claim would tell the story of the events relating to the dispute which could be understood by anybody unconnected with the project, without having to refer to any other document or person. All the factual matters were fully set out at the beginning of the document with copies of all relevant documents such as correspondence, site meeting minutes, diary entries, Architect's or Engineer's Instructions and the like bound together in an Appendix, cross referenced to the text. Legal arguments with supporting legal cases would follow the factual matters. A fully detailed evaluation setting out the claimant's financial entitlement was located at the end of the document, before the Appendix. The Claims I produced became well known in the industry and were said to strike fear into the hearts of many on the receiving end. In time others began offering the same service and my format became the industry standard.

CHAPTER TWO

TAKING ON STAFF

3.8 I had been in business for about six months and reached the stage where, due to the volume of work I was undertaking, I couldn't manage it all myself. In my opinion it would be extremely difficult to build up a business using only freelance consultants, who are very useful in dealing with a work bulge, but not helpful in building up client relationships. I decided to advertise for permanent staff, a trainee and an experienced quantity surveyor. I received several applications and among those interviewed for the trainee position was Paul Cookson. He was 18 years old and I took to him immediately as a result of his opening remark to the effect that he had attended a significant number of interviews and hadn't been offered a job and assumed the same would apply with regard to the position I was trying to fill. Not what one would have thought to be a winning line, however it appealed to me. Paul turned out to be a first class trainee who learned quickly and was willing to undertake whatever task was asked of him. However, when they were handing out good luck Paul was at the back of the queue, as the turn of events never went in his favour. At the time there was a television advertisement which featured a man for whom matters never went well. After the short scenario forming the story line in the advertisement in which some disaster befell the man, a voice-over was heard to say

"How does he do it Stanley?" Paul became known by all as Stanley. He came into my office on one occasion for a chat. It seems that his mother married just after Paul was born and Paul took his stepfather's name of Cookson. However the name on his birth certificate was that of his mother. Paul was intending to apply for his first passport and wondered what he should do as he had to submit with the application form his birth certificate on which his mother's name appeared, but wanted the name Cookson to appear on the passport. I looked into the procedure for a name change and it appeared that a person could change his or her name whenever he or she wished. However the advice was that evidence may be required to prove the name had been changed. This could be done either formally by what was known as Deed Poll or less formally by means of an announcement in one of a specified list of periodicals and in the list appeared the Manchester Evening News. Paul decided to go for the informal method and I drafted an announcement for him to have inserted. During the evenings Paul was employed at a local casino as a croupier and after about two years of working for me he tendered his resignation as he had secured a full time job as a croupier. I heard no more from Paul for about ten years when I received a phone call from his mother. It appears that Paul had married a Chinese lady and acquired a job as a croupier in South Africa. At the time intermarriage between Chinese and Europeans was to say the least frowned upon by the South African Authorities. Paul had come onto their radar no doubt due to him having a Chinese wife and questions were being asked as to why the name in his birth certificate differed from that in his passport. I thought to myself at the time "How does he do it Stanley?" I advised Paul's mother to contact the Manchester Evening News and secure a copy of the insert announcing Paul's change of name and send it off to him. I never heard from him, or of him, again.

3.9 Of the experienced quantity surveyors I interviewed, Mike Wills stood out head and shoulders above the others and

I had no hesitation in offering him the job. Mike had been working for Inman and Partners in the Midlands and at 25 years of age, with nine years' experience behind him, was well versed in all quantity surveying matters. As I was still securing quantity surveying work, Mike took control of that aspect of the business and also got himself into line with the dispute resolution services. Mike proved to be excellent in every respect and was still with the company forty years later. From my first day in business my wife Wendy had been the receptionist and secretary. However this only lasted for six months as she became pregnant with our daughter Beverley and so left to become a full time mother. For most expectant fathers, particularly as this was to be my one and only offspring, the day your child is born lives with you for ever. Even England losing to Poland in the World Cup on that day didn't prove to be a damper. For the remainder of the two years we spent in Manchester we made do with temporary receptionist/secretaries. The only other member of staff recruited during this period was Angus Morris, a young Scotsman who, having some experience as a quantity surveyor, slotted in between Paul and Mike.

3.10 During the 1970s the United Kingdom had been subject to high inflation which can be seen from the following chart:

Year Annual Rate of Inflation

1970 6.4%
1971 9.40%
1972 7.10%
1973 9.2%
1974 16.0%
1975 24.2%
1976 16.5%
1977 15.8%

1978 8.3%
1979 13.4%
1980 18.0%

During the 1970s the trade unions were ever vocal concerning wage increases, which were consistently less that the rate of inflation. The National Union of Mineworkers (NUM) was particularly vociferous in its claims for pay increases on behalf of its members The NUM called an all-out strike which commenced on 9th January 1972 and involved the closure of 135 Coal Board pits and 85 private mines. Pickets were manned at power stations, steelworks and coal depots. Dockers also gave support in refusing to unload coal from ships. As the mid-1970s approached, inflation was beginning to look like a runaway train. In an effort to control inflation the government capped public sector pay rises and publically promoted a capped level on pay in the private sector. This caused unrest among the trade unions as wages regularly lagged behind price increases. By the middle of 1973 the National Union of Mine Workers was again requiring its members to work to rule which resulted in coal stocks dwindling. This led to an increase in the price of coal. The 1973 oil crisis also put pressure on the price of coal. The oil crisis resulted from an embargo introduced by OPEC (Organisation of Petroleum Exporting Countries) on 16th October 1973 which affected USA, United Kingdom, Japan, Netherlands and Canada and resulted from the USA providing support to Israel during the Yom Kippur war. This had a serious effect on the oil price in the world market which increased from 3 dollars per barrel to 12 dollars per barrel. By the end of 1973 the miners had dropped from first to eighteenth in the pay league and following unsuccessful claims for a substantial pay rise voted for a strike which commenced on 9th February 1974. Edward Heath the Prime Minister, at his wits end, decided to challenge the NUM by calling a general election on 28th February 1974 using the slogan "Who Rules the Country?" The voters gave their answer by electing more Labour Party candidates than Tory. Unfortunately the Labour Party didn't command an overall majority and therefore operated with a hung parliament. This was followed by the restoration of the normal working week on 8th March 1974, but certain restrictions on the use of electricity were retained. The Labour Government negotiated a settlement with the NUM who ordered the striking miners back to work at the end of March 1974. There were two aspects of the settlement in addition to a pay rise. A scheme was implemented to compensate miners who suffered from pneumoconiosis together with a miners' superannuation scheme. A second general election was held in October 1974 when the Labour Party was elected with a four seat majority.

A further miners' strike took place in 1984. The government, led by Margaret Thatcher, announced on 6th March 1984 its intention to close 20 pits in the immediate future with the loss of 20,000 jobs, together with a further 70 pits at a later stage. This resulted in a mass walk out and a strike which was made official by the NUM on12th March 1984. The strike however was ill timed as it was the beginning of spring when the need for coal was less than when the 1974 strike took place and also the coal stocks at the time were more than adequate. The miners also found in Margaret Thatcher a much tougher opponent than Edward Heath. The most sensational event that took place during the strike was the "Battle of Orgreave" which occurred on 18th June 1984 at the Orgreave Coking Plant in Rotherham involving 5,000 miners and 5,000 police. 51 picketers and 70 policemen were injured that day. South Yorkshire Police eventually paid out £425,000 in compensation to strikers who were arrested. The strike came to an end on 3rd March 1985 when Arthur Scargill, the NUM president, accepted defeat and the miners went back to work.

3.11 I received a telephone call in late 1974 from Brian Hill, the Chief Quantity Surveyor at Holland Hannen and Cubitts. At the time Cubitts, in common with many other contractors, was working on two year fixed price contracts. Inflation by that time was running into double figures, well above the financial provisions included in the price, which often led to projects making losses. Brian was looking for ways to boost the financial recovery on these contracts and started to examine carefully the performance of the Architect with regard to the timing and content of the Architect's Instructions. He realised that success in making claims for late issue of instructions and additional work relied upon the evidence he was able to produce with regard to the effects in terms of delay to the progress and completion of the work and additional cost. To succeed with this type of claim it was essential for the contractor to produce good quality site records and supporting correspondence. Brian asked if I was prepared to present a one day training course to his site staff on the need for retaining good records, producing appropriate correspondence and the format they should take. It seemed obvious to me that one of the rules of survival in business is never to let a rival provide services to a client if it can be avoided. Worried that if I said the task was outside my skill base, Brian would find somebody else to undertake the task, I responded that it would present me with no difficulty to put on the training course. In my own mind I was fairly confident that although I had never undertaken anything like a training course before, I would cope. A few days later Brian was back on the phone advising me that the course had to last for two days, as this was a condition laid down by the Construction Industry Training Board (CITB) from which they were seeking a grant. I advised Brian that this would cause no problem at all. A few days later Brian was again on the telephone to advise me that a CITB representative would be present through-out the course to ensure it met with their standards, again being a condition of the award of the grant. My response was to say that the presence of the CITB representative would be more than welcome.

3.12 My decision to undertake the two days' training for Brian Hill turned out to be one of the best business decisions I ever made. Training and lecturing became a key part of the services we provided and was a lead in for many of the business opportunities that came our way. I got on very well with the representative from the CITB and at the end of the two days he said he would like a word with me. It seemed that the CITB in the North West ran training courses for construction management and would I be interested in taking on the role of trainer? They were late afternoon/evening courses run on the first Monday in every month except for holiday periods. My predecessor as trainer was Vincent Powell Smith, a very colourful and well known barrister, but his term of office had come to an end and a replacement was required. The venue was Warrington Technical College and the format comprised a start at 4 pm with a cup of tea. I was advised that the course should comprise a 30 minute introduction to enable the trainer to set the scene and then the delegates should be set work in groups, after which there would be discussion. There was no set time for finishing, it was a matter of drawing matters to a close when the trainer considered the delegates were starting to lose interest, which in my case turned out to be about 8.30 pm, after which there was then beer and sandwiches laid on. These training courses were very successful and many of the delegates came every month. The North Wales branch of the CITB also occasionally held these training courses in Chester and Rhyl, where again I acted as trainer. These courses were the result of a local initiative on the part of the CITB management, who no doubt when attending the courses gave of their own time. Unfortunately after about two years, due to changes introduced by CITB HQ which were unpopular with the local management, disillusionment set in and the courses came to an end. I gave one more lecture for the CITB after those in the North West were terminated and that was at their headquarters in Kings Lynn. When asked if I was prepared to give the lecture I agreed as was my norm. I knew that Kings Lynn was in the east of the country, a little beyond Lincoln was my recollection. When I came to drive to Kings Lynn from Cheshire it became clear there was a long way to go after passing through Lincoln before Kings Lynn came into sight.

3.13 A delegate on one of the CITB courses approached me saying that he had recently attended a course involving construction contracts and law run by Shaws Linton Courses Ltd. He told me that they were looking for another trainer and if I was interested to ring Richard Martin the MD, whose telephone number he provided. I duly rang Richard and arranged to meet him at a hotel near Hyde Park. I liked Richard immediately we met. He explained that they ran various courses including those on construction contracts and law at locations all around the country from September to May. After about half an hour's chatting he offered me a job to act as one of their trainers, to which I readily agreed. I was a trainer for Shaws Linton Courses for nine months per year usually three or four days per month from 1974 to 1982. The courses were held as far north as Newcastle, down to Southampton in the south. Shaws Linton Courses was owned by Tony Swash. I only met him on one occasion when he acted as administrator at one of their courses which was held in Bristol where I was the trainer. Tony explained that he considered that a company styled Swash would not prove successful and so he used Shaws which is an anagram of Swash, Linton being his wife's maiden name. He seemed a very precise man which was illustrated by my request at the beginning of the day for him to enquire as to the times of the trains which would take me to London at the end of the afternoon. I also asked him to order me a taxi. At lunch time he advised that a London train was due to leave Bristol at 5.30 pm, however due to possible traffic congestion he didn't advise going by taxi. It seems he had walked from the venue to the railway station which he timed at 15 minutes. He therefore advised that if I left promptly at the end of the course, which was scheduled to finish at 5.00pm, there would be adequate time to walk to the station, for which he gave me directions, and catch the 5.30 train. Even though I worked for Shaws Linton Courses for eight years this was my one and only contact with Tony Swash. I ceased working for Shaws Linton Courses in 1982 when we at James R Knowles started to run our own training courses. Eventually we ran them all over the country and also in East Asia, Australia and the Middle East. They acted as an excellent marketing tool and in addition produced significant profits.

3.14 It was the ambition of most quantity surveyors to sit the necessary examination and become a qualified member of the Royal Institution of Chartered Surveyors (RICS), a passport to good job opportunities. This was before polytechnics and later universities began running degree courses in quantity surveying with degree entry into the RICS becoming the norm. The RICS had a good set up which was controlled from the headquarters in Great George Street in London. Entry was open to all the surveying disciplines such as land surveying, mining surveying, building surveying, as well as quantity surveying, which had more members than the others. As an RICS qualified quantity surveyor, one was entitled to be styled as a Chartered Quantity Surveyor, a badge which was worn with pride. The RICS had a branch structure with the whole of the country divided into separate branches. When I worked in Shrewsbury I belonged to the Salop, Hereford and Mid-Wales branch; whilst in Manchester it was the Greater Manchester branch. Each branch had its own chairman, secretary, treasurer and committee which met regularly and organised meetings of professional interest for its members. There was also a well-attended and much enjoyed annual dinner. This was all very popular with the members who could see something they were getting for their annual subscription. The RICS also produced a magazine of general interest for all members. A decision was taken in 1974 to produce a second magazine designed specifically for quantity surveyors entitled The Chartered Quantity Surveyor. They were looking to appoint members who were prepared to write regular articles on contract and legal matters and I volunteered along with Cliff Cowen whom I knew well. It was decided that we would write our articles on alternate months, however at a very early stage Cliff withdrew from the arrangement and I took over writing a 1000 word article which I fulfilled each month for eighteen consecutive years. There was no internet in those days and hence up-to-date information was difficult to acquire. My articles covered recent legal cases which affected construction, new standard forms of construction contracts and recent amendment to standard construction contracts. The articles were well read and hence greatly assisted in the publicity of my services. An added bonus was that I was paid £130 for writing the articles, which remained at this level for the full eighteen years. I have however since written many articles for technical magazines and never been paid as much as a penny.

3.15 In 1992 the RICS decided upon a major change in that they completely disbanded the branch system. By then degree entry had become the norm and there was a need for Continuing Professional Development (CPD). It was also decided that there should be no different identities for the several disciplines within the RICS. Members were advised that they could no longer style themselves as Chartered Quantity Surveyors, all would be known as Chartered Surveyors. In place of the various disciplines the RICS set up separate Faculties and members were asked to choose which faculty or faculties they would like to join. Of the faculties on offer I decided that the Construction Faculty and the Dispute Resolution Faculty were the most appropriate. In the process of change, the RICS ceased to produce the Chartered Quantity Surveyor magazine. The branch structure was sadly missed by members as the branch meetings provided a forum for them to get together and discuss matters of mutual professional interest. CPD training Courses were organised centrally on a commercial basis by the RICS in competition with other training organisations. The branch meetings have not been replaced and are sorely missed.

CHAPTER THREE

EXPANSION

3.16 Work often comes from unexpected sources. Our offices in Canada House in Manchester were on the ground floor, and another tenant, Poole Dick and Partners, a firm of Quantity Surveyors, on the top floor. Dennis Dick was the senior partner and one of his fellow partners was Peter Barlow, who became senior partner when Dennis retired. Peter came into my office one day in 1974 with regard to an enquiry he had received from Worthy Thompson, a small building contractor, based in Denton, a sub-district of Manchester and whose owner was Bill Thompson. It seems that Worthy Thompson was in dispute with the Borough of Trafford in relation to the construction of a new school and needed professional help. Poole Dick was not an expert in dispute resolution and in any event the Borough of Trafford was a client and so they declined the offer to undertake the commission. Peter thought that I may be interested and provided me with Bill Thompson's telephone number. This was right up my street and hence I arranged to meet Bill with whom from the outset I got on with famously. We met at Bill's office where he explained the problems involved with the project which related to delay and disruption caused by the late issue of design information by the Borough of Trafford and that he needed to secure a substantial payment from them which they had declined to make. Bill indicated that there were a great many files relating to the project and that his in-house quantity surveyor, Harold Jepson, would produce them and provide me with any assistance I may require. Harold was in his early twenties and being very sharp saved me a great deal of leg work. A few years later Bill became insolvent and Harold came to work for me, a position he held for about twenty-five years. The dispute related to an overrun on the completion date due, according to Bill Thompson, to the late issue of drawings by the Architect employed by Trafford Borough Council. Worthy Thompson's costs as a direct result were considerably more than they would have been if the work had finished on time and therefore Bill considered that Worthy Thompson was entitled to be reimbursed these additional costs by his client. I produced one of my legendary claim documents which was submitted to the council. After an exchange of correspondence which was inconclusive I managed to arrange a meeting with the Chief Quantity Surveyor of the Borough of Trafford. There were only three of us at the meeting the Chief Quantity Surveyor, Harold and myself. We went through each item in the claim and whilst the Chief Quantity Surveyor agreed with a few of the additional cost items, he gave the thumbs down to many of the others. We were getting to the end of the list of cost items, the penultimate one being the shortfall in the head office recovery due to the overrun for which I had claimed a somewhat large amount. This is a controversial item, but receives support in the leading text book Hudson's Building and Engineering Contracts, a copy of which I noticed resided on the Chief Quantity Surveyor's book shelf. The solution I suggested was that we should accept whatever was indicated in the Hudson text book. The Chief Quantity Surveyor expressed the view that I must have known what was stated in the text book to have made the suggestion. He indicated that he didn't know what was included, but if it was recommended in a text book, he would have no difficulty in justifying it to the auditors. We agreed a final payment of £35,000 which was a considerable sum in those days and more than the £30,000 for which Bill had hoped.

3.17 The lease was coming to an end at Canada House and a decision had to be made whether to renew it or move to other premises. The workload was steadily increasing and I was considering taking on more staff. This being the case I made a decision that a move would be the best option. What area of office space would we require and where, required a fairly quick decision. I had been giving some thought to the problem for a week or two and Wendy my wife suggested we move to Knutsford. My first reaction was to dismiss the idea on the grounds that the likelihood of there being offices to let in Knutsford which would meet our needs was remote. It is never a good policy to argue with one's wife on such matters and she immediately produced the local newspaper in which offices in Knutsford were advertised to let. They were located in King Street, which is the main street in the town, over a row of shops, opposite the Angel Hotel, with good car parking at the rear. The rent was easily affordable and the accommodation comprised seven rooms which would hold a dozen or so staff plus a small reception room, and I decided that this accommodation would be ideal for our future growth. Knutsford is a small picturesque market town located in Cheshire and is recorded in William the Conqueror's Doomsday Book (1086). The centre of Knutsford is situated on an incline with two main streets running parallel, Princess Street known as Top Street and King Street known as Bottom Street due to their relative positions on the incline. There are a few famous names associated with Knutsford. It was here that Mr Rolls first met Mr Royce and what a great team they turned out to be. Elizabeth Gaskell, the famous writer, in her book Cranford wrote about life in Knutsford where she lived for many years. She married a Unitarian minister and when she died on 12th November 1865 she was buried in Brook Street Unitarian churchyard in Knutsford. King Canute, according to local legend, when on one occasion he was in the area, crossed the River Lily which runs through the centre of Knutsford, but is little more than a stream now. Barbara Knox, the Coronation Street actress, resided in Knutsford when we first arrived, but later moved to Mobberley a village located nearby. Geoff Pullar, a star cricketer who played with distinction as an opening batsman for Lancashire, Gloucester and England in the 1950s and 60s made his home in Knutsford until he sadly passed away on Christmas Day 2014. Geoff had an impressive batting average for England of 43.86. He was the first Lancashire player to score a century for England at Old Trafford in a Test Match and in 1959 he scored three centuries for Lancashire against Yorkshire. He was always known as Noddy, due to his practise of taking a nap in the dressing room. Geoff being an opening batsman, from time to time found that his batting duties were over in the early part of his team's innings, which left him time for a snooze whilst his team mates carried on at the wicket. Cricketer's earnings were modest in those times and after his playing days were over Geoff opened a sandwich shop in Top Street. Some years later I arranged for a taxi to collect me early one morning from my home. It was dark when the taxi arrived as so I was unable to see the driver's face. It is my practice to sit next to the driver to enable us to have a chat during the journey. On this occasion the driver mentioned that he had in times past owned a sandwich shop on Top Street and supplied my firm with his products. My response was to ask whether the shop was the one which had at one time been owned by Noddy Pullar. The response was "I am Noddy Pullar." Noddy had sold up and gone into the taxi business. I became very friendly with Noddy thereafter and was very saddened when I received the news that he had died.

3.18 With the increase in workload, it became clear that I needed to take on experienced staff. Mike Wills assisted by Angus Morris were doing an excellent job, but we were unable to cope comfortably with the workload which was growing and I was reluctant to rely on freelance consultants.

During the next twelve months I recruited three top line employees whom I felt were capable of building up relationships with clients and securing repeat business. I was delighted that Richard Davies, my old colleague from L C Wakeman and Partners, agreed to join me and also Bill Minnitt and John Wood. Bill turned out to be a really good work gatherer. He was friendly with Eddie Walmsley, the secretary of the National Federation of Building Trades Employees, North West Division who invited Bill to attend one of its meetings. It seems that the Federation used Freedmans, a London-based company of solicitors, for providing contractual and legal advice. A significant amount of the advice was given over the telephone to members for which they received a lump sum annual fee, but if matters became more involved then the legal processes took their normal course with the usual fee arrangement applying. This process was due for its annual renewal which would be confirmed at the forthcoming meeting. When the matter was being discussed Bill suggested that the Federation may wish to consider using James R Knowles, a local firm, in preference to Freedmans a London-based firm. It was decided that both Freedmans and ourselves be invited to submit a proposal for providing the service. Bill and I discussed the matter and I indicated that we should offer the telephone advice for a nil fee. My logic was that most of the queries raised by members over the telephone could be answered without any research, as they would normally relate to the standard construction contracts with which we were very familiar. This should not take long but may lead to a more detailed involvement for which a fee could be charged. Freedmans in their submission required a fee for the telephone advice and so we were given the commission. Over the next few years this commission provided a significant amount of work and only came to an end when the Federation started to employ its own in-house specialists. John Wood came from Macclesfield Borough Council and brought with him extensive knowledge of how local authorities operate. Being a good pub darts player he organised sessions to enable us all to relax for a while at lunch time, with the dart board secured behind the door in his office. I recruited Richard Burke, another experienced operator with whom John shared a room and worked on a number of projects over several years. In those early days in Knutsford we were also joined by George Goodchild a former partner in a quantity surveying practice and Derek Eccles who had been the Chief Quantity Surveyor for Balfour Beatty, both of whom brought considerable expertise to the company. I was keen only to recruit experienced staff who could be left to get on with the work without supervision and had the ability to secure repeat business.

3.19 Due to my lecturing for Shaws Linton Courses Ltd and the article writing for the Chartered Quantity Surveyor, the name started to become known countrywide and hence we received enquiries from various locations some of which were dealt with by me. I recall a telephone call I received from John Foxall of Shrewsbury Building Contractors requesting me to attend at his office as he was experiencing a tricky contractual problem. From my days of working in Shrewsbury I was aware of Shrewsbury Building Contractors but hadn't met John. A great deal of their work was for Shropshire County Council whose offices were located in Shrewsbury adjacent to the Column, a famous landmark in the town. The Column is 133 feet 6 inches high surmounted by a 17 feet high statue of Lord Hill, built between 1814 and 1816. John's company had a contractual problem in relation to the construction of a new school for the County Council. The work had a time over-run of twenty-eight weeks which had resulted in the project making a substantial loss. It seems that during the course of the work the Architect had issued a substantial number of variations to the design which had involved additional work and hence the delay to completion and additional cost. John had sought an extension in the time for completion plus payment of money to cover the additional costs. John had written to the council and met some of its officers but he had come away empty handed. It seemed to me that John had a requirement for one of my notorious claims which I duly prepared and John submitted. Within approximately four weeks a reply arrived from the County Architect's Department granting a full extension of time of twenty-eight weeks but nil in respect of the money claim. John was delighted by the extension of time but disheartened with regard to the money. However I assured him he would in due course secure a payment which would satisfy him. A meeting was duly arranged with Mr Bunker who was the County Architect, John and me. Mr Bunker explained that the extension of time was granted to ensure that Shrewsbury Building Contractors didn't have a liability to pay liquidated damages for the delay and that it had been granted by the Architect's Department almost as an act of charity. I explained to Mr Bunker that in granting the extension of time, his department was recognising that the variations his Architects had issued were responsible for causing the delay to the completion; this being the case there was no alternative to the County Council paying Shrewsbury Building Contractors the cost of the delay. However Mr Bunker was not convinced, explaining that the granting of the extension of time was intended only to relieve Shrewsbury Building Contractors of the obligation to pay liquidated damages resulting from the delay. After the meeting John, who over the years had been on the receiving end of blank refusals by the County Architect's Department's staff to his reasonable entitlements, was delighted that I had given Mr Bunker what we would now refer to as a hard time. John said he would be happy to pay my fee just to witness the County Architect getting his comeuppance, even if Shrewsbury Building Contractors received no payment at all. Shortly thereafter the task of resolving the matter was transferred to the County Council's Chief Quantity Surveyor, Dave Barker, who settled the matter to John's satisfaction.

3.20 From the outset I had undertaken the book-keeping, dealt with salaries and PAYE and managed the bank account. The year-end accounts and auditing were undertaken by Percy

Westhead and Co which was owned by Roy Ham. Roy was a friend who had lived close to me during our boyhood and it was natural for me when looking for an accountant to turn to him. However the time was swiftly arriving when I would need to appoint an in-house accountant to undertake book-keeping, deal with the salaries and manage the bank account, and with this in mind I inserted an advertisement in the Manchester Evening News for a part-time accountant to work 25 hours per week. An elderly gentleman by the name of Arthur Shaw arrived at my office for an interview and opened the conversation by saying "Well lad how many years are you behind with the accounts?" He went on to cross-examine me for the next half hour concerning the financial affairs of the firm and then announced that he would take the job. As he was the only applicant I had little choice but to appoint him. Despite his brusque manner I took to him and considered that his experience was just what we needed. Arthur was 63 years of age when he joined and over eighty when he finally retired. He loved working for the firm and handed in his notice to me with tears in his eyes. It seems he could no longer climb the stairs and as there was no lift he felt it time to go. His dedication to the firm was unmatched. I recall saying to him on one occasion that there was no need for me to worry about the financial health of the firm as he did more than enough for the two of us. By the time Arthur retired we had appointed a Finance Director and didn't replace Arthur.

3.21 When we had about fifteen employees on our books I received a visit from Chris Templer, a representative of Equitable Life Assurance Co, who was looking to sell me a company pension scheme. I wasn't much enamoured with company pension schemes as at the time, a transfer of pension arrangements, when a person changed his employer, was difficult without a reduction in the likely pension pay-outs. In addition I didn't want to employ people who stayed working for the firm to ensure they would receive a maximum pension. I therefore explained this as politely as I could to Chris and bade him farewell. In view of the problems Equitable life Assurance got themselves into in later years by guaranteeing sums to be paid out after pension age, which they found impossible financially to fulfil, it was just as well that I decided to bypass a company pension scheme. However I did make an exception and paid Arthur Shaw a pension until he and later his wife had passed away, which was financed out of cash flow. Arthur was the only former employee ever to receive a company pension.

3.22 I was ambitious, but never developed a business plan of any sort whatsoever. My plans were all short term made on the hoof. I decided that expansion would be best achieved by opening branch offices. My theory was that few companies would wish to appoint a consultant who had to travel many miles, involving unnecessary expense, if there was an alternative locally. We had several clients in Liverpool and Manchester and I was familiar with the construction industry and its participants in both areas and took the view that branch offices in these two cities was the direction in which the firm should be going. To my way of thinking recruiting people from outside the company to manage these offices was too much of a risk. However I needed persons who could attract business, and as Richard Davies had experience of running the Liverpool office of L C Wakeman and Partners and was first class in every respect, he was the obvious choice to manage our Liverpool office. It had never been in my thinking to share the ownership with any other person. It seems that another owner would only be necessary if additional capital was required, which couldn't be secured by borrowing, or he or she brought to the party some special expertise which I didn't possess. Neither of these applied and therefore the thought of a joint owner never arose in my mind. However when it came to running a branch office the thought occurred that, as many of the clients would arrive as a result of the efforts of the local manager, there may be a temptation for him to go on a frolic of his own, leave the company and take the business with him and therefore joint ownership may be the answer. I informed Richard Davies that I was considering creating the Liverpool office as a stand-alone business and would he like a share of the ownership; an offer which he immediately politely declined. This set the pattern for the future and whilst I opened several branch offices later in my career, until we moved into the overseas market, I refrained from offering a branch manager any share in the business. Richard would need good help if the office was to succeed and to do so recruited George Anderton and Vince Deane, both of whom were excellent choices. The office in Liverpool was very successful. Shortly after the Liverpool office was established I opened an office in Manchester and appointed Bill Minnitt as the manager. Bill, having good contacts with the National Federation of Building Trades Employees and its secretary Eddie Walmersley, secured from the outset a good flow of work. Bill was not the best qualified consultant we employed, but he had an air of confidence which clients found attractive. Bill appointed Ray Melling as his number two, who when Bill left some years later to plough his own furrow, took over as the manager.

CHAPTER FOUR

THATCHER YEARS AND FALKLANDS WAR

3.23 Major changes were taking place in the government of the country with the arrival at 10 Downing Street of Margaret Thatcher. She became prime minister when the Tories won the 1979 election and remained in post until November 1990. The government policy, of which she was the main instigator, was to reduce the involvement of the state in people's lives and increase individual self-reliance. Her government followed a radical programme of privatisation and deregulation, reform of trade unions and tax cuts. She was instrumental in putting a stop to the government financing loss-making industries which led to many people employed in the manufacturing industries facing the dole. It is said that over a period of three years in the early 1980s over two million were put out of work by this policy. On the opposite side of the coin the Tories under Margaret Thatcher, were responsible for stripping away government regulations which had restricted businesses and as a result made them more efficient. Privatisation of state industries was high on her agenda which resulted in the sell-off of water, power and railways. One of her most popular policies was the sale of council homes to the tenants, often at well below market value. The decision to close many of the uneconomical coal mines led to great opposition from the National Union of Mineworkers and resulted in the year-long strikes which took place in 1984 and 1985. What she learned from this strike was instrumental in her introducing legislation which curbed flying pickets and closed shops. One of the first actions she took when coming to power, anticipating trouble with the unions, was to substantially increase the pay of the police, as a result of which she became very popular with them. Mrs Thatcher was the daughter of Alf Roberts, a grocer from Grantham, and learned at an early age that expenditure should not exceed income. She considered this principle was as valid in respect of government policy as it was for her father's grocery business. With this in mind she set out to make sure that the government balanced its books. Unfortunately this policy wasn't followed by successive governments, who were more interested in introducing popular vote-winning policies, which involved giving away large amounts of tax payer's money, much of it to those who could live well without it. The annual government expenditure in 2013 was £100 billion in excess of income with the total government debt standing at approximately £1.3 trillion. There was an annual interest payment on the debt of £46 billion, which equates to the total sum of money spent on defence and just short of the total spent on education. Margaret Thatcher who died 2013, must have turned over in her grave.

3.24 The most momentous event which occurred during the Thatcher years was the Falklands war. For many years Argentina had claimed sovereignty over the Falkland Islands, referred to in the Argentine as the Malvinas, on the basis that they had been acquired from Spain in the 1800s. As the United Kingdom had occupied the territory for 150 years they claimed sovereignty to be theirs. There had been alarm at the landing of some Argentinean scrap metal merchants and marines in South Georgia, one of the Falkland Islands, on 19th March 1982 and the raising of the Argentine flag. As a result of this provocative action, HMS Endurance was dispatched to South Georgia. Shortly after, a crisis meeting was held headed by Margaret Thatcher, at which the Chief of Naval Staff, Admiral Sir Henry Leach, advised that Britain could and should send a task force if the islands were invaded. On 2nd April 1982 Argentina invaded the Falkland Islands, hoping to divert attention away from the economic crisis which had badly affected the country and resulted in civil unrest. There was a token resistance, organised by the Governor Rex Hunt, which proved unsuccessful. A decision had to be made by the British government as to what response should be made and it was decided to recapture the Falkland Islands which surprised the Argentineans. On 6th April 1982 the British Government set up a War Cabinet which met daily to provide political oversight of the campaign. A task force was rapidly put together employing whatever vessels were available. The nuclear submarine Conqueror set sail on 4th April and two aircraft carriers, Invincible and Hermes in the company of escort vessels left Portsmouth a day later. Ocean liners S-S Canberra and Queen Elizabeth II set sail on 7th April and 12th May respectively, followed by other ships. The British had 42 aircraft which were quickly assembled on Ascension Island compared with 122 mobilised by Argentina. A decision was taken to mount an invasion which commenced on 21st April when troops first landed on South Georgia, which was recaptured without too much trouble. Air and sea battles took place before a landing was achieved on the main islands. HMS Conqueror sank the General Belgrano on 2nd May when 323 men were killed. Two days later the British lost HMS Sheffield following an Exocet missile strike, when 20 of the crew were killed and 24 severely injured. On 21st May the British Amphibious Task Group made a landing on the beaches of East Falkland, which became known as bomb alley by the British troops, due to the low level air attacks by the Argentinean air force. However they managed to secure a beach head, the intention being to capture Darwin and Goose Green before going on to Port Stanley, the capital. Unfortunately, due to a lack of adequate anti-aircraft defences, the British lost HMS Ardent on 21st May, and on 2nd June HMS Antelope and MV Atlantic Conveyor which was struck by two Exocets. On 27th and 28th May after fierce fighting Darwin and Goose Green were taken. It was in this battle that Lieutenant Colonel H Jones lost his life at the head of his battalion, while charging into a well prepared Argentinean position. He was posthumously awarded the Victoria Cross. Port Stanley was the last part of the Falklands to be attacked and was heavily defended. However the British forces overcame the resistance and a cease-fire was ordered on 14th June when the Argentineans surrendered. The outcome of the war was never a foregone conclusion. In his book My Secret Falklands War, Sidney Edwards recounts that he was appointed by the British Government to secure a South American ally. The South American countries were all solidly behind Argentina except for Chile. They didn't wish to step out of line, however as they were in dispute with Argentina over the Beagle Channel, they provided assistance in a clandestine manner. Chile offered total co-operation within what was practically and diplomatically possible. Mr Edwards, with the co-operation of Chile, co-ordinated long range radar to detect Argentine troop movements. The Chileans also allowed the use of their airports by British fighter planes. Mr Edwards considers that without the assistance of Chile, the British would have lost the war. In an effort to evade the British air defence the Argentine pilots released bombs at low altitude which failed to explode as a result of the bombs' fuses not having sufficient time to arm before impact. Thirteen bombs hit British ships without detonating and as a result Lord Craig, the retired Marshal of the RAF, is said to have remarked "Six better fuses and we would have lost".

3.25 Mrs Thatcher's downfall resulted from her support of the Poll Tax and her ambivalent attitude towards the European Union. The Community Charge, the official title of the Poll Tax, was a system of tax first introduced into Scotland in

1989 and Wales and England in 1990 and replaced the rate system which was a method of charging tax on the assessed rental value of the property. Rates were levied by local authorities which, together with grants paid to them by the government, provided the necessary finance to run the services they provided in their area. By way of contrast the Poll Tax was levied at a rate fixed by the local authority on every adult in the country, except for the unemployed, who only paid 20% of the tax and students who paid nothing. The sum charged per head varied dependent upon the local authority, some councils charging a great deal more than others. It resulted, by and large, in families living in large houses, normally the wealthy, paying less in poll tax than they had in rates, with families living in small houses, usually the poor, paying more. The tax was hugely unpopular and led to a riot in London in 1990 when 340 of the rioters were arrested and 45 policemen injured. There were also disturbances in other parts of the country. Many people who rented property didn't pay the tax as they were regularly on the move and efforts to pursue them for the money often proved fruitless. Margaret Thatcher and her government accepted defeat and the Community Charge was replaced by the Council Tax in 1992, which was very similar to the rating system, but with properties being placed in bands based on capital value not rental value. It is surprising that a politician as astute as Margaret Thatcher would support a tax which in all probability was likely to result in there being more of the electorate who would be financial losers than winners.

CHAPTER FIVE

OPENED OFFICES IN SHEFFIELD AND LONDON

3.26 I have always regarded myself as a professional person first and businessman second. Making large sums of money was never my motivation. I spent little time examining the books of accounts and seeking methods of cutting cost. My pride lay in the quality of the work we produced and with that in mind I was always anxious to recruit the best people available which often meant paying over the odds in terms of salary, but in the end in my opinion it worked out beneficial. I was fortunate in my recruitment drive as those interested in undertaking dispute work were driven in my direction as I was the only company offering that type of service and thus able to take the pick of the crop. When interviewing candidates I was looking not just for professionals with the right sort of knowledge and experience, but those who demonstrated an entrepreneurial outlook as I needed others who were capable of helping to build up the business. Due to the type of work we undertook, I enlisted only experienced personnel and was very fortunate in recruiting over a ten year period some very exceptional people. I had three offices up and running but with no particular plans in place for further expansion, my policy was to examine opportunities as they presented themselves and if none came along to create some. Common sense usually had a part to play in my decision making but from time to time, looking back in retrospect, it seemed to have flown out through the window.

3.27 I operated the firm using few systems and even less rules and regulations. I liked the managers and staff to use their own initiative when faced with a problem; I certainly didn't encourage them to keep ringing me, but I was always willing to offer advice if asked. Where wrong decisions were made, there were no recriminations, but usually where appropriate, a chat to see why matters had turned out the way they had, together with a bit of friendly advice. We billed all clients monthly which was unusual for professional organisations at the time. Quantity Surveyors billed when certain tasks had been completed, such as the production of the Bill of Quantities. The Royal Institute of British Architects laid down in their standard fee agreement the various stages during the design and construction process at which the client should be billed. Solicitors tended to often bill in advance with new clients and well after the service had been provided with regular clients. Billing monthly reduced the need for much working capital and as many of our clients were contractors whose financial position could be less than ideal, it left us less exposed to losses in the event of insolvency. I was not in favour of no-win no-fee as it was bad for cash flow and increased the exposure to not being paid. Contractors are usually more inclined to pay fees in order to keep us keen and interested in recovering money on their behalf. Once the contractor had been paid to settle the dispute, our services were no longer required and therefore we became a low priority when it came to payment. Branch offices produced their own invoices but the fees were rendered to the Head Office from which all salaries and bills were paid. We produced monthly management accounts, usually within fourteen days of the end of the month, which indicated whether we had made a profit or loss. Each office was a profit centre which made it easy to identify those offices which were making good profits and those which were not. We were therefore usually on top of the accounting situation and there were rarely any great surprises when our year end accounts were produced. Due to expansion and hence an increased workload Arthur acquired an assistant, Oriel Henthorne, who proved very effective and worked well with Arthur.

3.28 I happened to run into Tony Callard on Manchester Railway station, shortly after he and Neville Deakin had opened an office in London. On enquiring how it was progressing he, with pride in his voice, advised me that it was doing so well that they intended to take on more space. I pricked my ears up at this point; although I had no plans to open an office in London, my conversation with Tony got me thinking. Tony was due to pay his London office a visit the following day and invited me to go with him, an invitation which I readily accepted. His office was located in Dryden Street, Covent Garden where he rented desk spaces and it was Tony's intention to take on two more. Services such as providing a main reception together with a receptionist, cleaning and the like were organised by the landlord. Desk areas which were rented were surrounded by shoulder high partitions which meant that privacy was limited, but there was a conference room which all tenants were entitled to use. Those wishing to vacate were required to give three months' notice. If I was going to expand into London, which had not crossed my mind prior to meeting Tony, this seemed like the ideal solution. One of my theories is that delaying making a decision doesn't result in a better one being made. On visiting the premises with Tony, I decided there and then to take the two desk spaces which were available. I had no work, or staff, in London, but I felt that this current shortage shouldn't cause too much of a problem. Quite by chance a few days later, I bumped into Phil Brady, who had worked for me in Liverpool in my LC Wakeman and Partners days. It seems Phil had moved to London to take up a position which wasn't working out and he was looking for a change. Phil was an honest, hardworking type of man and I felt he could do a decent job for us in London. I contacted him a few days later and arranged to meet him at the new Dryden Street offices. He was a clever sort of chap and as a result became known to his colleagues as Joe 90 after the TV character who was said to be the cleverest boy in the world. Having spent an hour or so together at the Dryden Street office, I offered Phil the post of manager which he accepted. We now had an office and a manager, all that was required was some work. It soon started to arrive, the most colourful client being Finers, a small building contractor run by Miss Finer who was very nice but whose bite proved to be worse than her bark. As the workload increased, after about six months of opening we recruited Gerry Newall, another senior consultant, by which time I considered the office was well and truly established.

3.29 To use the well-worn phrase, I was busy putting myself about. My commitment to Shaws Linton Courses Ltd took me all round the country and I was never slow to let the delegates know what my day job involved. It seems from comments made to me that my monthly articles which appeared in The Chartered Quantity Surveyor were well read. This led to invitations for me to speak at Royal Institution of Chartered Surveyors' branch meetings and conferences which I readily accepted. However I considered reviewing my policy of go anywhere as a result of two events. I found myself one evening in a room over a pub in Lincoln on a wet February evening, giving a talk to about twenty people with a three hour car drive home ahead, which was not attractive. Shortly thereafter I presented a one day conference in Newcastle followed the next day with a one day conference in Bristol with a seven hour drive between the two locations. I was a little more choosey concerning the lecturing engagements I took after that.

I had for many years been involved with the activities of the Royal Institution of Chartered Surveyors as a committee member and for a year acted as the chairman of the Salop, Hereford and Mid Wales Junior Organisation and later chairman of the Greater Manchester Quantity Surveying Branch. I was also one of four representatives of the Institution who sat on the Joint Contracts Tribunal, which was responsible for writing and publishing the standard forms of construction contract. They were always in the process of redrafting some contract or another and I was appointed as chairman of the drafting committee charged with rewriting the Prime Cost Form of contract. All of this helped to publicise the work of my company. Clients were very receptive to the one stop shop system we operated for resolving construction disputes, which greatly assisted in securing work. The use of the traditional method of resolving disputes required the appointment of solicitors, practising barristers, together possibly with a quantity surveyor, architect and engineer acting as expert witnesses. We undertook all of these activities under the one roof. All of this assisted in attracting clients to our doors. We had been operational for about two years in London and required more staff and consequently I recruited Colin Archibald whom I had met when working for LC Wakeman and Partners in Liverpool. At the time Colin worked for James Nisbet and Partners who occupied offices in the same building as me, and was looking to move to the south of England and so I offered him a position in our London office which he accepted. After about eighteen months Phil Brady became homesick and returned to Liverpool. We had no opportunities for him in the Liverpool office and so he left the firm and I appointed Colin Archibald to replace him as manager in London. Mike Hall I had known for some time, as he was a regular delegate at the CITB afternoon/evening courses I ran at the Warrington Technical College. He worked for HH Robertson, a well-known roofing and cladding specialist, and I must have made a good impression on him as he had me appointed to resolve some of HH Robertson's disputes. He had moved south together with house and home to take up the position of Southern Area Manager for HH Robertson, but the job didn't work out to his satisfaction and hearing I was recruiting gave me a ring and was subsequently appointed. The third person I appointed about the same time was David Somerville, a Scotsman who had spent the whole of his working life on the contracting side of the industry. He had held some high powered jobs but felt that at his time of life, he was approaching fifty, he needed a new challenge. All of them turned out to be first class acquisitions.

3.30 I had known Glyn Roberts for a number of years. When working for LC Wakeman and Partners, we had undertaken work for Grosvenor Estates in respect of a development in Sheffield where George Longden and Sons had been the main contractor and who employed Glyn. Now that the office in London was established with the bit well between my teeth I had been giving thought to further expansion, as I felt there is no standing still, you either go forward or backward. Having existing clients in Sheffield, I liked the idea of an office there with Glyn becoming our manager. However I didn't wish to poach staff from a client and decided the best approach, as a first step, was to have a meeting with Glyn. He was keen to undertake the position but I explained my reluctance to poach him from a client. Longdens were owned by Whitecroft, a manufacturing company based in Manchester and it appeared there was some animosity between the directors at Longdens and those at Whitecroft to whom the Longden's directors reported. Ken Shaw, Glyn's boss, was very understanding about Glyn's desire to work for me and said he would leave with his best wishes.

3.31 Glyn having joined us, we needed an office as soon as possible. I was anxious to have one fairly near to the centre of Sheffield. My logic was that with more businesses being located near city centres, we would be in a better position to secure work from city centre clients. Glyn found vacant premises in Dronfield, which turned out to be over 10 miles from Sheffield and probably favoured by Glyn as it was fairly near to where he lived. Some years later we moved office to Cathedral Walks near the city centre. There was no visible increase in the workload, which put a dent in my theory. Our first employee was Vicky, Glyn's sister, who became our receptionist/secretary, followed by Barry Clayton who responded to an advertisement. Barry stayed with us for approximately 18 months and then moved back into contracting, where he had worked before joining us. I got the impression that he was not cut out for full time involvement in dispute resolution. Three other recruits Les Birkitt, Roger Louch and Brian Turnbill joined within two years of our commencement in Sheffield and made significant contributions to the firm's development over a number of years.

3.32 Glyn was good at sniffing out opportunities. Skye Edge was a residential development constructed by Sheffield City Council and located at the top of an escarpment, hence its name. However the development was bedevilled by construction faults which led to a great deal of protest from the tenants and as a result the development became notorious throughout the town. Glyn noticed a report in the local newspaper in April 1984 to the effect that the Council intended to appoint a barrister to investigate the causes of the problems. He rang me suggesting that he put my name forward to the Council to undertake the task. The net result was that I was called to attend an interview and subsequently appointed to undertake the investigation and prepare a written report. Having secured the commission, the task was then to get started. It was likely to involve the painstaking job of inspecting every dwelling and preparing a brief report regarding the faults and arriving at a conclusion as to the cause. We therefore required an Architect and somebody to manage the process including organising access and keeping the client informed. I was giving some thought as to who should be involved just as Mike Hall joined the company. I had no immediate task for him to become involved with and so decided to allocate him to the Sky Edge project. I would oversee the task and become involved as was necessary to justify me being appointed in the first place. Mike is a busy sort of a person and in no time at all he had located an out-of-work Architect living in a council flat in Bradford. There cannot have been many Architects who fitted that profile and I had severe doubts as to his suitability. I decided that the first task was for the three of us to walk the site. When we were about halfway round a voice hailed us from a balcony "You lot down there would you like to come up and see the problem?" I am not sure how he knew what we were involved with but news travels fast. We went to his flat which had a spectacular view. Unfortunately the wind was blowing through the gaps around the window which resulted in the curtains billowing into the room. It seems that this was a regular problem which occurred on the estate. The Architect produced a satisfactory condition report which I incorporated into the report I submitted to Sheffield City Council. It seems the problem arose as a result of poor workmanship, which was reflected in the report. After a few weeks had elapsed I was called to a meeting of the housing committee at which there were about twenty-five present. I took Mike Hall with me in case there were questions which I was unable to answer. The first question came from a rather agitated man who enquired as to what my reaction would be if given a report such as mine, twenty minutes before a meeting was scheduled to commence, and expected to have read it and be in a position to ask questions. My response was to say that I hadn't been invited to attend the meeting to answer that sort of question. The meeting otherwise was conducted without incident. Sheffield City Council let a contract to undertake the remedial work with which we had no involvement.

3.33 The office in Knutsford was getting crowded and I considered we needed to move. We were located over a row of shops and I thought this wasn't the image we wished to convey. There was a purpose built office block, Wardle House, located a few yards down the road in King Street which had been constructed for Wardle Storey, who manufactured seat covers for the automobile industry. The office comprised three storeys and at the time Wardle Storey occupied the ground and first floors and were seeking to let the first floor. Following an inspection it seemed ideal and I had no hesitation in taking on the lease. As time progressed we took a further lease for the ground floor. The top floor was occupied by a company owned by John Knox, who at the time was the husband of Barbara Knox, the Coronation Street actress. He wished to move and as a result we secured from him the final two years of his lease. Some years later I purchased the whole building from Wardle Storey.

CHAPTER SIX

SCOTLAND AND THE IRISH DIMENSION

3.34 There are a few defining moments in the development of a firm and one of ours occurred when Paul Jensen joined the company. Paul was the Chief Quantity Surveyor for Lyjohn, a building construction company based in Ellesmere Port. He attended several of my courses at Warrington Technical College and I got to know him well. He, like me, had qualified as both a Quantity Surveyor and Barrister and in a like fashion to Mike Hall had arranged for his company to use my services. To my delight he approached me and asked if there was a vacancy and if so he would like to be considered. There was no vacancy, but I had no hesitation in offering him a job. He is one of those types of people who whatever he says is believed. The staff loved him as they had no hesitation in asking for his advice on a contractual problem which was causing them uncertainty. He was a good communicator and excellent lecturer. When he first arrived I was looking for a project on which to employ his expertise. At the time we were advising Monk and Company, a construction company based in Warrington, in respect of a dispute they had with South West Water Authority. The dispute didn't get resolved and was moving in the direction of arbitration. We needed somebody to lead the arbitration and Paul was the man for the job. There was no settlement and the case progressed to a hearing. Paul hadn't undertaken any arbitrations before, but was confident that he could handle the commission. When the hearing commenced the Water Authority was represented by a QC and also a junior barrister as the system of engaging a QC involves employing in addition a junior barrister. Paul in his usual style undertook his task with absolute confidence; it wasn't evident that this was his first experience of advocacy, but he went on to secure a good result for Monk and Company.

3.35 I received a letter from a Scotsman, Ian Strathdee, applying for a position we advertised in respect of senior dispute resolution staff in London. I invited Ian to attend an interview in Knutsford. He turned out to be in his late twenties, a very pleasant individual, without, at face value, a great sense of humour. In my normal style I had decided in the first couple of minutes of the interview that I would offer him a job. One of my first questions was to enquire why a Glasgow based person would be applying for a job in London. He explained that he was out of work, due to the insolvency of his last company, and looking for a position, and as there was nothing on offer in Glasgow he applied for positions which were on offer elsewhere. As we chatted my mind started working in the direction of an office in Glasgow. The longer the meeting progressed the more attractive the idea of an office there became. Finally I asked Ian if he would be interested in managing an office in Glasgow if we were to open one. He asked about our prospects of work in Glasgow to which I responded in a most positive manner. It must be rare for a person to attend an interview for a senior position in London and return home as the manager of a none-existent office in Glasgow. Ian joined the company in January 1983 and soon found suitable premises. He remained as our head man in Scotland for 20 years. There were a number of building contracting companies operating in Glasgow who had heard of us and our reputation and so we soon started to attract work. Ian had a friend, Peter MacGillivray, whom he was anxious for me to meet and consequently it was arranged for me to meet Peter at his office. He operated as a one man band working for Receivers and Liquidators of defunct construction companies. Peter's role was to finish off final accounts for projects on which the contractor had been working before the insolvency occurred. The total of the final account, when money paid to the contractor prior to the insolvency was taken into account, would show up any money due for payment. When the money was claimed from the building owners, it would often be met with a counterclaim based upon defective work, late completion and the additional cost incurred in finishing off the work, where the insolvency had occurred. Peter's role was to sort out these matters and recover as much money as possible on behalf of the Liquidator or Receiver. Peter's office comprised one room with wall to wall filing cabinets ram jam full of files. When first appointed Peter took over all of the defunct contractor's files and as he was working on several different cases he accumulated a vast number. Ian was anxious to recruit Peter to which I had no objection and agreed on condition that Peter disposed of some of the files before joining us. Peter was a life-long supporter of Morton FC who played football in the Scottish League. He attended all the home matches and the only guarantee at the end of a long season was an air of disappointment. They did from time to time secure promotion from the Second Division but this was often followed by relegation shortly after. Peter was a good Scotsman through and through and one of his proud boasts was that prior to joining our firm he had never set foot outside of Scotland and after joining, despite attending a significant number of meetings held in Knutsford, he never spent as much as a penny in England. He always travelled by air from Glasgow to Manchester and arranged to be picked up at the airport. Peter proved a first class member of staff in every respect and stayed with the company for over fifteen years. Ian was a go-getter and over the next couple of years recruited a number of senior consultants including David Carrick, Nick Longworth, Keith Milne, Keith Urqhart, Willie Hamilton, and Robin Macgregor who all played major roles in the company. We later opened offices in Edinburgh, Stirling and Aberdeen all of which were influenced by Ian. Ian was very good at providing a dispute resolution service and was also a very sharp businessman. Some of our Scottish clients referred to him as rhino as he charged for everything. Year on year we made good profits in Scotland which was in no small way due to Ian's drive. Looking back I made a few really good appointments of which one was Ian. I also made some very poor ones but as they say "No names no pack drill".

3.36 I received a phone call from the secretary of the Royal Institution of Chartered Surveyors Belfast branch, inviting me to speak at a branch meeting to be held at Belfast City Hall. The secretary indicated that if I accepted the invitation he could guarantee a hall full of members. At the time the Troubles were at their height and bombs were regularly going off with people killed and injured, but none-the-less, never being one to resist a challenge, I agreed. I booked a room at the Europa Hotel whose owner had spent more money on repairing bomb damage than on the purchase price. When I arrived on the afternoon of the meeting which was scheduled to be held in the evening, I was a little shocked to see the extent of the fortification outside the hotel. Everything however went off without a hitch; there were no atrocities during my visit and true to the promise of the secretary, the hall was full to capacity. Shortly after, I received a call from a representative of the Northern Ireland Housing Executive; whether this was as a result of my delivering the lecture I never discovered. A great deal of the housing requirement in Northern Ireland was provided by the Executive, which as a consequence employed a large number of employees. They were anxious for their technical staff to get up to speed with the provisions of the standard forms of construction contracts and intended to run a number of two day training courses to achieve this aim. The Executive employed all their own technical staff and didn't use any outside consultants, consequently they estimated a requirement for twelve two day courses. They were looking for an outside organisation to present the courses and the Executive had two organisations on the short list, but unable to decide which one to appoint. They concluded that the fairest way of making a choice was to hold a competition. Each organisation would present the two day residential training course at which there would be invigilators present, who would then decide the winner. I considered that it would need two or three of us to present the course. I felt capable of undertaking the task alone but thought that the invigilators would feel uncomfortable in appointing a one man team. Paul Jensen was an obvious choice to be a member of the team. A decision as to the third member was a little more difficult. Peter McGillivray had undertaken a limited amount of lecturing since joining the firm and I thought that as there is an affinity between the Scots and Irish, he would make a good choice. I prepared the course content and all the lecture notes and hand-outs and sent them to Paul and Peter for vetting and suggestions for alterations. The course involved morning and afternoon sessions and on the first day there was a final session after dinner. I felt that having worked all day on the standard forms of contract, a light relief in the last session was called for. About this time John Cleese had produced a video entitled "Meetings Bloody Meetings" lasting about 45 minutes which I had seen and enjoyed. I decided that the final session would be devoted to showing the John Cleese video. The dates were fixed when the competing teams were to present their training courses. The opposition was headed by Chris Willis, a very likeable and funny man. Humour, if appropriate, usually goes down well when introduced into a training environment, and so I was under no illusions that we were in for a tough battle. Chris was the son of Arthur Willis, who wrote a text book which became the Quantity Surveyor's bible and Chris was responsible for producing the updated version. It was decided that I would undertake the first day's training and Paul and Peter the second. Any organisation in any way connected to the government was regarded by the IRA as fair game and as the Executive fell into that category, security was therefore a high priority. The two courses were intended to be blueprints for the remainder and, in keeping with the security arrangements, we were not informed in advance as to the venue where the course would be held. I arrived in the early evening at Belfast airport, where I was met by a man in an unmarked car, who drove me to the hotel where the course was to be held. I stayed for a second night at the hotel as it was too late after showing the video to catch the last plane to Manchester. The course went well and we were declared the winners. Following the competition, Paul, Peter and I presented ten more two day courses which we found enjoyable and with never a hint of trouble.

3.37 As a result of my visits to present courses to the Northern Ireland Housing Executive, I developed a liking for Belfast. All the people I met were polite and friendly and the countryside was exceptionally beautiful. My contacts began to build up and my thoughts turned to the possibility of opening a Belfast office. Apart from Beirut, which at the time was a total war zone, Belfast, which to any right thinking person was a snake pit of violence, political intrigue and religious bigotry, must have been one of the last places on earth to be considered as a location for opening an office. However this was not part of my thinking. During my involvement with Northern Ireland I had become acquainted with Fergie Bell, who ran a small firm styled Fergus Bell and Associates. Fergie undertook basic quantity surveying, dispute work and anything else which vaguely fell within his sphere of knowledge. I thought that Fergie may be interested in throwing in his lot with me. We talked the matter over and in no time we reached an agreement which involved him continuing to trade as Fergus Bell and Associates and eventually changing the name to James R Knowles. Nothing earth shattering happened and Fergie carried on as before except that he had the financial backing of a much larger company. After about eighteen months I raised the matter of a name change which didn't meet with Fergie's plans and so we agreed to part company. In retrospect I think the whole idea of trying to run a successful business in Northern Ireland was a bad one and that despite the lack of clear vision on my part we escaped lightly from the experience.

3.38 Our involvement in Northern Ireland took place during the period of the Troubles, which began in 1968 and ended with the Good Friday Agreement in 1998. The heart of the Troubles was a conflict between the Unionists who wanted Northern Ireland to remain part of the United Kingdom and the Republicans whose desire was to be part of the Republic of Ireland. There was also a religious dimension as the Unionists were overwhelmingly Protestant and the Republicans Catholic. During the thirty year period 3,600 people were killed and 50,000 severely injured. There had been a great deal of tension between the opposing sides for a long time and matters had not been helped with the Unionists dominating the Northern Ireland parliament for over 50 years. This led to public unrest and disorder on a growing scale and became so great that the British Government sent in troops in 1969 to restore order. Matters worsened, resulting in the British Government introducing internment, which amounted to imprisonment without trial. The situation deteriorated even further with the killing of 13 people by the Parachute Regiment, referred to as Bloody Sunday. This led to even greater disorder and consequently in 1972 the Northern Ireland parliament was suspended and replaced with direct rule from Westminster. Attempts were made to restore self-government, the first being the Sunningdale Agreement which was entered into in 1973 and gave the Republic of Ireland government a role in the internal affairs of Northern Ireland, referred to as the "Irish Dimension". However this agreement proved impractical and collapsed, although it did sow the seeds, which eventually resulted in a settlement which lasted.

This was followed by the Anglo Irish Agreement which was entered into in 1985. Unfortunately this was opposed by the Unionist community and Sinn Fein which was the political wing of the IRA. The only parties to lend their support were the SDLP and the Alliance Party. Eventually the IRA accepted that the war they were pursuing was unwinnable and in 1994 declared a cease fire. Negotiations continued with a view of a lasting peace. Bill Clinton, at the time the USA President, took an active personal role, which led to US Senator George Mitchell being appointed as chair of the peace talks. This led to the Good Friday Agreement, which was entered into by the UK Government, the Irish Government and eight Northern Irish political parties and came into force on 2nd December 1999. Unlike the previous Agreements this was to last, however many significant issues remained to be resolved, not least the decommissioning of Republican and Loyalist weapons. With the passage of time, all outstanding matters were agreed, or became irrelevant.

CHAPTER SEVEN

CRAWLEY AND WINCHESTER OFFICES OPENED

3.39 Colin Archibald recruited Sue Hellings to work in the London office. Sue started her career as a typist, but later decided to look for a new opportunity. She chose the law, qualified as a barrister and commenced practising from chambers. After a few years she left to start a family, reached the stage where she could go back to work and applied to us for a position. As far as I am aware she didn't tell anybody working for the firm her reason for not returning to practising at the bar. Sue was talented, abrasive, sometimes funny and an asset to the firm. She brought to the southern part of the firm the sort of knowledge possessed by Paul Jensen and was always pleased to provide legal advice to anyone from whom it was requested. She stayed with us for approximately five years and then went to work in Hong Kong. We kept in touch but ultimately she emigrated to Australia and disappeared off my radar screen. Colin approached me when I was on one on my visits to the London office enquiring if I had considered opening an office in Crawley and if this was in my thinking he would like to be considered for the position. I barely knew where Crawley was located and so the answer was in the negative. It seemed to me that Colin, in making the enquiry, was experiencing a problem with working in the London office. When I asked why he would prefer a position in Crawley, his answer was that it was nearer home. I didn't find this a convincing answer but considered that if the situation were to remain unchanged he would probably leave. Approximately eighty percent of the reason why an office is successful is the choice of manager who will either make or break the office. This became obvious when managers left and offices they managed began to go downhill, taking the profits with them. In Colin I had found a good manager who could run an office profitably and so I decided in a very short space of time to open a Crawley office with Colin as manager. The office was very profitable for about ten years but when Colin left to start up his own business the office was never the same again. Replacing Colin as manager of the London office didn't create any problems as Mike Hall filled the position admirably.

3.40 Following one of my courses for Shaws Linton Courses Ltd which had been presented at a hotel in Southampton I received a phone call from Richard Brazier, who had been present at the course and was a director of Brazier and Sons Ltd, a Southampton based contractor. They had receive a claim from a subcontractor in the sum of £65,000 which was disputed and it looked as if the matter was likely to be referred to arbitration. I made a trip to Southampton, met Richard and his brother Phillip, who together explained the details of the case to me. I spent some time reading through the papers and concluded from what I had seen and heard that the subcontractor's case was weak. Time passed, correspondence with the subcontractor was exchanged and eventually a notice of arbitration was served. The first day of the hearing arrived, and the subcontractor's representative, a one man quantity surveyor/claims consultant, commenced his opening address. It was obvious from the first few sentences of his opening address that he was very inexperienced. After about five minutes the arbitrator stopped proceedings. He knew me and explained to the subcontractor's representatives that Braziers were being represented by a barrister, which could leave them at a disadvantage. He offered to suspend the proceedings for a few weeks if the subcontractor wished to secure the services of a barrister. The proceedings quickly came to a temporary halt to be reconvened a few weeks later. In order to appoint a practising barrister, as opposed to me who operated as independent consultant who happened to be a barrister, the subcontractor had to appoint a solicitor, who in turn appointed the barrister, this being one of the rules of the game. Richard Brazier started to receive correspondence from a firm of solicitors, who, following the aborted hearing, had been appointed by the subcontractor. Richard in turn decided to hand over to his own solicitor the task of corresponding with the subcontractor's solicitor. Richard's solicitor in turn decided to appoint a practising barrister, as dealing with an independent consultant who happened to be a barrister was outside his experience. I was gradually squeezed out of the task of representing Braziers, to become the background adviser. When the hearing restarted all were present who attended the first hearing plus two solicitors on each side and two practising barristers on each side which greatly added to the cost. I had advised Richard, once I had read all the papers, that he should win the arbitration but if he lost the case the award would be in the region of £20,000 to £25,000. The arbitrator's decision when it arrived was just in excess of £22,000 which greatly disappointed Richard. I could have explained that if I had run the case in preference to the practising barrister and solicitor, the adjudicator's decision would in all probability have gone the other way and at much less cost. It did cross my mind to do so, but I decided there was nothing to be gained by this action.

3.41 The hearing took place in Winchester, a town which I found greatly to my liking and the idea of making visits on subsequent occasions proved very appealing. My thoughts began to focus on opening an office in Winchester, which refused to go away. From my experience of opening offices I had reached the obvious conclusion that its success or otherwise was almost wholly dependent upon the qualities of the person appointed as manager. Rather surprisingly their contractual and legal knowledge appeared fairly well down the list of necessary attributes. However as managers had to double up as fee earners, a minimum amount of knowledge was essential, but wisdom and common sense, the ability to make decisions fairly quickly, a personality which most clients found pleasing, the ability to secure work from leads and obtain repeat business and an ability to manage staff fairly and firmly were also essential. When taking a decision whether or not to open a new office, whilst the location was important, the availability of a person who would make a good manager was the deciding factor. David Somerville, who had worked in the London office for about two years, ticked most of the boxes and as he lived nearer to Winchester than London he seemed the ideal person to appoint as manager, if he was willing. When I broached the subject with him, David jumped at the opportunity. The office in Winchester was very successful for two good reasons. In David Somerville we had a very good manager who in turn recruited Richard Hawkins who proved to be an admirable successor when David retired. We suffered in some of our offices in not having a ready replacement when the person first appointed left. Having a succession plan is not always easy to arrange, as those appointed to be in line for succession can become impatient for promotion and leave.

CHAPTER EIGHT

RUNNING OUR OWN SEMINARS

3.42 I received a telephone call in the early part of 1982 from a gentleman who introduced himself as Michael Milne. He was a director of a company styled Eden Construction Ltd who operated out of an office in Carlisle. Michael explained that his company was looking for somebody to run a one day seminar relating to contractual awareness for their staff in Carlisle. We discussed the programme and agreed on a date for the event. The seminar went well and shortly after I received another telephone call from Michael with a request that we meet. I was intrigued as to why Michael wished to see me as if he required another seminar it could easily have been arranged on the telephone. At the time Michael lived in Malvern and worked out of Eden Construction Ltd.'s office in Cheltenham. When we met, Michael quickly came to the point which was to enquire if I was interested in opening an office in his area, preferably somewhere like Tewkesbury; should this be the case he would be interested in being appointed as the manager. The idea of an office in this part of the country had never entered my head and this I explained to Michael. However never being one to scorn an opportunity I said that whilst there were no plans to this effect I would give it some thought. At the time we had eight offices some of which were still bedding in and therefore I decided that I could give this opportunity a miss and advised Michael accordingly. Michael however was not easily put off and he made a few subsequent calls to try and persuade me to effect a mind change. I took to Michael and was impressed with his never give up attitude and finally I agreed to his suggestion. However I didn't take to the idea of an office in Tewkesbury, still being of the opinion that given the opportunity, an office is more likely to succeed in a large town rather than a small one. Cheltenham could never be described as a large town but it was much bigger then Tewkesbury. It was therefore agreed that I would open an office in Cheltenham and that Michael would be the manager.

3.43 We rented offices in Ormond Terrace, Cheltenham commencing in September 1982. Michael was quick off the mark and soon secured work as an expert witness on a dispute which was heading to arbitration and also some claims work. After he had been in post about one year he made a suggestion which, following its implementation, made a huge difference to the manner in which we projected ourselves to our clients and prospective clients. I was still, after eight years, touring the country lecturing at seminars for Shaws Linton Courses Ltd. Michael suggested that we should run them ourselves to enable us to retain all the profits and not just my lecture fee. Whilst it was a good suggestion, my reservation was as to who in our firm would be responsible for their organisation, as I was too busy to take on the task. Michael suggested that they could be organised from Cheltenham. We were approaching late spring with the summer break on the horizon and it presented me with no problem to bring my arrangement with Shaws Linton to a close. Michael recruited Penny Jackson, who later became Penny Milne, his secretary at Eden Construction. Penny took on the task of organising the seminars. She is a very well organised lady and performed the task with great success. We needed to decide upon a subject matter, date, location and price per delegate. The choice of subject matter was mine and I considered "Are You Up to Date?" to be the most suitable. There was no internet and the only available sources of information relating to construction contracts and law were two text books, Hudson's Building and Engineering Contracts and Keating on Construction Contracts. These books were updated about every four or five years and so I thought that a seminar bringing delegates up to the minute information would be popular. Michael and Penny recommended Cheltenham Race Course as the venue, to which I readily agreed. Michael had recruited John Dobson who offered to undertake some of the lecturing. I wasn't very enthusiastic concerning this idea as I was unaware of his capabilities and being anxious to get everything off to a good start was inclined to refuse the offer. However I reconsidered the proposal and gave him one lecture to present. We were all surprised, to say the least, at the numbers of bookings we started to receive, following our mailshot. By the time the day prior to the seminar taking place had arrived we had received 183 confirmed bookings. The evening prior to the day of the seminar Michael, Penny, John and I decided to pay a visit to the venue to ensure that all was ready for the next day. When we arrived, the lecture hall was in the final stages of being set out classroom style, as I had requested, which involved rows of tables at which the delegates were to sit. Unfortunately the room was long and narrow, which meant that those seated towards the back of the hall were a long way from the stage. I explained to the person in charge that I was not too happy with this arrangement and he suggested that the setup could be changed as the chairs were capable of being converted in order for them to be suitable for a lecture hall style. This would involve bolting small purpose-made wooden plates, which they had in store, to the armrest of each chair, so they could be used by the delegates when taking notes. This involved removing all the tables and then bolting the wooden plates onto over 180 chairs. It was then after 8pm, with at least two hours' work ahead, but there was not a hint of complaint from any of the men involved, who had no doubt been about ready to go home. The seminar went without as much as a hitch and was well received by the delegates. From the smile on Michael's face at the end of the event, the profits we made from the day were obviously healthy. The "Are You Up To Date?" seminar was to be repeated the following day in Winchester and so after the close of the seminar in Cheltenham I made my way there by car. We had received 55 bookings, which was much less than Cheltenham. The only difference between the two seminars was that John didn't show any appetite to give his lecture in Winchester, and also the length taken up by the lunch break. If there is only one lecturer for the full day I have advocated a lunch break of one and a half hours. This provides the lecturer with a decent time for recovery and in any event many of the delegates like time to catch up with phone calls and networking. The lunch, which had been arranged by David, consisted of five courses, plus coffee. The service was slow and David seemed under no pressure to try and get the staff to speed matters up. Having drawn the morning session to a close on programme at 12.30 I was expecting a start at 2pm. However due to the number of courses and the slow pace of those serving the meals, we didn't get underway in the afternoon until 3 pm, which left me with two hours into which I had to project three hours of information. Throughout my lecturing experiences I have always finished on or slightly before the scheduled time for completion. If the seminar over-runs the time for completion, delegates begin to leave and the interest of those remaining starts to wane. Despite the long lunch period I felt under no pressure to finish late. When the seminar was over and the delegates had left, I quizzed David concerning the five course lunch and the two and a half hours it took to serve. His response was to explain that in his opinion the success of a seminar depended mainly upon the quality of the lunch and if providing a first class lunch took up a little more time then so be it.

3.44 Ian Strathdee was never slow to exploit a profit-making opportunity. Having heard of the success of "Are You Up To Date?" in Cheltenham he rang me to enquire if I would be prepared to present the seminar in Scotland, to which I readily agreed. He appointed his secretary Morag Gordon to undertake the tasks performed by Penny in Cheltenham. The Garfield House Hotel which is located in Stepps, just outside Glasgow, was chosen as the venue. This was the first seminar of this size which had been held at the hotel and of course our Glasgow office staff were also on a learning curve. The venue held a maximum of 120 delegates and in no time at all we were sold out. Ian, not being slow off the mark, had arranged a date with myself and the hotel to put on a repeat performance which attracted a further 60 delegates. Peter MacGillivray, who had shared the lecturing duties with Paul Jensen and me for the Northern Ireland Housing Executive, presented two of the lectures and no doubt the sound of a Scottish accent provided some comfort to the delegates. From a standing start we had arranged four seminars, attracted 429 delegates and made a handsome profit. If only all of our new enterprises were so successful; but still one cannot expect to hit the jackpot every time.

3.45 We had been receiving a significant number of enquiries from the North East of the country and my thoughts moved in the direction of an office in the area. I was acquainted with Ron Bailey who lived in that part of the world and decided to ask him to open an office for us. I left the details to him and he arranged to rent a small office in Morpeth. Progress in getting the office up and running and into profits was too slow for my tastes and whilst I continued to consider there was scope for a profitable office in the North East, the formula we were using wasn't working. I decided to recruit somebody with a bit more fire in him than Ron and interviewed Andy Dunn, a Scotsman, with a view to recruiting him. Andy was the Chief Quantity Surveyor of Wimpey in the North East and obviously the sort who wasn't inclined to take prisoners. I appointed Andy with instructions to find us an office in Newcastle-upon-Tyne which he quickly accomplished. Andy was larger than life and a big family man. In no time at all he had recruited his wife Marion as his

PA/Secretary together with his son Stuart and his wife, to form the Dunn clan who ran things their way. What few rules we had in the firm were usually ignored by the Dunn clan. However as they consistently made good profits it was usually ignored. I have been heard to say that if Andy Dunn had no work, Newcastle office would still break even. Andy had a gallows sense of humour, which he would need to have being a lifelong supporter of Hamilton Academicals who played in the Scottish League and whose idea of success was to avoid finishing bottom of the league at the end of the season. Andy wasn't slow at noticing the profits being made on running seminars and so rang me to request that one be presented in Newcastle. The event was organised by his wife Marion a very nice lady, but one with nothing to learn from the average sergeant major, hence it ran with smooth precision. Some of the offices developed specialities and Newcastle became experts at putting together claims relating to open cast coal mining, which proved very lucrative. Andy secured a client by the name of Harry Banks, who became one of his all-time favourites.

3.46 Glyn Roberts rang to advise me of an opportunity with which he had become involved. He had been in contact with Eric Rigby who ran Silkstone Construction, a medium sized builder based in Barnsley. It seems that Silkstone Construction was in dispute with three local authorities, being the city councils of Wakefield, Barnsley and Leeds. Claims had been submitted by Silkstone Construction, all of which had been rejected and they were considering referring them to arbitration. Eric had enquired of Glyn if we would be interested in running the arbitrations of behalf of Silkstone Construction. I met Eric at his home in Barnsley to discuss the disputes and our possible involvement. There were some fifteen projects in all, five against each authority and Eric was considering commencing arbitrations on all fifteen and wished to know if we were in a position to handle them all? Eric had all the appropriate files in his lounge and after a quick perusal

I informed Eric that we could handle the lot. The claims were not of a high quality, but I decided that in the first instance we would try negotiation with the opposition and see where this would lead. I chose to meet the Quantity Surveyors responsible for the Leeds projects. The meeting was over fairly quickly as I was informed that in their opinion there was no merit in any of them. This seemed to leave arbitration as the only option. Having said that, often the first reaction to a claim is rejection and with persistence, agreement can often result. I had been impressed by the up and at 'em approach of Andy Dunn and decided to hand over to him the process of arriving at a settlement if possible on the five Leeds projects which would be satisfactory to Silkstone Construction, or if not he was to take all five disputes to arbitration, leaving him to decide the strategy. Within about three months Andy was on the phone informing me that he had settled all five disputes in return for a payment to Silkstone Construction of £800k. I had some difficulty in taking in the news. When the payment was received by Silkstone Construction, Andy had a blown up photograph of the cheque, which he had framed and hung on the wall in his office. George Goodchild had been with the firm for a few years at the time we took on the Silkstone Construction disputes and, being an experienced man who always kept his feet firmly on the ground, I decided to ask him to take on the Wakefield disputes, but as Paul Jensen was snowed under with work, intended to use the services of Sue Hellings if matters were referred to arbitration. George decided to refer one of the disputes to arbitration which we won comfortably, following which the local authority indicated that it wished to resolve the remaining four disputes by negotiation as they obviously had no appetite for any further arbitrations. The disputes with Barnsley I decided to handle myself and got matters underway before Andy and George had concluded their handling of disputes. Barnsley appointed the late Brian Green to represent them. Brian was well known to me and we enjoyed a good relationship. He had started his career as a lecturer at Salford University and then gone into practice where his main source of work was advising insurance bondsmen and as a result became known in the industry as the bondsman's friend. He advised me at an early stage, that Barnsley had no intention of settling the disputes by negotiation as they considered the claims had no merit. I made a tactical error in deciding to start all five arbitrations more or less at the same time. I thought we had the resources to handle such an extensive workload whereas Barnsley didn't and as a result would cave in. It turned out that I was wrong in that our resources were not sufficient to run five arbitrations successfully at the same time. We reached a settlement but it was nowhere in the same league as the Leeds deal. In all Eric received on the fifteen disputes over one and a quarter million pounds. Unfortunately with the first one being settled at £800k Eric got in his mind that this would be a blueprint for the other two which turned out not to be the case. Had the settlements been in a different order with the Leeds deal coming last Eric would no doubt have been delighted. As it was he walked away slightly disappointed having contacted us when he had no offers on the table and left after our work was over one and a quarter million pounds better off.

CHAPTER NINE

OPENING UP OVERSEAS

3.47 My thoughts had never stretched to opening an office overseas, but that was about to change. I received a letter from Mike Charlton in 1984 who had been working in Singapore as the local manager of Frank and Vargeson, a Quantity Surveying practice, but had returned to the UK due to a slowdown in work. He attended an interview, at the close of which I offered him a job which he accepted. Contractors and subcontractors who found themselves in a dispute situation and required professional help, once they had appointed us, expected a start on their problem to be made within a day or so. There was as a result no lead-in time; a prompt start was therefore essential if repeat business was to be secured. Architects and Quantity Surveyors, once they have received a commission, usually experience a delay before they are required to make a start, followed by a workload stretching way ahead and are therefore able to staff up as appropriate. We, on the other hand, with commissions often taking at best a few weeks, only recruit more staff, if the general workload is increasing, to meet an anticipated need. When Mike Charlton arrived we had no work on which he could make a start; fortunately Ian Strathdee telephoned to advise me that he had just received a commission with regard to the liquidation of a contractor based in Perth, trading under the name of

McAdam, where our assistance was required. Peter McGillivray usually dealt with insolvency work in Scotland but was too busy to take on the commission; Mike appeared to fill the bill admirably. Following Mike's return from Perth he advised me that everything had gone off well except for the hotel where he had stayed, which was of exceptionally poor quality and inhabited by dubious looking Russian ladies. It seems that the client had been left to select and book the hotel which was contrary to the basic rule which I applied for myself, being never to let a client book your hotel room for which he will be paying the bill, as inevitably it will be one of the items on which cost cutting will apply. A year or so after Mike had commenced working for the firm he mentioned that he fancied a return to the Far East, as the life-style suited both himself and his wife, Christine. About that time I had on three separate occasions been chatting to solicitors who had offices in Hong Kong, where, they advised me, disputes in relation to construction work on which they were working were booming. This set me thinking that if it was good for solicitors, why not us and as we had a person of known ability who was keen to return to the Far East, it seemed appropriate to look further into the matter. As my knowledge of Mike was slim I decided to ask David Somerville, a wise old owl in whom I had a great deal of confidence, if he would like to spend a couple of weeks in Hong Kong and let me know if there was sufficient potential for us to open an office. The cost of scheduled airline travel at the time was extremely expensive and so David went on a Thompson two week holiday which filled the bill and was a great deal less expensive. When he returned his report was that there was great potential for our type of work acting for local Chinese contractors and a few UK contractors who had a Hong Kong set up. He had met David Myles the MD of Henry Boot Ltd, the Sheffield-based contractor, who undertook to use our services in relation to a new Container Terminal at Kwai Chung on which they were working, subject to us having an office in Hong Kong. I suggested to Mike that he might be interested in going to Hong Kong for six months to see if he could get an office established and he readily agreed. In no time at all everything fell into a place and an office was established. The office soon became the jewel in the crown and in my opinion the decision to open an office in Hong Kong was probably the best business decision I ever made.

3.48 Hong Kong is located off the southern coast of China and comprises Hong Kong Island and an area of land on the mainland referred to as the New Territories. In its time it has grown from being a fishing village and then a salt producing site, a military port and finally an international financial centre. There was a vibrant trade between Britain and China in the early 1800s, but there was an in-balance of trade in favour of China. In an effort to rectify the in-balance Britain exported opium to China, which was legal in Britain and produced in vast quantities both there and in India. This met with strong resistance from the Chinese, which led to the Opium Wars. Britain was the victor in the first of the Opium Wars and as a result annexed Hong Kong Island in 1841. The New Territories were leased by the British in 1898 for a period of 99 years. Between World War I and World War II, many Chinese citizens took refuge in Hong Kong. Following the bombing of Pearl Harbour, the Japanese invaded Hong Kong, where the locals were overwhelmed and surrendered on 23rd December 1941; Christmas of that year was thereafter referred to as Black Christmas. Hong Kong was liberated on 15th August 1945 and developed into an economic miracle.

3.49 I received a phone call from a Mr Morris, who asked if he could visit me at my office. We agreed a date and time and when he duly arrived he was carrying a large suitcase. I thought for a moment that he was a travelling salesman and the suitcase contained samples of his wares. He explained that he and his wife lived in Salford and had purchased a cottage in the Lake District. They were both keen ballroom dancers and had visions of long weekends and holidays spent in the cottage practising dancing. However the cottage required to be renovated and in particular there was a need for laying a timber floor suitable for ballroom dancing. Mr Morris appointed an Architect and contractor to carry out the work. Unfortunately when complete, the work wasn't to Mr Morris's satisfaction. In particular the timber floor in his opinion wasn't up to the standard he required for ballroom dancing. In the opinion of Mr Morris the contractor had failed to construct the works, and in particular the timber floor, to the requirements of the specification. Having given me an outline of the problem Mr Morris asked if he could show me something and ask a question, to which I readily agreed to provide an answer. At this point he opened his suitcase which contained a set of drawings, a specification and the contract. "My question is this" he said. "Am I entitled to have the work carried out in accordance with the specification?" I tried to explain that the answer to the question was yes, but to go on to explain that the way in which specifications are often written they are not always followed to the letter. As far as he was concerned the building contractor was obliged to follow the specification and had failed to do so. Mr Morris then advised me that he was in dispute with the builder, a small time operator based in the Lake District, and the matter had been referred to arbitration. He had appointed a firm of solicitors which he had dismissed and appointed a replacement which he had also dismissed. The purpose of him coming to see me was to offer me the task of representing him in the arbitration. With two solicitors as casualties I didn't fancy my chances of seeing the arbitration through to a satisfactory conclusion and therefore politely declined the offer. However as the dispute concerned the quality of work undertaken by the contractor, he would need an expert Architect to provide evidence and we could provide such a person. He explained that without a legal representative he was at a loss as to the road he should take, as an arbitrator had been appointed and some action on Mr Morris's behalf was required. I suggested that he represented himself and the Architect I intended to provide would assist him in his task. We employed an Architect, Brian Crabtree, in our Manchester office, whom I knew to be a good operator and when Mr

Morris agreed to my suggestion I contacted Brian and explained what his role would be. With the exception of the occasional telephone conversation with Brian, I had no further involvement with the commission. Some four months after we had been appointed I received a phone call from Brian and from the tone in his voice I knew there was a problem. It seems that the arbitration was being held at a hotel in the Lake District located near to the cottage. The hearing was underway and in addressing the arbitrator Mr Morris had referred to some notes which he had recorded in his diary. The arbitrator explained that as Mr Morris had referred to notes made in the diary, it should have been disclosed to the contractor's representative prior to the hearing, as part of the arbitration process. As Mr Morris didn't have the diary with him, he was instructed by the arbitrator to go home to Salford where the diary was kept and bring it with him to the hearing the following day. When he arrived home he was tired after the long journey and with a return trip still to come that evening decided to have a rest before starting back. He switched on his electric blanket, lay on the bed and was tragically electrocuted. When he didn't return, his wife, who had been staying at the hotel and hadn't made the trip back to Salford, went home and found her husband dead. The arbitrator immediately suspended the hearing. Mr and Mrs Morris had no children or relatives who lived nearby and so she turned to Brian for assistance in sorting out her financial affairs. Brian being a very caring person provided what support he could. The hearing was never restarted as shortly thereafter Mr Morris's Architect died, followed by the builder, who also passed away. A monetary casualty was ourselves who didn't receive payment of our fees as Brian explained that Mrs Morris's financial position was such that she couldn't afford to pay. Rather than get involved in a long dispute with a grieving widow, I organised a credit note to be raised for the full amount. The finale to the story is that a short time later Mrs Morris married again and as far as I am aware lived happily ever after. Brian, who had become emotionally involved with the whole episode, wrote a book of the events entitled "The Morris Dancers".

3.50 The expansion of a business such as mine is reliant upon a number of factors without which it will shrink and die. One of the key ingredients is the employment of top class consultancy staff who can attract business and keep clients happy to ensure repeat business. I was lucky in starting up a one stop shop before others arrived on the scene and was thus able to attract top ranking staff in substantial numbers. The trick then, with others entering into the market place, was to keep them happy, motivated and retain them. After working for the firm for a year or two, these top class people no doubt started to ask themselves what prospects there existed in staying where they were. Many were studying for legal qualifications and receiving financial support from the firm and probably wouldn't wish to move until they had secured the qualification for which they were studying. However finding positions higher up the ladder was difficult. The offices were all small to medium and after the branch manager, there was no intermediate position for the ambitious to move into. To some extent opening new offices gave an opportunity for promoting the more ambitious to become managers. By the mid-80s we had ten offices in the United Kingdom plus Hong Kong and I felt there was room for more, which would provide opportunities for promotion. Les Birkett, who had been recruited by Glyn Roberts to work in the Sheffield office, was ambitious for promotion. Les came from Leeds and was an avid Leeds United supporter. I recall him being devastated when Leeds United sold Eric Cantona to Manchester United in 1992. Les' great strength lay in preparing contractual claims on behalf of contractors. He had a manner with him which instilled confidence on the part of his clients that Les would deliver the goods. It is my opinion that the greatest asset to achieving a successful result is confidence, without which the outcome is likely to be less than satisfactory. When explaining a client's case to him I usually spend 90% of the time explaining the good aspects of his case and the remaining 10% of the time on any downside. This leads to enhanced morale which is of great assistance in achieving a satisfactory result. There are those who advocate keeping the client's expectations down to a minimum, but this can lead to a turnoff when one is looking for a substantial amount of input from the client and his staff. I decided that even though we had a Sheffield office, as it was in Dronfield in Derbyshire, a Leeds office in Yorkshire with Les at the helm stood a good chance of success. I discussed the matter with Glyn who was disappointed at the thought of losing Les, but bought into the idea. Rowlinson Construction was a client for whom I had personally undertaken commissions and they mentioned a company trading as Barnes Brothers based in Bolton who needed our type of service. They were owned and run by two brothers, Tom and Brian Barnes and I rang to make an appointment to meet them. I thought this would be a good client for Les to get his teeth into, assuming we could secure a commission. As the meeting unfolded it was obvious that Tom and Brian had come up the hard way. They were very pleasant with Les and me, and engaged us to prepare some construction claims for them, which was right up Les' street. As we were leaving the office I said jokingly to Les that if he didn't get a good result on the claims, Tom and Brian would probably break his legs. After that Tom and Brian were referred to collectively as Old Break Your Legs. Fortunately Les managed to get a good result and the Barnes Brothers, who soon became well-liked by us, remained as clients for many years.

I received a letter from Dr David Chappell, an Architect who was employed lecturing in construction matters at a technical college in the Midlands. David's name was known to me as he had written a number of very good text books. He had given up practising as an Architect due to his interest being in construction contractual matters. He was looking for a change from lecturing and wished to become involved in construction disputes at the coalface. David lived in Leeds and was pleased to join Les in the Leeds office. As the work-flow increased, Les recruited a few more disputes consultants, one of them being Robert Evans a very talented Architect. He was excellent at diagnosis and if for example there was very severe cracking in the wall or the presence of water where it should not have been, Robert would very soon identify the cause and provide a solution. His solutions were often quite simple and he developed a reputation for solving difficult construction problems inexpensively.

3.51 In the early to mid-80s we were still running successful seminars under the title of "Are You Up To Date?" Contracts were consistently being amended and the JCT had completely revised its suite of standard forms in 1980. We ran seminars introducing JCT 80, as the new contract was styled, as a separate seminar subject. I purchased all the leading text books and information relating to court cases involving construction law. Unfortunately I had no system for storing and retrieval of the information. They were piled in heaps on the floor of my office and any spare shelves I could find. Locating any particular document became far too time consuming and I realised something had to be done. I took the decision to recruit a librarian and advertised the position. Of those who responded, there was only one worth interviewing. Ann Glacki was currently employed in a library at a technical college and had become disillusioned with the job. It seems the students liked to use the library as a place in which to hang out and drink coffee, with little interest in reading and learning. When Ann arrived, we occupied the ground floor and first floor of Wardle House in Knutsford. There was a large open area on the ground floor which was allocated to Ann. She soon got into her stride arriving at 7.00 each morning and news of her arrival was sent round the firm, which created great interest. At an early stage she suggested it may be of assistance to the technical and legal staff if she produced a weekly bulletin, which set out a summary of recent legal cases and magazine articles which may be of interest. I really liked the idea as it would save people like me a great deal of time wading through heaps of information to arrive at the nuggets. This bulletin became very popular with the technical and legal staff and Ann's reputation grew. What staggered me was Ann's ability to read through a long legal case report, digest it and produce a couple of pages summary. In each copy of the bulletin there were often several of these legal case summaries. Ann suggested that we might like to consider inviting subscribers from outside the firm to purchase her bulletins. I was not too keen on the idea at the start, as we would be giving away information which had been expensively garnered. However I changed my mind on the basis that it would give us publicity and we know all publicity is good publicity. Ann decided that we should offer the bulletins on an annual subscription basis. Ann entitled the bulletin BLISS (Building Law Information Subscriber Service). We secured almost one hundred subscribers which provided a useful income. Ann continued to produce and sell the BLISS bulletin to our subscribers for the next twenty years.

CHAPTER TEN

EXPANDING THE MARKETING EFFORT

3.52 We were enthusiastic about the need for effective marketing and selling, but our methods had no structure. The seminars we ran in Cheltenham, Newcastle and Glasgow were bringing in enquiries. Managers of course had their personal contacts. My monthly articles, which appeared in The Chartered Quantity Surveyor, together with seminars and talks I gave to companies, trade associations and professional bodies were also helping. We had repeat business, but many of our clients would only have one dispute every four or five years. We realised there was the need for a company brochure, which was produced by Mike Milne the Cheltenham office manager. Our marketing efforts included the occasional flurry of mail shots and it was generally considered that we required a company logo, which would appear on our letter heading and any documents we sent out from our offices. Some deep thought was given to the logo and Bill Minnitt suggested that a company seal which appeared on many legal documents would make an appropriate logo. All who had been involved in the discussions concerning the choice of logo agreed. When it went into production the logo appeared on the letter heading and documents leaving the office, in black and not the red usually used for company seals. Somebody remarked that the logo looked more like a Pontefract cake than a seal and henceforth the logo was always referred to as the Pontefract cake.

3.53 By the time the mid-eighties had arrived, we had offices in Knutsford, Liverpool, Manchester, London, Glasgow, Sheffield, Crawley, Cheltenham, Leeds and Newcastle in the UK, plus Hong Kong. My ambitions were to open more offices and if they were to be successful I considered that we needed to beef up our marketing. I decided that what we required was a professional full time marketing manager. This would add to the overheads but I felt in the long run it would pay for itself, and so the process began to recruit a suitable person to fill the post. It never crossed my mind to seek any advice as to the most suitable type of person to meet our needs. I intended to locate the manager in the Knutsford office to enable me to keep an eye on what was going on and so placed an advertisement in the Manchester newspapers. I didn't receive any applicants with experience of working for a professional firm, which is not surprising as I wasn't aware that at the time professional firms employed marketing staff. I appointed Ian Phoenix, who had extensive experience of marketing with major companies including ICI and his track record looked impressive. The managers of some of the branches were keen to employ specialist marketing staff in their areas and eventually five Regional Marketing Co-ordinators were employed in London, South West, North West, Yorkshire and the North East and Scotland. I was fully conscious that the secret of success was good marketing and selling and therefore having appointed Marketing Co-ordinators we needed to get the best out of each one of them, and to help in this regard we held regular meetings at which they and I attended. The intention was that co-operation be engendered, good ideas pooled, and successes shared. The Co-ordinators advised me that we needed a new logo, company sales brochure, national database of clients and companies to be targeted and a mission statement. Experts were drafted in to design the brochure and logo and temporary staff employed to produce the databases. All this came at a considerable cost; for example the logo design cost of over £20,000 was never going to be good value. I wonder what the average taxpayer felt when it was made known that the design of the logo for the 2012 London Olympics cost in the region of £400,000? When Ray O'Rourke acquired Laing he was asked who he intended to appoint to design a new logo, which would reflect his newly combined company Laing O'Rourke. His response was to say that he would design it himself, which he did on the back of an envelope, and this was for one of the largest construction companies in the country. Mission statements were generally regarded in the private sector as meaningless drivel and a waste of time and money. They still however appear in the public sector on the sides of buses and refuse removal carts. The only mission statement which has impressed me is the one used by First Class Hire, a Knutsford-based taxi firm. In each of its cars, all Mercedes, appears a notice which reads "Travel in Comfort Arrive in Style" which in any event was scrapped after a few years. In general terms employing the Regional Marketing Co-ordinators was a qualified success, however there is no way of knowing what the effect would have been had we not employed them.

3.54 I worked well with Ian Phoenix and the Regional Marketing Co-ordinators, all of whom were women. I was always anxious to meet each of the Marketing Co-ordinators at an early stage of their employment, to let them know that effective marketing was regarded as crucial by the man at the top of the organisation. One of them, who will have to remain nameless, at our first meeting asked me who she had to sleep with to secure work for the company. I was taken aback by the question but managed to retain my composure and responded to the effect that it was not part of the company's marketing strategy. She may have been joking, or just liked to shock, or of course it may have been a serious question. I liked to attend as many face to face meetings as possible with key decision-makers of organisations, who I considered were in a position to provide us with work. Arranging for the meetings to take place was always difficult. I didn't have the time to spend on the telephone, which is usually necessary to set up one of these meetings and I had difficulty in finding any person in the company capable of undertaking the task successfully. However Helen Walker joined the company as the North West Regional Marketing Co-ordinator and she proved to be very successful at arranging these meetings. She was so good I was never slow at telling people that in my opinion, if required, she would successfully arrange a meeting with the Pope or the Archbishop of Canterbury. The secret of her success she put down to persistence. Our marketing activities proved expensive, but were they good value for money? The well-worn expression that half the money a company regularly spends on marketing is wasted, but one never knows which half that is, seemed applicable to our level of expenditure.

3.55 I am not a golfer but it was suggested by the marketing staff that as so many of our staff and clients were keen golfers, we should organise a golf day. I discussed it with Ian Phoenix who liked the idea. It was agreed that I would ask George Goodchild, a very keen golfing member of the staff, if he would provide advice to Ian Phoenix as to how the event should be organised. George agreed to undertake the task with some enthusiasm. The most prestigious golf course in the area around Knutsford is Mere Golf and Country Club and George suggested this should be the venue. The managers and senior staff were asked to submit names of those clients we should invite. On the day of the event the weather was fine and all involved had a marvellous time. We held a dinner in the evening at which the prizes were handed out and a speaker arranged. What came as a surprise to me was the number of prizes which were presented. I am used to sporting events where there is one winner and only one prize. George explained how golf was different from other sports and this was reflected in the number of prizes awarded. All involved agreed that the day had been very successful and that it should be repeated. We ran the golf day from 1989 until 1995. The cost however was in my opinion out of proportion to the amount of work we were likely to secure as a result of the event, which in any case was impossible to measure. We normally had about 40 to 50 guests and each four included a senior member of staff, which represented a significant loss of fee earning time. I was advised that over half of those who had accepted invitations, cried off at the last minute and sent a substitute, who may or may not have been in a position to provide us with work. I decided that the golf day was not value for money and so the golf day held in 1995 was the last one. The Premier Football League had only just been established and I thought as a marketing exercise we could sponsor a match. This was towards the end of 1992 and in the previous season Liverpool had won the FA Cup and Leeds United were the league champions. Enquiries were made as to the cost of sponsoring one game at each club, which turned out to be expensive but affordable. It was my idea, but if I am being honest probably didn't represent good value for money. At the Leeds game an announcement was made that the match sponsor was James R Knowles of Knutsford, which was met by loud booing from the crowd. My claim to fame in the football world is that we are the only professional organisation ever to have been booed at Eland Road. With the experience of the golf days and football sponsorship, it was agreed that the big ticket events probably didn't provide good value for money, although it was difficult to prove one way or the other.

3.56 For some time I had been considering Birmingham as a place in which to plant our flag, as it was a vibrant and growing city with a great deal of ongoing construction work. My experiences had taught me that the success or otherwise of an office was dependent upon the abilities of the manager. The right choice would almost guarantee success, with failure likely if the wrong person was appointed. I liked to promote people from within the company, as I was in an ideal position to know their strengths and weakness and it also sent out the message that promotion came from within, which might encourage people to stay rather than seek better positions elsewhere. John Wood had been employed in our Knutsford office since 1979 and as it was 1986 I'd had plenty of time to assess his abilities. He had impressed me and I decided to enquire if he would be willing to relocate to Birmingham and take on the role of manager. There was an "I would like to think about it" response; it was not a matter of snatching my arm off but I shortly after received a positive acceptance of the role. Once a manager had been appointed, it was the policy to let him make all the key decisions relating to the office. In the first instance this would include the location of the office and initial staffing arrangements. If advice was required then I was available to have an input. When deciding to open an office in Birmingham I had in mind a location somewhere near the centre. LC Wakeman and Partners, my old firm, had its head office located in Edgbaston, two miles from the city centre, where I had worked for a couple of years, which seemed ideal for us. Following his appointment John advised me that he had chosen an office in Sutton Coldfield, some fifteen miles from the centre of Birmingham, where he proposed taking a lease. I didn't argue as it was John's job to make the office successful and I didn't wish to impose my ideas on him. The office got off to a good start with a few commissions from existing clients which John undertook whilst he secured clients who were based near to his new location. As time progressed he recruited a very good team of consultants which included Mike Rycroft a former chief quantity surveyor at IDC who were the opposition on Liverpool Head Post Office, our first commission. John also recruited Tony Phillips, David Barker, and Roger Jewell all of whom were very experienced and made significant contributions to the growth and success of the office. John appointed Lyn Danks as the office administrator who worked very well with all our staff and clients. Having seen the success of the seminars run in Cheltenham, Glasgow and

Newcastle, John and Lyn followed the formula and approached me to provide my normal service. I noticed on one occasion that the mailing for the seminars included the Isle of Man and suggested that it was a waste of time and money as nobody would be prepared to travel from the Isle of Man to the Midlands to attend a seminar. However it never pays to be too adamant when offering an off the cuff opinion, as we attracted delegates from the Isle of Man which effectively shut me up, which John never let me forget. We held seminars in Sutton Coldfield and Birmingham which proved to be a great success in making good profits and attracting new clients. I was still obsessed with the idea that offices in the centre of towns and cities would prove better locations for attracting business than elsewhere. I thought that perhaps a sub-office in the centre of Birmingham could be successful. John agreed, probably because I had made the suggestion, but with little enthusiasm. It was decided to go ahead with the plan and Tony Phillips, a good old fashioned Brummie with appropriate local accent, was approached by John to establish whether he would be willing to take on the role of managing the sub-office. Tony, who could always be relied upon to see the down side of any proposition, turned the proposal over a few times and finally agreed. Prior to joining us he had been employed by Birmingham City Council which would have provided him with a substantial number of good contracts. The office ran for about three years and could be described as a qualified success. It seems that there are more miles of canal in Birmingham than in Venice. Tony owned a narrow boat and liked to take advantage of the vast number of Birmingham canal miles. He was coming to the end of his career and decided to retire when he reached sixty to allow him to spend more time on his narrow boat. We didn't consider it worth our while to replace Tony and so the sub-branch was closed down.

CHAPTER ELEVEN

EXPANSION INTO SOUTH WALES AND SOUTH WEST

3.57 By the time the mid-80s had arrived, the accounts department had grown considerably. It had started with Arthur Shaw and expanded with Oriel Henthorne, Brenda Bates, Jean Goodchild and a credit controller John Glimond. Arthur was by then in his mid-70s and I considered that as the company was continuing to grow, we needed to appoint a young Financial Director. Recruitment procedures were put in place and as a result I called Patrick Lineen for an interview. He was in his late twenties and currently working in Belfast for one of the big accountancy firms. After the usual handshake and five minutes of chat I had decided he was the man for the job and at the end of the interview offered him the position, which he accepted. This was the beginning of a long and successful partnership which lasted for over fifteen years. One of Patrick's first self-allotted tasks was to improve the payment record of our clients. The average period of time taken by them to pay our fee accounts, when Patrick arrived, was 103 days. Patrick set about improving this situation and in addition to giving strict instructions to John Glimond, whose job it was to chase up outstanding debts, he wasn't beyond getting on the phone to clients, who had owed substantial amounts of money for some time, to request payment. Patrick was even known to visit a client and collect the debt. His longest trip was to New York to collect a debt of £400,000. This didn't always go down well with some of the managers, who thought that aggressive fee collection would frighten clients away. My view was that if we were unable to collect money on our own behalf, how effective would we be in collecting money on behalf of our clients? The result of Patrick's efforts was to bring down the average period of time taken by our clients to pay our fees to below 50 days. I don't recall there being any noticeable departure of clients resulting from our improved debt collection, but our bank balance looked much healthier.

3.58 Patrick revised the production of management accounts which usually appeared quarterly, two or three weeks after the end of the month, to monthly management accounts. They were eagerly awaited by me and all of the branch managers as they highlighted the company's performance and that of each office. Our year-end was 31st July but I was never on tenterhooks awaiting the arrival of the year-end accounts as the information in terms of company profits varied little from what could be seen in the management accounts. Patrick introduced cash flow forecasting and budgeting systems which together with his other improvements ensured I enjoyed more peaceful nights. We banked with National Westminster and by chance the manager in the Knutsford branch was Brian England. Brian was a pupil at Boteler Grammar School at the same time as me. He was a good footballer and secured a regular place on the left wing in the school team. When in full flight, as part of his running style, Brian nodded his head and as a result was nicknamed Nodder. When discussing banking matters with Patrick, we always referred to Brian as Nodder. My management style involved expanding the firm which invariably involves an outlay of money. We always made a profit at the end of each year and so provided we acted sensibly, very rarely did we experience serious cash flow problems. However I was keen to expand the firm and opening on average one new office a year was a drain on cash. But my golden rule was that I would never undertake a financial risk which would bankrupt the firm if it failed. We couldn't survive merely on cash flow and from day one we had worked on an overdraft. We were well served by Nodder with regard to overdraft facilities, but not wishing to have all the eggs in one basket, arranged for the firm to borrow money using an invoice discount system. This involved borrowing money with the unpaid fee accounts acting as security. The system operated by money being transferred into our bank account on the raising of an invoice. As we billed all our clients monthly, we usually received a big influx of cash at each month end. When the clients paid up in respect of the invoice, the money went into a special account for the benefit of the invoice discount company.

3.59 We had a car policy from the outset. All our senior consulting staff were provided with a company car. I set a purchase price which applied to everybody and within that price the new member of staff could have the car of his or her choice. It was the job of Oriel Henthorne to purchase the chosen model of car. It was not a company friendly policy, because whilst most cars chosen were fairly standard, others bordered on the unbelievable. Disposal of the car, in the event of staff leaving, was never easy and whilst the intention was always to make a vacancy in the firm attractive, had I my time to go over again, I would have operated a different policy. One of Patrick's first decisions, after starting work with the firm, was to sell the whole car fleet and lease all the cars back, referred in the financial world as sale and lease back. From a company tax point of view this was more advantageous than purchase, and it assisted with cash flow, as we received a large payment once the sale and lease back had been completed with the finance company.

3.60 I was never keen to lead the race when it came to the introduction of technology and on the other hand I was anxious not to be at the back of the field. Following Patrick's arrival, in the mid-1980s we purchased an IBM System 36 on which the accounts were produced. When this became obsolete we purchased a Sonata System followed by a CCS System. By then we had all our time recording, management accounts and year-end accounts produced on computer, which saved considerable amounts of time and allowed the system to operate with less staff. As we were growing rapidly there was no necessity to make any of our accounting staff redundant, neither was there a need to recruit any additional staff.

3.61 The Cheltenham office was one of our great success stories. Michael and the team he gathered around him provided a first class service and of course the seminars were bringing in new clients. There was never any suggestion of discounted fees. We had a company-wide fee scale made up of hourly rates from which Michael and his team were never prepared to deviate. Michael, in the early days of the Cheltenham office, decided that a legal/contractual journal would be a useful reference document and also provide the company with good publicity. With this in mind he produced the Knowles Quarterly Review which he edited for many years. Expansion was still the company policy and a suggestion was made that we open an office in Bristol, which received agreement of all concerned. We needed a manager and Simon Bayliss, one of Michael's team, was selected. After about two years Simon decided that he would like to become a solicitor and left to join Neil Jones and Company, a Birmingham firm. We required a replacement and as there was nobody employed in the Cheltenham office we considered suitable, it was therefore necessary to look elsewhere. As our policy was to recruit from inside the firm, the name of Malcolm Roberts came up on my mental radar screen. Malcolm was a quantity surveyor, who joined the firm in 1985. He was a keen rugby player who turned out for

Davenport RUFC (later renamed Stockport) each Saturday during the season. After his playing days were over he became a long distance runner and took part in several London Marathons. Just after Malcolm started with the company he and I were involved in an arbitration, acting on behalf of GR Morris, a Stockport firm of building contractors, who were in dispute with a local Housing Association. With the hearing due to start on the Monday, I asked Malcolm to work with me over the preceding weekend to get ourselves ready for the off. I think weekend working was a foreign country for Malcolm, however he didn't complain. Brian Green was the arbitrator and the opposition Housing Association was represented by a team made up of a firm of solicitors and a practising barrister. Most of the disputes in which we were involved invariably were settled before a hearing took place and therefore I could be best described as an occasional advocate, and this was Malcolm first experience of working on an arbitration. However despite Malcolm and I being much less experienced than the team acting for the Housing Association, we secured a good result for our client. Michael was happy for Malcolm to be appointed as the new manager of the Bristol office, which took place in 1989. Malcolm ran the office in Bristol successfully for many years, however in 1999 he became involved as project manager with a major new development for Cadogan Estates in London, which lasted until 2003. He then took on the role of Major Projects Director, his most memorable case being the Dubai Festival City audit for Gordon Moffat our Dubai office manager. During Malcolm's absence from the Bristol office, Tim Sills and Helen Bentley jointly took over the day to day role of office manager.

3.62 Cheltenham office had secured a commission from Cwmbran Development Corporation, with regard to four remedial works projects, which included removing and replacing the outer skins of blockwork on 778 houses. Michael recruited Mark Entwistle, who although born in Devizes, was a very Welsh Welshman, who being dually qualified and experienced was very suitable. His working life had been very varied, having at one time worked on a milk round. However when he arrived on the scene in 1985, his previous job, prior to joining us, had been that of a lecturer at Gwent College of Higher Education. He was steeped in Welsh rugby, in fact he considered Cardiff the world's capital of rugby. From being a boy in short trousers, Mark had committed to memory the name of every rugby player who had been selected to play for Wales. I am not sure whether we considered an office in Cardiff was desirable and that Mark would be the ideal manager, or as we had Mark on the staff in Cheltenham it would be advisable to open an office in Cardiff and appoint him as manager; whichever occurred, an office was opened and Mark was appointed as the manager. To enable an office to begin to make a profit, it is usually necessary to employ a manager who, in addition to performing the manager's role, must be a good fee earner, plus two or three senior fee earning staff. Mark recruited Stan Knill, Terry Fitzgibbon and Julie Traynor, all dually qualified, and hence the office quickly moved into profits. Mark proved very effective and the office in Cardiff became very successful and, according to Mark, after Knutsford and Glasgow, developed into the third largest office in the UK, until being overtaken by London. One of Mark's claims to fame was the development of in-house training for our client's staff; Cardiff City Council being a good example, for which Mark and his team trained 100 members of its staff on construction law and contractual matters. From time to time we meet persons who are larger than life. Clive Hughes, a client of the Cardiff office, fell into that category. In the early part of his working life Clive, whose language was enough to make a brothel keeper blush, had been a lorry driver. He was ambitious and managed to work his way up into owning a haulage firm, from which he moved into building contracting and finally became a developer. He had a development involving the design and construction of a factory in London, which went wrong, following which he contacted Mark. An Architect had been appointed by the building owner to supervise the construction and turned out to be a nit-picker, whilst the building owner could see no person's point of view but his own. The combination of the two led to a major dispute on the project, with Clive looking to us to recover for him a large sum of money. The dispute wasn't resolved and so Clive commenced an arbitration, with Roger Dyer being appointed as the arbitrator. Once the arbitration had got underway Clive decided he would like me to be involved, a sort of minister without portfolio. The hearing was held at Baden Powell House in London. Shortly after the hearing commenced it was decided that a meeting would be held to try and effect a settlement. At the outset of the meeting the factory owner announced that he would settle the dispute if Clive withdrew his claim entirely and reimbursed all his legal fees which amounted to hundreds of thousands and that this was not negotiable. Clive's company had by then been acquired by Dares Estates who decided that rather than go on with the arbitration they would close the company down, and hence the arbitration came to an abrupt end. This was a lose lose for all concerned except, I imagine, the factory owner's legal team.

CHAPTER TWELVE

MORE AND MORE SEMINARS

3.63 After the war was over in 1945, on most Saturdays during the summer months my brother and I were taken to the seaside. Sometimes it was our father who was the chaperone, when he would take us to New Brighton, which involved a train journey from Warrington to Liverpool, followed by a ferry from Liverpool Pier Head. This was very popular with us as there was a fairground in New Brighton which always received our custom. On other occasions our mother would book a coach trip which on Saturdays went to Blackpool, Rhyl or Colwyn Bay. I am not sure why we opened an office in Colwyn Bay, but it could have been as a result of my desire to take a trip down memory lane. Fortunately we were able to appoint Terry Williams as the manager and when he left the company Nick Gurney took over, both made good managers. A significant amount of the work we undertook was for Housing Associations, which regularly became embroiled in disputes with local building contractors. I recall that over the fourteen years in which the office traded we either broke even or made a small profit. In addition it provided me with the opportunity of making a few very enjoyable trips to Colwyn Bay, which enabled me to relive a part of my youth.

3.64 Suzanne Cash, an arts graduate, joined the company in the early part of 1987 as the marketing assistant to Ian Phoenix. She was bright and hardworking and Ian, conscious of the successes of the seminars we were holding in Cheltenham, Winchester, Glasgow, Newcastle, Sutton Coldfield, Birmingham and London, suggested that Suzanne should take charge of those to be held in the North West. Suzanne proposed Haydock Park Racecourse as a regular venue which turned out to be a good choice. It was my role to choose the subject matter, design the course, produce the seminar notes and undertake the lion's share of the lecturing. I was aided in the lecturing by Paul Jensen, who was a natural and well informed; being a scouser he was also funny, with a great delivery. His down-side was that he didn't like preparing the lecture notes. I therefore came to an arrangement with him whereby I would prepare the notes for his lectures. At the time lecture notes provided for the few seminars given by other organisations comprised a page or two of bullet points. As our name appeared on the front of the document, I decided that our seminar notes would be very informative and read like a book. Our main subject in the early days was "Are You Up to Date?" and my intention was to make the notes useful for reference by delegates at a later date. Paul had his own style and his lectures never followed the sequence of the course notes. I recall on one occasion Paul pausing partway through a lecture to jokingly enquire if any of the delegates knew the stage he was at in the notes, as he had no idea.

3.65 We were regularly attracting 50 to 100 delegates at our seminars and so an effective PA system was essential. Most of the venues we used didn't have a built-in system and so made arrangements with outside organisations to rig up a temporary system. I usually arrived at about 8am on the morning of the seminar to test the PA system, which was usually being erected about this time. After some adjustment, the system was usually in good order by 8.30 when the engineer left. It was not unusual for the system to fail to operate properly at some point before the lunch break, which involved a hasty phone call and the company's engineer arriving at lunchtime to attend to the problem. If we were lucky the problem would occur close to lunchtime but occasionally we were left with no effective PA system by 11.00 am; but whenever the problem arose the engineer never appeared before 12.30. Lecturing to 50 or more delegates without a PA system operating properly proved to be hard work. During the 1980s and 90s Norman Collier, a popular comedian, who regularly appeared on TV, had an act where he imitated a chicken. His act also included telling a joke, during which the PA system would break down, leaving Norman's lips moving but no sound. There was an occasion, during one of my lectures given at Haydock Park, when the PA system ceased to function, leaving me with lips moving and at least for those delegates seated at back of the hall, no sound. A voice piped up "It's Norman Collier", which brought the house down.

3.66 We had been running seminars in Cheltenham, Winchester, Glasgow, Newcastle, Sutton Coldfield, Birmingham, London and Haydock Park which all began in 1983, usually two per year in each location and sometimes three. It was left to the local office to produce the mailing list and arrange for the mailshots to be sent out. We found this method of publicity brought a much better response than advertising the event in a building magazine. Towards the end of the 1980s I began to think this to be an inefficient way of promoting the seminars and it would be more efficient to run them as a roadshow advertised on the one booking form, organised centrally, with the local office providing the staff at the venue on the day of the event. This idea was met with a lukewarm response, particularly by the local administrative staff who enjoyed the organising process. I decided none the less to proceed with my idea and appointed Suzanne Cash to be the central organiser. We needed a change from the usual subjects of Are You Up to Date, Preparation of Claims, JCT and ICE Contracts and Recent Legal Cases which had been our stock in trade for five or six years. At the end of each lecture there was a short period for questions and also thirty minutes at the end of the afternoon. These question periods were usually lively and the same queries kept coming up time after time. I decided to design a seminar devoted entirely to the questions I was regularly asked and styled it "50 Contractual Nightmares and Their Solutions" referred to thereafter merely as The Nightmares. I made sure that each of the contractual problems I was to deal with during the seminar was set out clearly on the booking form, thus providing delegates with what they would be getting for their money. We put on the first Nightmares roadshow in 1990 at five locations lasting a week, starting at Haydock Park Racecourse on the Monday and finishing at Norwich on the Friday with Cheltenham Racecourse, Leeds Castle and Blenheim Palace in between. We attracted over one hundred at each event except Norwich which fell just short of the hundred. We were still running this subject or a variation on the theme to large numbers of delegates in 1992. During the period from 22nd of September to 28th October of that year we ran 26 half-day seminars, two per day at the same venue. In the morning I presented 30 Critical Contractual Problems and Their Answers and in the afternoon 31 Crucial Contractual Issues and Their Solutions. In total we attracted 2,682 paying delegates which averaged over one hundred delegates for each seminar. On the altar of efficiency I gave all the lectures, which comprised four, lasting forty-five minutes each prior to lunch and three in the afternoon. The delivery of seminars in the 1980s and 90s comprised the lecturer standing at the head of the hall delivering his lecture like a sermon, with no input from the delegates, except for questions at the end. In the 1990s PowerPoint presentations became all the rage and we were all advised that they were a must. I never took to the idea, as I felt that if a lecturer's presentation had a major input from PowerPoint, the delegates would be left either reading what was on the screen, or listening to the lecturer; they couldn't manage both. My lecturing style didn't comprise much in the way of producing facts and figures, as to my way of thinking, this could be sleep-inducing. My system when explaining a contractual, or legal issue, was to provide a great deal of examples, based upon the facts of a legal case or a commission we had in the office. If the facts of the legal case seemed to me a bit dull, I would invent a few which were more interesting. I recall Sue Hellings, the former practising barrister, who came to work for the firm, collaring me at the end of one of my lectures to advise me that in relation to a legal case I had described, which explained a legal point, the facts of the case I had given were incorrect. She seemed a bit nonplussed when I explained that I had altered the facts of the legal case to make them more interesting. I was always careful to look down the list of delegates and tailor some of my examples to the trades or professions represented at the seminar. From the early days of my lecturing activities, whilst always producing very detailed seminar notes for the delegates to take away with them, I didn't follow a script but relied on a list of about a dozen or so bullet points to keep me on the straight and narrow. The object was always to get the attention of the delegates at the start and keep it until the lecture finished. I considered that if I lost the attention of a large section of the delegates, we might as well all go home.

3.67 We were regularly running two and sometimes three roadshows per annum with the locations usually close to existing offices. An administrator from the local office was detailed off to provide the administration for the day and the local manager acted as chairman. Following our successful run of seminars for the Northern Ireland Housing Executive I decided we should try sending the roadshow across the Irish Sea to Belfast and Dublin. Mike Hall was proving to be a good lecturer and he agreed to accompany me on the trip and take up some of the lecturing work. As we had no office in Belfast at the time, Suzanne Cash accompanied us to perform the administration functions. The seminar was scheduled to take place in Belfast at the Chimney Corner Hotel and all was well until 3.00am on the morning of the event, after we had all gone to bed, when we were instructed by the hotel management to vacate our rooms immediately as the hotel had been fire-bombed. I thought fire bomb or no fire bomb I need to collect my papers together which were scattered around the room, get myself properly dressed and don the overcoat before leaving my room. It was on the ground floor and if the worst came to the worst I considered an exit via the window would be appropriate. It was February and even though I was wearing an overcoat I was extremely cold, as we were left standing in the car park waiting for the emergency services to arrive. It was easy to recognise those for whom this was not the first such experience, as they were the ones wrapped in blankets. The emergency was over by 6.00am when we went back into the hotel to be provided with hot coffee. We received a few calls between 7.30 am and 8.30 am from delegates, who had seen a report of the firebomb on the television, enquiring as to whether the seminar had been cancelled. The fire damage had affected those parts of the hotel where the seminar was to take place, but the hotel management were able to find alternative rooms for us to use; fortunately the kitchen and dining room had not been damaged and so the seminar was held as planned. We travelled from Belfast to Dublin on the train which had been featured in a TV programme entitled the World's Leading Railway Journeys and it lived up to its billing. Unfortunately it was dark during much of our journey but in later years I travelled on the train in the daylight and found the views from the windows to be magnificent. I had decided that we should hold the Dublin seminar at the world famous Jury's Hotel. Suzanne was impressed with Jury's in particular the telephones which were located in the bathrooms. Without a telephone in the bathroom however, one could on occasion be faced with a dilemma. Being caught short during a telephone call made in the bedroom where a discussion concerning a lucrative appointment was moving in one's favour could prove unfortunate; or finding oneself in the bathroom attending an ablution of some urgency, when one is expecting to receive a phone call from a much fancied member of the opposite sex, and when the phone rings in the bedroom, could result in a great deal of disappointment. The problem however is solved if there is a telephone in the bathroom. I presented the Belfast and Dublin seminars in each of the succeeding six years which proved a great pleasure. We ran ten or more seminars on each roadshow for fifteen years with me lecturing on most of them, which took up thirty or so days per year. When lecturing for trade associations, professional bodies, local authorities and companies both in the UK and overseas is added to the lectures I gave on the roadshows, some 50 to 60 days per year of my time was taken up lecturing, which doesn't include the time taken up preparing the detailed lecture notes. The course appraisal forms were always marked good or excellent and so I kept on going; the fact that I found them enjoyable may also have been a contributing factor.

3.68 Transferring the running of the seminars from the administrators at the branch offices to Suzanne Cash who was based in Knutsford produced one casualty. Ian Strathdee, who was responsible for our Scottish operations, and based in Glasgow, advised me that he could no longer justify employing Morag Gordon, who was responsible for the organisation of seminars which were held in Scotland. I was advised by Ian that he was expecting me to give Morag the bad news. On my next visit to Glasgow I took Morag on one side and told her of our intention to dispense with her services. Morag is a lovely lady and it was a task I disliked intensely, however in ladylike fashion she responded by telling me that she had been expecting to be given her notice. A couple of weeks later I received a very nice letter from Morag advising me that she had been able to secure a new job very close to her home, news which delighted me.

3.69 Our main method of publicising the seminars was by mailshot and inserting drops in construction magazines. As the strike rate of bookings to mailshots was less than 1% it was usual for us to organise two mailshots per roadshow of about 50,000 each, plus 100,000 drops in three construction magazines. It is hardly surprising that we soon became a household name in the industry. We put together a database from clients and prospective client lists, which produced a thousand or two names; nowhere near enough. Trade association lists were obtained, containing the names of contractors and subcontractors, which together with lists of members of professional bodies, eventually produced the necessary numbers. Suzanne Cash spent a significant amount of her time imputing into the database and we employed temps to help with the task. Once we had produced a database of sufficient names and addresses, it was necessary to keep it updated as companies were often on the move, or going out of business. Eventually we employed a person fulltime to manage the database. Initially we employed a mailing firm to despatch the mailshots, until we purchased our own mailing machine and brought the task in-house.

CHAPTER THIRTEEN

EXPANSION IN MIDDLE ENGLAND

3.70 It crossed my mind that as our seminars were very popular with delegates, if recorded on video, they could be sold at a profit. However the process would have to be unobtrusive. Suzanne was charged with finding a company that could meet our requirements and she was able to locate Van Martin, who operated with a hand-held camera which fitted the bill very well. We sold untold numbers of these videos which helped our profits and assisted with our marketing efforts. The numbers attending each of our seminars averaged about 60 during the 1990s, however nothing lasts for ever and they suffered a downturn from about 2000 onwards. They ceased to show a profit at this stage, but we continued running them as they kept our name in the eyes of clients and prospective clients.

3.71 Quality Assurance (QA) became a must-have, beginning in the late 1980s and early 90s and is defined as:

"a method designed to prevent mistakes or defects in manufactured products and avoiding problems when

delivering solutions or services to customers. QA is applied to physical products in pre-production to verify what will be made meets specifications and requirements and during manufacturing production runs by validating lot samples and meets specified quality controls."

It was introduced to succeed quality control which didn't seem to be as effective in eliminating manufacturing errors as desired. Whilst QA was introduced to improve the quality in manufacturing process it was adopted into the service industry and was subsequently heralded as essential. I undertook some reading on the matter and was sceptical as to whether it would be of any advantage to us, but conscious that some commissions may be lost if we hadn't been QA'd. Managers were expected to use their discretion concerning any processes they employed, as they were expected to show a profit. They were all experienced, high quality people and so I didn't feel it to be one of my tasks to instruct them as to how they should carry out their roles. Therefore it was left to each manager as to whether or not to adopt QA. Suzanne Cash who was responsible for the seminars decided to introduce QA into her department. This required a QA consultant to be appointed to set up the systems. We instructed Keith Winter, who had been one of our clients in the days when he worked for a contractor, but had later become a QA consultant. The process of becoming QA'd took in the region of six months. From a casual viewpoint the process involved a great deal of form filling and box ticking and quality checks. The process involved self-audit every six months and external audit every three years. If one were to measure the process by applying a cost benefit analysis the installation costs of employing a QA consultant were high, which was added to with the additional time taken complying with the process; it would therefore be fairly easy to calculate the costs. To evaluate the benefits would involve assessing how good was the seminar department before the introduction of QA compared with their quality post-QA. The answer would have to be there was no difference. The department was excellent before becoming QA'd and so it continued post-QA and therefore we received no benefit. Having successfully become QA'd the seminars department was entitled to a certificate to record its success. As Suzanne is a Liverpool FC supporter, I thought it would be nice if a Liverpool footballer made the presentation. I therefore rang the club to enquire if one of their players would be prepared to attend our office in Knutsford to make the presentation. They undertook to ring back which they did a few days later to inform me that none of the players were interested. We were fortunate in that George Goodchild, one of our senior consultants, knew Roger Hunt, who was a member of the England World Cup winning team of 1996 and he graciously agreed to make the presentation.

There was little appetite elsewhere in the organisation for QA with the exception of the marketing department in Knutsford and the Sutton Coldfield office. They took QA on board which resulted in no change to the excellent service each of them had provided prior to becoming QA'd.

3.72 With the success of most of the offices we had opened in mind, I was convinced that the fastest way of growing the firm was to open even more offices. The key of course was to find the right person to appoint as manager. Roger Louch, who had been recruited by Glyn Roberts to work in the Sheffield office, lived in Nottingham and it occurred to me that this might be a good place in which to open our next office. I talked to Glyn and Roger about the possibility, following which I decided to proceed. In my usual manner I left it to Roger to find some suitable accommodation, appoint an administrator/secretary and to get started. The new manager usually took his existing work with him and commenced looking for new clients. Roger was joined by Brian Turnbill and together they were soon able to find a few new clients. An early client was the East Midlands Electricity Board which was experiencing difficulties on a contract to maintain every street light in Derbyshire. There was a three stage process starting with one of the Electricity Board employees engaged fulltime riding the streets of Derbyshire on a motorbike to identify lights which were not working. This was followed by an engineer who visited the malfunctioning lamp to identify the problem and decide the process necessary for its correction. Arrangements were then put in place to put the work in hand. In the majority of cases the problem was the need for a new bulb or parts, which had to be acquired from Derbyshire County Council's store. Inevitably there was none of what was required in stock resulting in wasted journey time and extra cost. As the contract ran for five years, the additional cost was extensive. We were appointed by the Electricity Board to prepare a claim and negotiate a settlement with Derbyshire County Council. Brian Turnbill was selected to undertake the task which involved searching through heaps and heaps of Electricity Board records which provided details of all the wasted journeys. The contract had been completed by the time Brian arrived on the scene and records were kept in a small outhouse in which Brian spent many a long hour; he referred to it as the bunker. Eventually the matter was resolved.

3.73 I received a telephone call from David Kent, an in-house engineer employed by Harrods. With the intention of increasing the sales area of its Knightsbridge store, Harrods had purchased a building at the rear. The plan was to transfer all those employed in the non-selling activities to the newly purchased building, leaving more room in the store in which to create additional sales areas. The building at the rear required a great deal of conversion work before the staff could be transferred. This work was well underway, but disputes were regularly arising with the contractors who were undertaking the construction work. The main bone of contention related to the construction of an underground car park, which involved the removal of a substantial amount of unforeseen obstructions at a considerable cost to the contractor. David had seen one of our videos which dealt with this problem and hence he was anxious to meet me to discuss the matter. The contractor had submitted claims running into many millions of pounds relating to the unforeseen obstructions together with other contentious matters. David must have been satisfied with our discussions as he indicated, on behalf of Harrods, that he would like to appoint us to deal with the claims. I advised David of my intention to arrange for a senior member of our staff to become involved right away. On my way home I was toying with the idea of whom I should allocate to the project. I knew that all staff in the London office were busy at the time but had doubts as to Roger's workload. It was soon established that he could accommodate the work and so I took him to meet David. The underground car park involved a great deal of exposed concrete. After only a short period of time Roger identified that there should have been a smooth finish to the exposed concrete in the car park, as provided for in the specification, whereas it had been left with a rough finish. Rough finished concrete is probably in order for most car parks, but this is Harrods. Roger found anomalies in the contractor's claims resulting in a major reduction, which, when the cost of creating a smooth finish to the concrete was deducted, left the contractor with no financial recovery at all from its claims. Harrods held a party to celebrate the finish of the construction work to which Roger and I were invited. Mr Al Fayed who was present at the party came and spoke to us all individually and proved to be very pleasant. The wife of one of Harrods employees was very ill and rather than wait for the NHS to attend to her Mr Al Fayed paid the cost of sending the lady to Switzerland for immediate treatment. He may have his detractors, but Mr Al Fayed showed himself to be a very compassionate man.

3.74 I had opened an office in Winchester due to my liking of the town and it had proved successful, so why not Cambridge? Mike Illidge, a former Chief Quantity Surveyor for Manchester City Council, was employed in our Manchester office and seemed a suitable candidate for the position of manager. I discussed the possibility with him and he seemed keen. All was agreed and the usual procedure followed to get the office up and running. Mike appointed Jeremy Hackett, a very experienced quantity surveyor, who in later years made a name for himself due to his much publicised criticism of the Royal Institution of Chartered Surveyors' membership fees which he styled as "Stop the Rot". It wasn't long before we received a major commission from a local metalwork supplier. They had received an order from British Nuclear Fuels to supply purpose made stainless steel panels for a nuclear waste storage vessel. The order was for approximately 500 purpose made panels comprising five different shapes. When the drawings arrived the differing shapes were not limited to five. In fact there were dozens of different shapes. Whilst the cost of the materials for each of the panels didn't vary much, the production cost dropped markedly for the second and subsequent panels of the same size and shape. With the number of differing sizes increasing from five to dozens there was a massive increase in the total costs of producing all five hundred panels over and above what had been allowed in the tender. Computers had been finding their way into office procedures in a number of ways and this including producing analysis reports. Mike had embraced the use of computers wholeheartedly and suggested that he could use his computer in the analysis of each of the 500 panels, indicating how the costs had increased due to the many different shapes. He produced a document a couple of inches thick, which I liked, knowing it would be unlikely that the opposition could produce anything which would disprove Mike's analysis. The claim was submitted to the main contractor and on to British Nuclear Fuels, who were responsible for the design of the vessel and finding the money to settle to claim. A long period of time elapsed and no response was received, the main contractor, each time an enquiry was made, indicated that a response from British Nuclear Fuels was awaited. Patience was becoming exhausted and I advised the client to issue a writ against the main contractor, which I considered would set the cat among the pigeons. It appears there had been several claims received by the main contractor from other subcontractors and suppliers working on the scheme and due to the issue of the writ, the main contractor got together with British Nuclear Fuels to try to resolve the matter. Within a short time our client received over two million pounds in settlement. The delight at the settlement was displayed in the black tie cocktail party arranged by our client, at which great praise was heaped on Mike and me. Mike remained as manager for a couple of years, but was experiencing domestic problems which had been hindering his move and with reluctance tendered his resignation. Stephen Pratt, who had been working in the London office, replaced him and he was joined by Tony Clarke, an experienced engineer.

3.75 Mike Charlton had set up the office in Hong Kong which soon became well established. He appointed Keith Lorriman and a little later, Eric Chung, a young local quantity surveyor who was a good acquisition as he introduced the company to some Chinese contractors who became regular clients. Others who joined in due course included John Molloy, Paul Barrett, Louise Popplewell and Gregory Tung with the numbers of technical staff increasing steadily over a period of years. I decided it was time I paid a visit and made arrangements to go in October 1986. Reg Thomas had recently joined us after spending a number of years working in Hong Kong for Sui On, a major local contractor. I thought that it may be helpful to Mike to have a visit from Reg and so he accompanied me. My wife Wendy expressed an interest in seeing Hong Kong and so she joined the party. In advance of my visit, Mike had indicated a desire for us to run a one day seminar during my trip, with me the principal speaker. He also secured the services of a local solicitor, Nicholas Gould, who worked for Lovells. I was impressed with the quick start Mike had made at recruiting staff and securing work for them as well as himself. I hadn't given much thought to the seminar before arriving in Hong Kong, but as it was scheduled for three days after my arrival, I had to quickly get up to speed. The Hong Kong forms of contract were based on those used in the UK and hence didn't present me with any difficulties. We had two hundred delegates booked to attend and I began to wonder if they would understand what I was saying. My only concession was to try to speak slower than normal, but otherwise it was business as usual. The seminar went down well, there were very few whose attention appeared to wander and they laughed in the right places. Every expat living in Hong Kong almost without exception employed a maid referred to as an amah who was usually a Philipino. Sunday was their day off and they liked to leave the home where they worked and congregate in the streets. They arrived early in the morning and stayed until it was dark sitting on pavements, shop doorways and any other space where a few of them could sit down together. They brought food with them for the day and except when eating they chattered non-stop producing a noise which was unbelievable. Many of the local Chinese liked to keep caged birds in their homes and could frequently be seen carrying the cages with bird inside around the local parks. This fulfilled two purposes; it provided exercise for the owner and a breath or two of fresh air for the bird. The other common sight in Hong Kong which involved the local Chinese was practising T'ai Chi which took place just after sunrise in most of the local parks. I visited Hong Kong each autumn for the next twenty years and Mike on each occasion organised a seminar where we rarely attracted fewer than two hundred delegates. Hong Kong soon became our most profitable office and it remained in top position for twenty years thanks in no small manner to the skill and efforts of Mike.

CHAPTER FOURTEEN

EXPANSION IN EAST ASIA

3.76 With our experience of setting up in Hong Kong and making profits I began to wonder if this performance could be repeated elsewhere in that part of the world. During the middle of 1988 I received a letter from Derrick Morris. Derrick was in his early fifties, born and educated in England, but in his early twenties had taken up a position in Singapore working for the government. He subsequently became a partner in Frank and Vargeson, the firm for which Mike Charlton had worked before joining us. Derrick had returned many years later to study for a law degree, following which he decided against returning to Singapore and bought a house in Devon. When he contacted me, he was working on a freelance basis for Neighbour Northcroft, a firm of quantity surveyors, but in view of his law degree would like to work for us. We agreed to meet and in view of both of our commitments, chose Gatwick airport, from which Derrick was due to depart on an overseas trip. It seems we had met on a previous occasion, at an arbitration, where Derrick had acted as advocate for one of the parties and I was the arbitrator. We agreed a deal and a start date and off Derrick went to board his plane. This may seem a bit hasty, but I knew there was a limit to the number of offices we could accommodate in the UK and we were reaching that limit. This left us with a choice of either standing still, or expanding our operations overseas. We had opened an office in Hong Kong, which was proving to be very successful and therefore growth in this area seemed a good move. Derrick had the right qualifications and experience and I liked him. This being the case, why wait, there may be other opportunities he was exploring, or rival companies considering making him an offer and my thinking was that if I left making the appointment for further consideration, the opportunity to engage his services could be lost. I wasn't sure in what capacity Derrick would be employed after he commenced working for us, however on his first day there was a need for him in the Manchester office and that was where he commenced his duties. He went home to Devon at the weekend and returned in time for a prompt start on Monday morning.

3.77 After working for the firm for a few weeks, Derrick rang to say he had received a call from an old Singapore client, who had some work he required Derrick to undertake. Derrick was checking to ensure I would be interested in him accepting the commission. There was no hesitation on my part in giving it full approval. Derrick returned two weeks later and came to my office for a chat concerning his recent visit to Singapore. He advised me that during his stay he had been working out of the office of an old friend, Terry Cleary, a one man band quantity surveyor. It seems that after many years of working for himself, Terry was looking to tie up with a larger firm. I immediately indicated my interest and by coincidence Terry was due to visit London in the near future and Derrick was able to arrange for us to meet. Terry had been in Singapore for well over ten years and by a very strange co-incidence, before leaving England, he had lived in Kingsley in Cheshire within a few hundred yards of where at the time I was living. Prior to our meeting however we had never set eyes on each other. Terry wasn't looking to sell his practice, he was happy to gift it in return for a steady job. I was now in the position of having Derrick on board with all his experience of working in Singapore and now Terry willing to make a present of his practice. I agreed a salary package with Terry and a date when he would commence. We parted after shaking hands on the deal with me undertaking to visit Singapore in the near future. With Terry now on board, Derrick spent an ever increasing amount of his time in Singapore servicing his old clients. He took a flat there and together with his wife June spent some time in the UK and the remainder in Singapore. The system worked well for all three of us.

3.78 The modern Singapore was established by Sir Stamford Raffles in 1819. Due to its location at the southern tip of Malaysia, it became a strategic location for trading and as a military base. When the war with Japan started, following the bombing of Pearl Harbour, the invasion of Malaya and Singapore was high on the Japanese hit list. The British expected an invasion of Singapore but anticipated that the Japanese would attack from the sea. Instead they advanced through Malaya. The Japanese tactics involved bombing the airfield to put the air force out of action and sinking the war ships to incapacitate the navy. The problem was that the leaders of the British forces considered the Japanese to be inexperienced in warfare against major countries like the British, and they would prove to be easy meat. The Japanese attacked across the straits which divided Malaya from Singapore and soon overwhelmed the British forces. 100,000 British soldiers surrendered to the Japanese army, many of them having never fired a shot in anger. Winston Churchill was said to be beside himself with anger when he heard the news. Of those captured at Singapore, 9,000 died building the Burma to Thailand railway. The island was liberated after Japan surrendered in August 1945. For a considerable period after the end of the war Singapore suffered from high unemployment, severe housing shortage and widespread corruption. After a period of partial self-government, in 1963 Singapore became part of Malaysia, but due to a series of disagreements left in 1965. Singapore was a democracy and in

1959 elected the People's Action Party (PAP) which formed a government. Its leader, Lee Kuan Yew, became the prime minister, a position he held until 1990. In the early part of his period in office, Lee Kuan Yew had a major struggle with the local communist party who were instrumental in creating unrest among the working population. He eventually overcame this problem due to the passing of appropriate legislation. As a result the working hours were increased, holidays shortened and employers given power to fire employees. Employers on their part were forced to make greater contributions to the Central Provident Fund (CPF) which was used for paying pensions. The government set out to attract investment capital and built a large number of factories where goods for exporting were manufactured. Ship building and ship repairs became an important industry; a container complex was constructed and the island became a base for oil exploration and extraction in the region. The net result was that there was full employment, good housing, better education and effective medical care. The corruption was to a large extent eliminated by the introduction of appropriate legislation.

3.79 It became the norm for me to visit Hong Kong and Singapore each autumn. I was anxious to ensure that my visits were not seen by the local managers as a time waster and so offered to speak at a seminar on each of my visits. From my reading of the tea leaves I came to the conclusion that my visits were most welcome as they helped swell the income and provided opportunities to secure new clients. My suggestion that a seminar be held in Singapore was met very favourably by Terry, but Derrick took a different view. He was of the opinion that there was no appetite for seminars in Singapore and we would finish up making a loss on the event; as it turned out we attracted eighty delegates. Terry was delighted, obviously due to its success, and for once when in disagreement with Derrick, he had been proved right. One of the aspects of my visits to Singapore was taking part with

Terry and Derrick in the hash, which is a run organised by the Hash House Harriers. Derrick had been a keen rugby player in his day and was still engaged in a run of five miles or so on a regular basis. Terry like me was in his late 40s and despite the hot and steamy weather still played football each weekend. Having kept up my twice per week six mile runs, which I began when in my mid-teens, I was very much up for taking part in the five mile hash. One of the members was appointed to lay a paper trail during the afternoon and all taking part arrived for a start at 5.00pm. A different trail was laid each week and from the off it was every man for himself. The trail often went through the semi jungle which occupied parts of Singapore and as it became dark at about 6.30pm it paid not to get lost. There were stories of runners spending the night in the semi-jungle, but none came to any harm. A lorry awaited us at the end of the trail from which beer and other refreshments were served.

3.80 The Hong Kong office under the direction of Mike Charlton was going from strength to strength. In a conversation I had with Mike, he suggested that he should be put in charge of the company's development in East Asia. I was happy with this arrangement and he soon came up with the suggestion that we open an office in Kuala Lumpur, to which I readily agreed. He employed Leonard Kok in the Hong Kong office and as Mike was very confident in Leonard's abilities and in view of his Malaysian origins, he seemed an ideal choice to be appointed as manager. Mike approached Leonard, who agreed to being transferred to a newly formed office in Kuala Lumpur, with him as manager. Leonard soon found some premises and appointed his formidable wife Susan as administrator/secretary. When autumn came round, it was time for my annual East Asia visit and the matter of running a seminar in Kuala Lumpur was raised. I readily agreed to give all the lectures and set about ascertaining what forms of contract were employed on Malaysian construction work. On the trip I had paid a visit to both Hong Kong and Singapore before moving on to Kuala Lumpur. The day of the seminar arrived all too quickly, however I never lacked confidence, even when, as then, there were in excess of 200 delegates, all of whom were Chinese or Malays with not a European in sight. The queue to register was so long it wound up the stairs and I understand the toilets couldn't cope with the numbers. I didn't like the set-up of the lecture hall, which was theatre shaped with a raised stage at one end. My normal procedure, whilst delivering my lectures, is to walk around the hall and occasionally pick on one or two unsuspecting delegates, and ask them questions relating to their business and how they were affected by the subject matter of the day. This method isn't practical when lecturing from a raised stage. The office in Kuala Lumpur made a profit most years which was very satisfying. During a period when work was hard to secure Mike Charlton and I discussed how to boost the performance of the Kuala Lumpur office during a slack period, with no end in sight, and both agreed that if we could persuade Reg Thomas, who had in his past worked in East Asia, to spend a year there it should improve the performance of the office. The presence of Reg gave a boost to the office performance for which both Mike and I were grateful.

3.81 Rod Martin had an interesting career with the company. He joined the staff in the Winchester office in 1995 having achieved dual qualifications and experience working as a quantity surveyor. He lived in Southampton, but none-the-less, being as keen as mustard, would go more or less anywhere. During his time with us, in addition to working in the Winchester office, he had spells in Edinburgh, Liverpool and London interspersed with working on various overseas projects. He had an unusual visit to Zimbabwe, where it had been arranged for him to work on a dispute for Sam Smith, a long-standing client of mine. The aircraft on which Rod was travelling had to be diverted from Blantyre, the airport at which it was scheduled to land, as the electricity bill hadn't been paid, hence power had been cut off, resulting in there being no effective landing lights. Another of his trips concerned the difficulties we were experiencing with a client who had a dispute in respect of payment for work being carried out on the Commonwealth Games Stadium in Kuala Lumpur. The client wasn't satisfied with the service he was receiving and made it very plain to me. I promised to send out a top class consultant from the UK to remedy the situation. Rod was on the aircraft within three days of my request for him to go to Kuala Lumpur. It was intended to be a one month project but Rod really took to the place and remained there permanently, taking over as manager when Leonard Kok left in 1998.

3.82 Malaysia as it later became known came under British control in 1874, which at the time comprised Sabah and Sarawak. The Japanese invaded Malaya in 1941 and defeated the British. During the Japanese occupation, British and locals formed resistance groups numbering about 5,000 who operated out of the jungle. They were made up mainly of Chinese communists who hated the Japanese due to their invasion of China in the 1930s. After the war had ended there was unrest among the local Malays and Chinese with the latter forming themselves into the Malayan National Liberation Army (MNLA) a communist grouping, many of whom had fought with the resistance against the Japanese during the war. A state of emergency was declared in 1948, after three planters were executed by the communists. It was referred to as an emergency and not a war, as Lloyds Insurers would pay out in respect of damage caused by an emergency, but not if the damage was the result of a war. In the same year the Federation of Malaya was formed, made up of nine states each with its own Sultan. The emergency lasted until 1960 when the communists were defeated. This was achieved largely by winning the hearts and minds of many of the local Malays. One of the methods of receiving their support was the setting up of 500 villages which were surrounded by high fences and had the effect of cutting off the supplies of food to the communists. The locals were given more rights, what would now be termed human rights, and gradually support for the communists faded, allowing the British to defeat them. After the British withdrawal, there was a further communist insurgence lasting from 1967 to 1989, which was referred to as the Communist Insurgency War, but again the communists were defeated.

3.83 Derrick Morris suggested Brunei as a place for us to indulge in further expansion in East Asia. One of his former colleagues David Gainsbury, was currently employed in Brunei and both Mike and Derrick recommended we set up an office there with David as manager. A visit to Brunei was arranged during one of my trips to East Asia, to give me an opportunity of meeting David, after which the office was established. Derrick liked to tell a tale regarding one of his visits to Brunei. He decided one evening to go for a run and left his hotel without being too familiar with the area in which the hotel was located. On his return, he had difficulty in opening his bedroom door, he checked the number on the door and on the key which corresponded. Whilst standing at the door wondering what to do, it miraculously opened and a lady who was completely unknown to Derrick appeared; it seems, in error, Derrick had gone back to the wrong hotel. Brunei was very much a stop and start place, as new construction work is dependent upon the plans of the Sultan. We held the traditional successful seminar, this time at the Sultan's polo club, and most luxurious it turned out to be. After a couple of years David, for family reasons, wished to return to the UK and so we decided to close the office as there was no suitable replacement for him.

3.84 As a result of having an office in Brunei we received a commission from Prince Jefri, the brother of the Sultan of Brunei. He had purchased a house in Park Lane, London which needed refurbishment. The Prince's representatives had arranged for the house to be refurbished and furnished, for which a final bill had been received in the sum of £30m. This was considered high and we were appointed to value the refurbishment and furnishing. We had no experience of the cost of furnishing and so we secured the services of an outside expert. I became involved and made a few visits to the house which had been furnished using the most exotic colours and fabrics; there is no accounting for taste it is said. We valued the work including the furnishing at £20m, which was reported to the client. The procurement method employed by the Prince when making a major purchase was to use the services of an agent. All the legwork was undertaken by the agent leaving the Prince to make the final decision. The agent then presented the bill to the Prince which included the basic cost plus the agent's fee. It was reported in the press that it was customary for the agent to add a 50% uplift to the basic cost of the purchase before presenting the bill to the Prince. This being the case, with a basic cost of £20m for the refurbishment and furnishings, plus 50% uplift, the final bill would be £30m.

3.85 Our other venture, with regard to offices in East Asia, was Shanghai where we had an office for a period; Dugald Findlayson was the manager. There was a construction boom at the time and we considered that there would be a market for providing quantity surveying staff to construction companies working on site. This was not our core business, but we had provided the service from time to time. We managed to secure work, but not in sufficient quantities to justify an office and so about three years after opening it was quietly closed.

CHAPTER FIFTEEN

TECHNOLOGY ARRIVES

3.86 Work started to arrive in the Singapore office to such an extent that Terry needed to recruit additional fee earning staff. He appointed Christopher Nunns, an ex-pat geology engineer, who brought with him knowledge and experience which proved very helpful. For a reason which never became clear to me, after about six years of success in Singapore, Derrick and Terry, who had always been the best of friends, got into a disagreement. It was obviously a serious matter as Terry submitted his notice and left the firm. He went to Hong Kong to work for Sue Hellings, who a few years earlier had been employed in our London office. Christopher Nunns was appointed as Terry's replacement, on Derrick's recommendation. Christopher owned a small yacht and offered to take a few of us out one Sunday. It was a most enjoyable day with a light breeze, but with the sea nonetheless smooth. Christopher, who was familiar with the waters, took us for lunch to a restaurant located at the mouth of a fast running river. It comprised a wooden shack with hinged sides which could be fixed in the open position to let in a breeze. There was a sloping roof covered with corrugated tin, on which two men were stationed, constantly hosing it down with cold water to ensure those partaking of lunch inside didn't fry. Christopher dropped anchor about thirty metres from the river bank and we went ashore in a small jolly boat which held three at a pinch, including Christopher who undertook the rowing. It took a few journeys from ship to shore and all was well on the way to the restaurant. However disaster almost befell us on the return journey. David Price one of the party, who is a big man, when scrambling aboard found himself with both feet in the boat but both hands on the jetty. With a fast flowing river, the boat moved quickly downstream before David could get himself fully aboard and he finished up in the drink. He clung on to the jetty but as he and I were the last to leave, I couldn't pull him out myself; fortunately there were a couple of locals available to lend a hand. David's escapade apart, my lasting memory of the day was the food, mainly fish, cooked over an open fire, the magnificent flavour of which I still savour.

3.87 I received a phone call in the late 1990s from Mike Charlton in Hong Kong, advising me that after a short illness, Derrick Morris had died. This came as a shock to us all, as Derrick was only in his late 60s, never known to be ill and fit as a fiddle. It was approaching Christmas and the funeral had been fixed for the day after Boxing Day. I had been staying in London over Christmas and planned to drive to Devon to attend the funeral. Unfortunately it had been snowing and so I set off early to ensure arriving in good time for the funeral, which was scheduled to commence at 2.00pm. At the time I didn't have a satellite navigation system in my car as they were not available on the market and so I worked out a route from the road map. Derrick lived on the edge of Dartmoor and when I was a mile of two from the village church, where the funeral was to be held, the car when halfway up a hill, due to the presence of snow, refused to go any further. There being no alternative, I got out of the car and started to walk. After a great deal of slipping and sliding and making slow progress, a man driving a four by four passed me and stopped on the brow of the hill. As I approached the car, the man poked his head out of the window and said "I know where you are going to, it's Derrick Morris' funeral". When I enquired how he knew, he indicated it was the black tie I was wearing which gave it away. He provided me with a lift to the church, by which time it was approaching 2.00pm, but apart from us, there was nobody else present. Shortly after our arrival June, Derrick's wife and their two daughters arrived and advised us that the hearse, when on its way from the chapel of rest, had become stuck in the snow. June expressed a view that Derrick must be up there laughing his socks off. After a while the man who had given me a lift said he couldn't wait beyond 3.00 pm, by which time nothing had happened and so he left and took me with him. Fortunately I was able to find a garage which possessed a vehicle capable of pulling my car out of the snow, and I was pleased to be able to return to London later that day. After a few days, I received word that news concerning the problem with the hearse had travelled quickly round the village and help had arrived to enable it to be dug out of the snow in time to allow the funeral to take place at 4.00pm.

3.88 In the mid-80s word processors came onto the market. Until that time most commercial organisations, including ourselves, used electric typewriters. The advantages of word processors were their flexibility and dexterity. It was a simple matter to correct errors, eliminate sections and reorganise the whole layout of a report. The ability to save documents in memory with very easy retrieval was also a big plus. It was accepted by all in the firm that we should change from electric typewriters to word processors as soon as possible. Fearing difficulties with the transition, I decided to employ an expert on the staff who had knowledge of computers in general and word processors in particular. Terry Bennett was recruited and proved to be ideal in that he was a hands-on practical person who was able to explain matters relating to word processors in a simple way, which could be understood by us all. His method was to visit each office in turn, following the arrival of the new equipment, to ensure it was installed properly and at least one person in the office understood how it should be operated. I recall having a conversation with Terry the day prior to his intended visit to the Newcastle office. I advised him that the first question he would be asked is "How do we switch it on?" which he considered to be incredulous. On his return he put his head round my door and said "You were right".

3.89 It had been the system for the fee earners to produce handwritten reports and claims to be typed by a specialist typist, or in the case of the smaller offices by the office administrator/secretary. With the arrival of word processors, the fee earners were anxious to secure a computer and instead of hand-writing their reports and claims, type them on a word processor. The production of spreadsheets on the word processor was simple, which acted as a real advantage to the fee earners. The changeover was gradual but I could see that the need to employ typists would soon disappear as reports and claims in their finished state would gradually be produced by the fee earner. It was not the intention to make any of our typists redundant but they would not be replaced when they left by their own volition. The first test of this policy came when Patrick Lineen, the Financial Director's, secretary left and he expressed an intention of finding a replacement. I explained it was the policy not to replace typists and secretaries, a decision which he either disapproved of, or considered it didn't apply to him. I suggested if he wasn't confident in his ability to use a word processor then perhaps the purchase of a voice recognition system may fill the bill. He agreed to this arrangement and mastered the equipment in three to four weeks. Many years later Patrick was big enough to admit that the decision not to replace his secretary had forced him to become self- sufficient, which had proved later in his career very much to his advantage.

3.90 I was becoming concerned at my own neglect at mastering the new technology. I had seen others in the company typing on word processors using two fingers whilst wearing a worried frown. This I decided was not for me and so I signed on for a six months, one morning per week course at Pitmans in Manchester, to learn to touch type. The course was straight forward in that they provided a word processor for each student and a Work Book and instructed us all to follow the Step-by-Step Guide and Exercises set out therein and if we had any questions, to consult the person sitting at the front of the class. I supplemented this with an hour's practice at home each evening, except for holidays. There was an examination at the end of the course which comprised typing a set piece. To pass, the candidate must type the set piece with no more than eight errors. I failed at the first attempt but passed second time. There was also an examination in Word which I passed with a distinction, probably because I had purchased a CD entitled Teach Yourself Word before taking the exam which by chance contained all the exercises which formed the basis of the exam.

3.91 In addition to work processing, computers were gaining a reputation for being able to solve most problems involving the management and processing of data. Project Management software had been introduced which caught my eye, as it provided for programme preparation and management and was said to be useful in the production of delay analysis a feature of most delay claims. Being the leading company in this field, I was interested in giving it a try because if we didn't, somebody else would. As it happened, we came into contact with an engineer, Brian Williams, who claimed to be able to use the new software and I was anxious to give him a try out. Voices from among the sceptics however were heard to murmur "rubbish in rubbish out". Whilst I understand that the accuracy of the delay information produced by the software is dependent upon the accuracy of the information fed in and that contractors' records are usually non-existent, or substandard, we needed to give it a try out. We had just received from a client a commission to prepare and submit a claim in respect of delays to a road bypass in Scotland and this seemed an ideal opportunity to try out our new man and his equipment. To cut a long story short, it was an outstanding success, the software worked well and our client received his money. Nothing breeds success like success and our client appointed us for a repeat performance but this time the project was located in Dubai. A team including Brian Williams set off for Dubai. The commission was scheduled to last three months but after six weeks the news I was receiving wasn't good. The project in Scotland involved a road of less than a mile long whereas the Dubai job involved a road dozens of miles long. It seems, due to the vast increase in data being fed in, the system couldn't cope. I had visions of Brian with an icepack on his head, hunched over his computer which was emitting smoke. Plan B was being implemented which involved using the traditional method of delay analysis. The project was being constructed by a joint venture company comprising our client and a local Dubai contractor. It seems about the time of our computer problem, there was a big fall out between the parties and our team were all dispatched home. The software for calculating delays improved and we had on our books one or two who were anxious to give it a try out. Danny Atkinson, employed in our London office and David Carrick and Billy Lowe in Scotland were probably the most successful in the use of computer aided claims. I decided in an effort to move things along we should employ a number of delay analysts, most of them coming from a planning background; the most prominent in England being Len Lea and Ian Dunbar. The difficulty is invariably a lack of accurate records which results in assumptions being made by the delay analyst. This being the case, it is quite possible for two experienced delay analysts, who have been provided with the same information concerning delays on a project, to produce completely differing opinions as to how those delays have affected the completion date. Some years later I was acting as an adjudicator in a dispute between a main contractor and a government agency. The project was subject to an 86 weeks' overrun to completion in respect of which the Architect had granted a 29 week extension of time. Each party had employed independent delay analysts. The expert's report prepared by the analyst acting on behalf of the employer, having produced a 65 page report, concluded that the Architect was wrong and in fact the contractor was entitled to no extension of time at all. The contractor's expert produced a report of similar length which indicated that the contractor was entitled to a full extension of time amounting to 86 weeks. In my decision I rejected both of the experts' reports and concluded that the Architect had probably got it right in granting an extension of time of 29 weeks.

3.92 Since we opened the office in Glasgow, Ian Strathdee had been doing a magnificent job. He wasn't slow at turning some of the seminar delegates into clients and soon required more fee earners, in addition to Peter McGillivray, who in any event was working more or less full time on the insolvency work which he brought with him when he joined the firm. Ian had very quickly recruited David Carrick, Robin McGregor, Nick Longworth, Keith Milne and Willie Hamilton and business boomed. It was my usual policy for managers who wished to introduce major changes for me to accept their recommendations, with little or no questions asked. It was my feeling that if it was their idea they would be under pressure to make it work. The only exceptions were where the idea required a substantial input of set up costs and working capital, in which case Patrick Lineen, our Finance Director, would be consulted. Ian explained that there was a great rivalry between Glasgow and Edinburgh and as a result there was little chance of securing work in Glasgow from organisations based in Edinburgh and if we had ambitions to undertake work there, we would require an Edinburgh office. I fully understood the logic as the same applies with Liverpool and Manchester. It was soon decided that we would open an Edinburgh office and offer the job of manager to Keith Milne. Ian felt that of those fee earners employed in the Glasgow office anyone would be capable of doing the job well, but as Keith lived in Edinburgh he would be the obvious choice. Keith accepted the position and soon had an office up and running. Early successes with securing work resulted in the need for more fee earners and Keith Urqhart was taken on. We did well in our Edinburgh office but it never became as successful as the Glasgow office. There was no good reason for this; perhaps the Strathdee factor was missing, or as both Keiths were English there could have been an element of prejudice involved. This was unlikely as after both Keiths left the company Willie Hamilton a true Scotsman took over as manager and the level of business generated by the office didn't change. Even the seminars we held in Edinburgh were never as well attended as those regularly held in Glasgow. Despite all of that, the Edinburgh office was successful and I had no complaints.

CHAPTER SIXTEEN

OPENED IN DUBAI AND KUWAIT BOTH WITHOUT SUCCESS

3.93 Few of our fee earning staff had a great interest in the production of computers aided claim. The exceptions in our firm were Mike Illidge, who managed the Cambridge office, Danny Atkinson in London and David Carrick in Scotland. To be able to make full use of computers required a basic understanding of how they worked and their capabilities, which Mike, Danny and David possessed. David became the guru in Scotland regarding all things computer. He lived in Stirling and floated the idea with Ian of opening an office there, which could be the computer hub in Scotland. Ian gave it his blessing and my only observation was that whilst Stirling may become the computer hub, it would have to carry out fee earning work and show a profit, which was accepted by both Ian and David. The office in Stirling ran for many years, remained small but usually showed a profit. Aberdeen, due to North Sea Oil, was a booming town and I was interested in providing our services to the oil industry. Archie Holmes had joined our staff in Scotland and as he lived in Aberdeen, it seemed as if an opportunity had come knocking at our door. To cut a long story short we opened an Aberdeen office but unfortunately we failed to attract business from the oil industry and despite running the customary seminar there we failed to secure sufficient business to merit keeping it open and it was duly closed. My one abiding memory of Aberdeen relates to the seminar we held and the hotel in which I stayed the night. It was February and being Aberdeen, as cold as it gets in the UK. Unfortunately the hotel policy was not to waste money heating the bedrooms and I was as cold as I have ever been. Needless to say all future visits by me to Aberdeen were during the summer months.

3.94 On the evening of 21st December 1988, the worst air disaster in British history occurred. A Pan Am Boeing 747 left London Heathrow, bound for New York's JFK airport with 243 passengers and 16 crew on board, but shortly after 19.00 hours, it disappeared off the Prestwick Air Traffic Control Centre radar screens. An explosion occurred on board and the debris crashed into the town of Lockerbie killing another 11 people who were on the ground. The explosion was caused by a bomb packed into a suitcase, which was smuggled onto the aircraft. Many of the victims were American college students, including 35 from Syracuse University, who were travelling home for Christmas. The debris from the aircraft was scattered across 845 square miles and the impact reached 1.6 on the Richter scale. After three years of investigation by the Scottish Constabulary and the US Bureau of Investigation, two Libyan nationals were charged with murder. Abdelbaset ali Mohamed al-Megrahi was jailed for life in January 2001, following an 84 day trial, but was released in August 2009 on compassionate grounds due to him having prostate cancer which was diagnosed as being terminal; he died shortly after. His alleged accomplice Al Amin Khalifa Fhimah was found not guilty. In 2003 Colonel Gaddafi accepted responsibility for the Lockerbie bombing and paid compensation to the families of the victims. Just days before the sabotage of the aircraft, security forces in a number of European countries, including the UK, were put on alert after a warning from the Palestine Liberation Organisation (PLO) that extremists might launch terrorist attacks to undermine the then ongoing dialogue between the USA and the PLO.

3.95 With our successful venture in opening offices in the Far East and as locations in the Middle East, such as Dubai, were experiencing a construction boom I thought perhaps it may be worth considering opening an office in that region. Words of wisdom were whispered in my ear that the main drawback to opening an office in the Middle East was the local legal requirement that overseas companies had to hand over 51% of the shareholding to a local Arab. This was a complete turnoff for me. However the wisdom whisperer suggested that the most effective way of securing work in the Middle East, in the absence of a local office, was to open one in Cyprus. I consulted the atlas to satisfy myself that Cyprus was fairly close to the Middle East. It is on the doorstep of Syria and Lebanon but some distance from Dubai which had first caught my eye following our aborted commission there a year or two earlier. Still nothing ventured, nothing gained and I decided that we would open an office in Cyprus. Jim English and Reg Thomas showed an interest in running the office and as I knew them to be very suitable they were appointed joint managers. In no time at all we were established in premises in Limassol in 1987. Reg and Jim suggested they organise one or two seminars in the places where we were looking to secure work. Dubai, Abu Dhabi and the Oman were chosen. Reg was a competent speaker and so it was decided we would share the lecturing tasks. The subject matter of the seminar was chosen and the programme arranged. We had to build in appropriate stoppages to provide prayer time to suit the Muslim delegates which was a first for me. Reg and Jim managed to secure mailing lists which overcame the first problem being that of publicity for the seminars. In view of the way in which the postal service worked in Cyprus, we were advised to have the bookings returned to a PO Box No. I was doubtful of the likely success of this method of securing bookings, as I considered expecting people in locations such as Dubai, Abu

Dhabi and Oman to send hard earned money to an organisation of whom they had no knowledge via a PO Box No. in Cyprus was expecting a bit much as it may appear to be a scam. However I needn't have worried, as we had over 100 delegates at each of the Dubai and Abu Dhabi seminars and 70 in Oman. Follow up seminars were organised in Dubai and Abu Dhabi but they were never quite as successful as those first ones. The original plan of securing work in the Middle East from a base in Cyprus never had much chance of succeeding. However Jim and Reg were able to secure work from contractors based in Cyprus, where the construction contracts and systems for organising construction work were similar to those which operated in the UK. The norm with commissions acquired in Cyprus relating to the preparation and submission of claims, was for a lump sum fee to be paid for the preparation of the claim and a percentage of the money paid to our client following successful negotiations undertaken by ourselves. Not a method which I favoured, as when clients have received the money we have fought for, they usually show no enthusiasm to pay us as by then we have become a nil priority. There was no difficulty however in collecting our fees when the claim document had been completed. It was the norm for the claim document to be sent to our client when completed leaving him to submit it for consideration and hopefully payment. Our clients would however only submit the claim when they considered that the time was right. This meant avoiding the times when new projects were scheduled to come out for tender. On many occasions the time was never right and so the claims didn't get submitted and as a result we didn't receive the success fee. The effect on our profit and loss for the office was most unfortunate as we made a loss from our efforts in Cyprus for most of the fourteen years during which we were present. Year on year Patrick Lineen, our Finance Director, suggested I close the office, but there is something magical about Cyprus, which seemed to get hold of me and due either to my stubbornness, or stupidity, or a combination of the two, the executioner's hands were stayed. Jim and Reg returned back to the UK after a few years and we appointed other managers to carry on the task.

3.96 As we entered the mid to late 1980s I had the feeling that we were reaching saturation point in the UK as far as branch offices was concerned. The effect of opening more offices in my view would be to dilute the work sources available to the existing offices. Growth must therefore come from overseas and if we were to follow the UK pattern then it meant more offices. Despite the failure to secure work in the Middle East from the Cyprus office, I was still convinced that an office in one of the Middle East countries would be the way forward. With our experiences in Dubai, despite the untimely end to our one project there, I felt this was the place to drop anchor. I was informed that there was an alternative to having an Arab partner when opening an office in the Middle East which involved appointing an Arab sponsor. In this case a fee is payable to the sponsor rather than a share of the equity and profits. From an economics point of view, in the early years when a new office is unlikely to turn a profit, a share of the non-existent profits is preferable to the substantial fee payable to a sponsor. Taking all into consideration, provided the fee was reasonable, paying a sponsor was for me the better option. What we needed however was a manager; cometh the hour, cometh the man, or so it has been said. Nick Longworth had been working in the Glasgow office for a couple of years and giving a good account of himself, from what I was able to learn from Ian Strathdee. Nick, in an earlier part of his career, had worked in Dubai and in a conversation he expressed an interest in returning. In view of the good opinion formed of him, I felt he was the man for the job. He was soon up and off with his wife Caroline alongside and in no time at all had established a new home and an office. Nick knew the territory from his time there and was soon knocking on doors looking for work. In keeping with most of our managers' early marketing efforts, running seminars was high on the priority list. Nick as far as I was aware hadn't trodden the lecture theatre boards before, but was more than willing to give it a go. Reg Thomas, who was based in Cyprus, and an accomplished lecturer, gave a hand. The three of us managed to cover a fair amount of ground on the seminar front. The numbers at the outset were good in that it was not unusual for there to be up to 200 delegates present. The numbers however, after we had run several seminars, began to dwindle. Profits from our standard dispute resolution work were not showing through in either Dubai or Cyprus and therefore a question mark began to hang over survival of these offices. When a company is running an enterprise which is a loss maker, there are two schools of thought as to the action which should be taken. One is to cap the losses by closing down the loss making enterprise, the other is to keep going, provided the enterprise looks capable of succeeding, and eventually with a fair wind it will start to make a profit, which will wipe out the losses. Patrick Lineen, our Finance Director, was a member of the first of these two schools of thought, whilst I was firmly in the latter. After Reg and Jim had left Cyprus and returned to the UK, Nick Longworth was given responsibility for both Dubai and Cyprus. After about three years Nick decided to return to the UK. He had got us up and running in Dubai and whilst not showing a profit had established our name in the market place, a position on which we were able to build in later years. Even though based back in the UK, Nick retained responsibility for Cyprus, however we closed the Dubai office.

3.97 I remained bullish about the prospects for expansion in the Middle East and when an opportunity arose to purchase a company who provided a similar service to us, my radar signals came on stream. Alan McArthur had established a profitable company in Kuwait, which he had run for a number of years. Due to family reasons he wished to sell up and return to the UK. Patrick, not willing to leave me to sort out such a delicate matter as the purchase price, decided to go to Kuwait himself and undertake the negotiations. This was fine by me as my skills don't include negotiating knock down prices. Patrick decided to take Ian Strathdee with him, as he knew Alan McArthur. I began to feel sorry for Alan, as I wouldn't care to take on the task of negotiating a price with Patrick and Ian on the other side of the table. The deal was done and it was a matter of deciding who was to replace Alan as manager. In this context the name of Bruce Parry an existing member of the Kuwait staff came to the fore and he was appointed as Alan's successor. This name rang a bell in my mind, as when in my late teens I had attended the Liverpool College of Building on a Day Release Course, where one of the other students was a Bruce Parry; could it be the same Bruce Parry? When I had last seen Bruce in the late 1950s, I didn't think for one moment that our next meeting would be in Kuwait in 1988. However neither Bruce nor I had any inkling as to what fate had in store for him in less than three years' time.

3.98 Kuwait is a strict Muslim country and hence no alcohol, bacon or pork is sold in the shops. However Bruce and his wife Edna were very partial to bacon for their breakfast and a glass or two of wine with their dinner and so Bruce went on regular smuggling trips to Dubai, where bacon and booze is readily available for purchase by non-Muslims. He had acquired for the task, a large Barbour coat with poacher's pockets, in which to conceal the bacon and a large suitcase in which he secreted the booze inside polythene bags, which made them invisible to the airport screening process. Each month or so, he would take himself off to Dubai, which is a short flight from Kuwait, to stock up with bacon and booze. He must have looked an odd sight walking round the streets wearing a large Barbour coat with bulging pockets, when the outside temperature was in the 90s. I suppose he was regarded by the locals as an eccentric Englishman, who is apt to pop up anywhere throughout the world.

3.99 On 2nd August 1990 the Iraqi Republican Guard invaded Kuwait. The Kuwait Armed Forces were soon overrun and within a few days Kuwait was declared to be the 19th Province of Iraq. There are various theories as to why the invasion took place, but it seems to have stemmed from Iraq's US$80 billion debt pile of which US$14 billion was owed to Kuwait. This level of debt had been built up by Iraq in fighting its war with Iran. To enable the debts to be repaid it was necessary for there to be maintained a high price per barrel for oil. This is where the conflict first began as Kuwait, throughout most of the 1980s, was producing more that the mandatory quota of oil imposed by OPEC, which had led to the price per barrel being extremely low. The reduced price of oil resulted in the revenues received by Iraq being much less than would be the case if Kuwait had adhered to OPEC's price ruling. Between 1985 and 1989 Iraq lost on average US$15billion per year due to the depressed level of the oil price and during that time suffered a crippled economy as a result of the war with Iran. It wasn't helped by Iraq accusing Kuwait of slant drilling in the Rumaila oil field. This oil field was shared between the two countries, each with its own section. Kuwait was accused of using advance drilling techniques to exploit oil from the Iraq share of the oil field, an allegation which was hotly denied by Kuwait, who considered it was a smokescreen to disguise Iraq's more ambitious intentions. Just prior to the invasion 100,000 Iraqi troops had been deployed along the Iraq/Kuwait border. In an effort to defuse the tension, OPEC officials announced that there had been an agreement between Kuwait and the United Arab Emirates to limit the production of oil to 1.5 million barrels per day. Despite the agreement the invasion still took place. In spite of months of sabre rattling by Iraq, Kuwait was ill prepared for the invasion and its ground and air forces were vastly outnumbered and quickly overrun; it was all over in three days, by which time about half of the Kuwait population had fled the country. The occupation of Kuwait by Iraq received international condemnation. The UN Security Council passed 12 resolutions demanding the withdrawal of Iraqi forces, but to no avail. Due to the continued occupation of Kuwait, a coalition of forces led by the USA launched a massive military assault on Iraq in January 1991. The offensive was referred to as Desert Storm and the coalition forces led by a USA General, Stormin' Norman Schwarzkopf, described as having a John Wayne swagger and a growl like a grizzly. Despite Iraq having the fifth largest army in the world, it was soon overrun and Kuwait officially liberated on 25th February 1991. Sensing that a defeat was on the way, Iraq set alight 600 Kuwaiti oil wells, which could well have been the reason for a subsequent oil price rise.

3.100 Bruce Parry was mild mannered, very polite and completely non-aggressive. Much to my surprise after the invasion took place when I made enquiries as to the fate of Bruce and the other members of the Kuwait office staff, I was informed that Bruce hadn't fled the country, as nearly all the other British and foreign residents, together with half the Kuwait nationals, had done. Bruce had a long running love affair with Kuwait where he had been living for many years and obviously had no intention of being driven out by the Iraqis. He was forced to hide, as capture by the Iraqi forces could have been at best unpleasant and at worst terminal. Bruce's wife Edna had left Kuwait and no doubt was extremely worried about his welfare, as were his two sons who were resident in England. I kept in touch with one of his sons who passed on what little news he had received. After seven months of occupation Bruce reappeared, however understandably he required significant time to recover and as a result our office in Kuwait never reopened. Bruce was quite rightly awarded the MBE in the Queen's honours list for his bravery.

CHAPTER SEVENTEEN

PROFITS IN THE MIDDLE EAST AT LAST

3.101 I met Gordon Moffat, a cheery Scotsman, in the late 80s in London and again sometime later in Singapore and had there been a vacancy in our organisation for a senior person at the time I would have offered him a job. In more recent years he had been operating on his own account in Dubai and showed an interest in joining us. This probably came as a shock to Patrick Lineen in view of the red figures produced in Cyprus and Dubai to date, but be that as it may, I had the bit between my teeth and wasn't for stopping at this stage. In 1997 I appointed Gordon, who had ingratiated himself into the local society, mainly through his passion for golf and a pint of beer, to be our manager in Dubai. Work started to arrive firstly at a trickle and then a little more strongly and so Gordon recruited Colin Smith and Graham Atherton, both expats with good contacts which helped to increase the flow of work. We started to secure major commissions, the most impressive being to review all the claims received by Sheik Mohamad on the world famous Burg Al Arab tower. By then the Dubai office had started to make a profit. Patrick was quickly on the warpath in seeking to have some of the profits repatriated to the UK. However two factors mitigated against a large flow of money from Dubai to Knutsford. Gordon was cautious to ensure that the Dubai office had adequate funds to pay its staff and bills, plus some in reserve for a rainy day. In addition Arabs, with some justification, had a reputation for being slow payers which adversely affected the cash flow. It is said that if you are involved in commerce and not prepared to wait 90 days for payment you shouldn't be operating a business in the Middle East. However as the office was making profits the pressure was off.

3.102 The office in Dubai, during the late 1990s and early 2000s, was very successful, leading to an expansion and employment of a large number of employees. I made at least two trips there per year and my usual instruction was for Gordon to arrange for me to meet some clients, or prospective clients. My visits were not a matter of a CEOs inspection, but an opportunity of opening a few doors and increasing the work-flow. During one such visit Gordon decided that a trip to Cairo would be appropriate as we were contemplating opening an office there. At the time we had a major commission involving the preparation of a claim and Gordon thought that a visit to the client's office would be appropriate, along with meeting a few prospective clients. It was about 11.00pm when we arrived in Cairo and during the taxi journey to the hotel I noticed that cars didn't stop when arriving at traffic lights showing red, unless it was obvious that an accident would result if they didn't. The reception area in the Intercontinental Hotel was a combination of check-in, bar and general meeting place and was heaving with people when we arrived after midnight. We fought our way to the check-in to be told that only one room had been reserved. I advised the check-in clerk that this was totally unacceptable and produced a hotel written confirmation of two rooms being booked. After a conversation with his senior manager the clerk apologised and advised us that we could have the Presidential Suite as well as the room they had reserved for us. There being a pecking order in the company, I took the Suite and Gordon the room. The Suite was magnificent, as in addition to a sumptuous bedroom there was a fully fitted kitchen, lounge, dining room and bathroom. We stayed for three days and from the morning following our arrival to our departure, I was regularly left messages to contact reception. Knowing that they intended to bounce me down to a standard room, I carefully avoided the reception for the three days of our stay. The idea of an office in Cairo was a non- event as it was the wrong place at the wrong time.

3.103 We were acting for Bechtel an American company who had a dispute with the Government of Dubai, relating to a major project which had been cancelled just prior to a start being made on site. The client accepted that some element of compensation should be paid, but the dispute concerned the amount of money which was due. A great deal of the design work had been completed and significant numbers of staff had relocated to Dubai from the USA. There were also significant cancellation charges to be paid as orders had been placed with subcontractors and suppliers. A claim had been prepared by our staff in Dubai and in the absence of agreement being reached, an arbitration notice had been served. The lawyers appointed by Bechtel to represent it in the arbitration proceedings were looking to appoint an expert witness regarding quantum and Gordon suggested that he put my name forward. I was, to say the least, a little reluctant due to my lack of familiarity with local Dubai costs; however Gordon indicated that I would receive all the assistance I required from our staff in Dubai, who would write the expert report on my behalf. When offered a commission, the word no doesn't appear in my lexicon and I was duly appointed. Under no stretch of the imagination was I an expert in relation to construction costs which were applicable in Dubai. Other than the cost of a taxi, hotel room and meal in a restaurant, I hadn't a clue of what anything cost there. I comforted myself in the knowledge that in nine cases out of ten disputes which were referred to arbitration settled before the hearing took place. This dispute unfortunately was the tenth and the hearing proceeded. My biggest fear was that it would soon be made clear that under no stretch of the imagination could I be described as an expert in construction costs in Dubai and be made to look a fool. Matters didn't improve when I discovered, on the first day of the hearing, that John Uff QC was representing the Government of Dubai. John was an old friend, but this wouldn't stop him from tearing me to shreds in the witness box. When discussing the evidence I was to give with my colleagues, I had noticed a construction price book, similar to Spons and Laxtons used in the UK, which set out in great detail construction costs and prices which were applicable in Dubai. In line with normal practice a QC doesn't act alone but has a junior barrister to assist him in his work. When it became my turn to give evidence, John's colleague undertook the task of cross-examining me. His first question, as expected, was to enquire as to my knowledge of Dubai construction costs. I explained that they were limited, but I had received a great deal of assistance from my Dubai colleagues. He then pointed out that the expert witness acting for the government was a locally based quantity surveyor fully familiar with the local prices. My response was to say that as the local construction price book was approximately two inches thick, it would be surprising if he was familiar with any more that a small fraction of the prices contained therein. In giving my answers, I addressed them to the arbitrator, as he was the person I had to convince. The arbitrator was a Swiss gentleman and from the look on his face seemed satisfied with my answer. To cut a long story short the arbitrator awarded our client a sum of money which was not far short of the sum claimed and I turned out to be one of the heroes of the hour. However the triumph was short-lived as the government refused to pay the arbitrator's award. The matter was referred to the local court for enforcement. Due however to procedural matters regarding the giving of oaths before the arbitrator and a failure on the part of the arbitrator to sign every page of the award, the court refused enforcement. This is now a landmark case in Dubai to which reference is regularly made.

3.104 With the success of the Dubai office we began to look elsewhere to plant our flag. Gordon Moffat suggested Abu Dhabi, which is an hour's drive from Dubai and was in the process of following the lead set by Dubai in building up large shopping centres and other commercial buildings, which would make it an ideal location for an office. He felt that claims would be as plentiful as coconuts on the palm trees and so we decided to open up there which we accomplished in 1999 when we appointed Steve Exelby as the manager. Despite his Danish name Steve was a thorough Englishman and a rabid supporter of Sheffield Wednesday. In no time at all the office was up and running. After a while Steve decided to move home to live in Dubai. Steve secured a very nice apartment overlooking the Dubai Marina, which I had the pleasure of visiting. Steve also made a bit of history in that the purchase of his apartment was one of the first by an expat after the rule that only residents of the United Arab Emirates, of which Dubai was one, could purchase property in Dubai, was changed. When Steve moved to Dubai, Alan Davidson took over as manager of the Abu Dhabi office and was later joined in 2003 by Hamish a very experienced operator with good local contacts who acted as joint manager with Alan. The number of staff built up and shortly after the arrival of Hamish we had ten employees.

3.105 Gordon was in favour of further expansion and Qatar was suggested as the next place for us to open an office. As usual Gordon had the ideal man to manage the office, this time it was Tom Sawyers, another Scotsman, and so in 2004 we established our third Middle East office. I was more that satisfied that my refusal to accept defeat had come good. After Cyprus and our early efforts in Dubai, it would have been easy to give up and go home with my tail between my legs. When added together, the staff in Dubai, Abu Dhabi and Qatar numbered in the region of 60. I was lucky in meeting Gordon again, as it was the result of his skill and knowledge that led to our success.

3.106 Our London office was jogging along having had three managers. Phil Brady followed by Colin Archibald and then Mike Hall. Rather unexpectedly Mike handed in his notice having decided to take up a position with a trade association. There was nobody employed in the London office whom I considered suitable to appoint as manager and so it became necessary to cast the net further afield. John Dobson had been employed in the Cheltenham office for some time and I had got to know him quite well. He had become the joint editor of Construction Industry Law Letter, a prestigious construction magazine with headquarters based in London, and seemed to enjoy visits to London and most things which were London related. I mentioned to Mike Milne, the Cheltenham office manager, that I was giving some consideration to appointing John as the next London office manager. Mike was supportive and felt if John moved to London it would not be too difficult to find a replacement. I didn't know how this would affect John's domestic arrangements but felt that if there was likely to be a problem it would be a matter for him to raise. John was very positive when I broached the matter with him and in no time at all he was in post. It didn't take him long to advise me that, in his opinion, the London office which was still located in Dryden Street, Covent Garden, where we rented desk spaces, seemed like the poor relation in the firm. He suggested that he look for new premises with which I was in full agreement. I realised this would push up the costs, but if we could secure better premises and aim high, London was the ideal place to undertake such as venture. Office space in the mid-1980s in London was very difficult to secure, as the boom in office development hadn't got underway at that time. Still John, not to be deterred, wore out copious amounts of shoe leather before coming up with an office location in Bedford Avenue, which we both considered suitable. We were on a short notice period in Dryden Street and so we were soon able to vacate the premises and bed ourselves in at our new location. John set about increasing the commissions and recruitment of senior fee earning staff. Geoff Brewer was one of the new arrivals having previously worked for a UK firm of consulting engineers in Paris and was to have a significant input into our growth in London.

3.107 After about three years John decided he would like to return to his home in Gloucester and was transferred back to work in the Cheltenham office. We needed a replacement manager and I had no hesitation in appointing Geoff Brewer. After about twelve months I received a call from Geoff to say he would like to see me fairly quickly and as I was due to pay a visit to the London office it was easily arranged. It was obvious from the outset that Geoff had big ideas which presented me with no difficulties. Geoff explained that he thought the office was too small and that we needed bigger and better premises. Ambition for the firm was always going to find favour with me and so I gave it my full approval to start looking. In no time at all Geoff had found premises in Bedford Square, a prestigious part of London. The snag was that the rent was £175,000 per annum, a big jump from the £20,100 we were currently paying. I told Geoff that I would require a little time to come to a decision. One of the difficulties, apart from the rent, was that the lease period extended to 25 years without a break clause. If it all turned to sawdust it wouldn't break the firm but for a few years it would leave a big dent in the profits. I spoke to Patrick and told him that unless he had very good reasons, I intended to give Geoff the go-ahead. Patrick was in no position to say yea or nay as neither of us had a crystal ball, but I had plenty of confidence that we would make a success of the venture. Geoff went ahead and secured the lease. Both Geoff and I realised that we would have to step up the marketing and selling effort to secure the level of work necessary to make a success of the move. I decided to throw in my energies in an effort to secure more work and to facilitate this. To send a message that it had my full backing, I purchased an apartment in London and had an office allocated to me. This all happened in 1988 and from then onwards the whole scene in our London office changed. Geoff considered we were big league and it needed to be demonstrated. He believed in the big ticket marketing events and as a result typical venues were The Ritz, and Harrods. A memorable event was held in Smith Square, where we put on a concert for our guests featuring the London Vivaldi Orchestra. A cocktail party held at the top of Tower Bridge which had a panoramic view of the Thames both up and down stream was also a very memorable occasion.

3.108 In keeping with the big ticket marketing events a river trip on the Thames aboard the Silver Dolphin was arranged to take place in August 1989. We were advised that the river authority only allowed two minutes for picking up passengers in the location where it was to take place. I arrived at the pickup point about five minutes before the due time; it was pouring down with rain and there was nobody in sight. I wondered if I had mistaken the date. Eventually the boat arrived and as if from nowhere people descended on the boat and scrambled aboard. It seems they had all been sheltering in doorways and anywhere else inaccessible to the rain. Despite the foul weather, the event went off well, but there was one occurrence which took the gloss off the evening. It seems that one of the guests, the worse for drink, had been enjoying himself goosing some of the ladies. Unfortunately when in mid-stream, it is a little difficult to ask a guest to leave.

3.109 Nearly all the guests who had been invited arrived for the river trip on the Silver Dolphin, which in view of the disaster involving the sinking of the Marchioness two days earlier, when fifty-one people died, was surprising. The Marchioness was carrying more than 120 young people for an all-night party and within minutes of setting sail it was in collision with a massive Thames dredger, the Bowbelle, which was on its way out to sea. The skipper of the Bowbelle, Douglas Henderson, had severely limited vision at the front of the boat whilst the skipper of the Marchioness could only see directly behind him by leaving the wheel and poking his head out of a hatch. There was a lookout positioned on the Bowbelle, but there was no intercommunication or even loud hailers to allow for verbal communication. There were three walkie-talkies on board, but they hadn't been used for some time. The only method of communication between the lookout and the bridge was by shouting, but as the distance between them was almost the length of a football pitch, communication between bridge and lookout was virtually non-existent. There was some controversy as to whether the Marchioness changed course into the path of the Bowbelle, but at the inquest it was held that there was no intention to change course and any deviation could have been due to the swell of the river. Passengers on the Hurlingham which was close by observed that the Marchioness was pushed over by Bowbelle and went under its bow before sinking. Many of the passengers were thrown into the river, whilst others were trapped below deck. There was a further catastrophe with regard to the rescue. The first alert occurred at 1.46 am which arrived at the rescue services base over the marine radio and broadcast "Wapping Police Wapping Police emergency pleasure boat is sunk Cannon Bridge railway bridge". Unfortunately the officer responsible for responding to the call thought he heard the broadcast as Battersea Road Bridge and sent the fire brigade to the wrong location. It was twenty minutes after the collision that the fire brigade received the correct location. Passengers on the Hurlingham rescued 20 survivors, officers on a police launch managed to drag 22 onto their boat, which was designed for three crew and two passengers, with a second police launch rescuing 15.

Geoff was tenacious at chasing up opportunities. I recall him getting a sniff of a possible commission in respect of the new British Library, which was a very prestigious project but with a catalogue of claims which had been allowed to gather dust. Geoff wouldn't give up until eventually he secured the work. We also held a great many seminars in London which were always well attended and produced work and good profits.

CHAPTER EIGHTEEN

DIVERSIFICATION AND OVERSEAS DEVELOPMENT

3.110 We opened two spin-off offices from London, being Brentwood and Weybridge. Bob Kingston who was employed in the London office and lived in Essex, was appointed as manager of Brentwood. The office was a bit low key but made modest profits. When Bob left, there was no suitable person available to be his replacement and so the office was closed. A slightly different story emerged when Roy Reynolds was transferred from London to open an office in Weybridge. Profits were good from the outset and when Roy left to start his own company, Paul Lomas Clarke took over and for many years carried on in the same manner. The intention was for the three offices to run separately but to co-operate in securing work, sharing staff and providing a good service which is what they achieved.

3.111 In the late 1980s the idea of diversification was in vogue. All the eggs in one basket was considered to be a poor recipe. When it was suggested that we might consider setting up a loss adjusting subsidiary I was all in favour. Armed with little intelligence as to how they worked or their potential profitability, I decided to advertise the position of manager and see what came to the surface. There were two really good applicants and being in a dilemma as to which one to appoint, I took the coward's way out and appointed them both which was in 1992. My thinking was that we would make Colin Dawson the Northern Region Manager and David Parker the Southern Region Manager and the company would be styled Knowles Loss Adjusters. After about six months Colin Dawson resigned, leaving David Parker to run the whole show. I considered that we should specialise in claims arising out of construction work and as David had been a quantity surveyor in the early part of his career, this seemed a sensible plan. David soon disabused me of this idea as being too restrictive. I took an interest in the early days to find out how the business worked. I was surprised at how small the fees were on most of the projects. David explained that as many of the claims were of low value, the amount of time spent on each claim had to be proportionate. We were able to keep some of the running costs low by using spare rooms in the London office in Bedford Square and in Knutsford where Knowles Loss Adjusters offices were established. David Parker was a human dynamo and quickly built up a sizeable clientele. David appointed Simon Smith as his No. 2 which worked well. After steady progress, by the year 2005 the numbers employed had reached 40 and the fee income £2.4m per annum.

3.112 Bert Hamilton, a likeable Irishman, joined the staff in the London office in the mid-1990s. In a conversation we had, he recounted his recent experiences of working in the USA as a project manager. The role of project manager had existed for some time in the USA, but had only fairly recently arrived on our shores. Bert enquired as to whether we had any plans to get into project management and if so he would like to be considered. David Parker was doing well with Knowles Loss Adjusters and showing profits and so I thought "why not?" It didn't take long for Mandeco to get off the ground with Bert at the helm. I had no idea of the significance of the name, which was Bert's choice, but an office wag styled it the Manchester Decorating Company. After a few weeks Bert came to see me and explained that he had undertaken a large marketing exercise comprising mainly of mailshots. From the results of research undertaken in the USA, Bert was convinced we should immediately recruit a number of staff in readiness for the anticipated surge in work. Bert suggested using psychometric testing, as a method of selection when choosing which of the applicants we intended to appoint. This method of staff selection had been devised by occupational psychologists and had originally been used in education psychology. It comprises a series of set questions for which there are a number of alternative answers provided, from which the applicants are required to make a choice. The questions deal with numeric reasoning, verbal reasoning and diagrammatic reasoning. The answers provided by the candidates are then compared with the standard answers, which dictates the candidate's score. There are many different sets of questions and answers from which employers can choose the most suitable, dependent upon the post on offer. For example the questions posed to a prospective managing director would differ from those relating to a school teacher. It seemed too much like the TV programme Who Wants to Be a Millionaire for my liking and I rejected the idea. Some years later, the Co-op Bank got into financial difficulties having lost £700m in the first half of 2013 and discovering a £1.5b hole in its balance sheet. The Reverend Paul Flowers was the chairman at the time and after the finances of the bank became public, questions were asked as to his suitability to be the chairman of a major bank. He was found to have had no experience of banking, prior to becoming chairman and had a history of drug and sex abuse. When those on the appointing committee were questioned as to why Paul Flowers had been selected the response was that they had used psychometric testing and of those under consideration for appointment to the post, Paul Flowers had finished at the top. Having read a report of this matter in the press, I considered I was justified all those year ago in rejecting psychometric testing. Bert recruited Pat Simpson and Ian Bell but unfortunately we were never able to make a profit. The reason appeared to be that the fees we were able to charge were either lump sum, or a percentage of the contract price. The fee would probably have been sufficient if the work had finished on time, but invariably the work overran the contract period often by many weeks and we were involved in providing services until the work was complete with no opportunity of increasing the fees. The purpose of a commercial enterprise is to make money and as Mandeco showed no prospect of making profits I had to close it down. This is no reflection on the abilities of Bert, Pat and Ian who proved to be good operators. However when commercial reality kicks in, there are often casualties.

3.113 We had from time to time provided clients with surveying staff to work under their control and supervision, which was widely referred to as body shopping. Expanding this service would require little in the way of set-up costs and if it proved unsuccessful, closing it down would be a fairly simple and inexpensive matter. I considered that there may be a spin-off benefit, as with somebody on the inside, securing dispute work from construction clients should be a fairly simple matter. I asked Suzanne Cash, who was responsible for the seminars, if she was interested in heading up what became known as Staff Placements, to which she responded positively. This would add to her workload but the intention was to appoint somebody to undertake the day to day tasks. She recruited Sue Harrop and we were then in a position to get started. We had many clients in the construction industry and they were the first port of call for providing the service. Sue Harrop was an aggressive type and was on the telephone in no time seeking out opportunities. The business started to grow and the numbers and locations where we were asked to provide surveyors widespread. For example we provided ten surveyors for Siemens, some of whom were located overseas and had surveyors on sites as far away as Ethiopia and Tbilisi. Most of the disputes staff we employed had joined us after working for many years with firms of Quantity Surveyors, Contractors or Consulting Engineers and were mature in years, most of them being over 45 years of age with grown up families. Staff Placements, on the other hand, attracted much younger personnel often who had children of an early age. This from time to time presented a problem, as members of our staff, working many miles from home, were often needed by their wives to deal with difficulties arising with their children. However this was not a major problem, but one which we hadn't experienced before. My hopes that providing a surveyor to work in a contracting organisation would lead to dispute work, proved groundless, as our contractor clients expected this type of work to be undertaken by the surveyor provided by Staff Placements. A further unforeseen aspect of the service was that our competitors recruited their surveying staff straight from college or university. Our policy was to ensure that the personnel we provided were experienced surveyors, who obviously were more expensive. The result was that whilst Staff Placements was a successful enterprise, the profits were somewhat thin. Having diversified into loss adjusting and body shopping successfully, I was out of ideas for any further forays into setting up new enterprises.

3.114 Bill Minnitt had in 1983 secured an arrangement with the National Federation of Building Trades Employers (NFBTE) North West Division to provide free advice over the telephone to its members. The NFBTE became the Building Employer's Confederation (BEC) and this arrangement continued. We went even further in an attempt to attract business in offering members a 10% discount on our fees, often referred to as the BEC discount. This came to an end when the BEC employed its own in-house lawyers, who would attend meetings and provide written advice to the members without making any charge, as it was all covered by the annual subscription. However it is said that as one door closes another opens. I was introduced to John Hood, the Secretary of the Suspended Ceiling Association. John was a very caring person and a member of the Church of Jesus Christ of Latter Day Saints originally known as the Mormons. John was not for ramming his religion down throats, but he lived his religion in his day to day life. I explained to him our free advice and fee discount service, which he liked the sound of and quickly got it established among his members. I went round the country giving talks to them and it soon became established. In like manner to the BEC advice service, it led to good fee earning work. Unfortunately John died and his position with the Suspended Ceiling Association was taken up by Jean Birch whom I got along with very well and we continued the arrangement I had started with John. The Suspended Ceiling Association was part of an umbrella association styled FASS, the Federated Association of Specialist Subcontractors, which represented many trade associations in addition to the Suspended Ceiling Association. John Huxtable was the director of FASS, whom I met through knowing John Hood. He was interested in the free advice and fee discount service, which soon became established among member companies of the Trade Associations which formed part of FASS. John however left his employment with FASS, his replacement being Ron Davies. Ron had his own tame firm of solicitors, who rather liked our arrangement with FASS as they, like us, could see it for the major opportunities it presented. Our relationship with Trade Associations thus came to an end, however we had secured a number of clients from the arrangement and provided services to many of them for years to come.

3.115 I received a telephone call from David Price in early 1985. He was the secretary of the Royal Institution of Chartered Surveyors, Junior Organisation, Liverpool and Isle of Man Branch and enquired if I would be willing to give a talk at a branch meeting to be held in Liverpool, to which I responded in the affirmative. The event went well and I thought no more of the matter until shortly after when I received a letter from David enquiring as to whether we had any vacancies, as he was looking to advance his career in dispute resolution. He was at the time in his late 20s, employed by GD Walford, a Liverpool firm of quantity surveyors, qualified as a Chartered Surveyors and studying for a law degree. I passed the letter to Mike Wills and asked him to deal with the matter. David was duly appointed and took up a position in our Knutsford office. He was a keen sportsman and supporter of Liverpool FC. He played cricket for Liverpool and when at his best had a golf handicap of three. His own football playing days had ended prematurely due to an injury. David kept his head down and got on with the job. Richard Davies, the manager of the Liverpool office, handed in his notice in 1989 as he was planning to start his own firm with two other members of the Liverpool staff, Peter Kerrigan and Terry Hughes, styling themselves Davies, Kerrigan and Hughes. In addition to losing three good fee earners, we no doubt lost a few good clients. I had to decide on a replacement, the bookies' favourite being one of the remaining consultants in the Liverpool office. However I made an inspired decision in appointing David, who I personally took to the Liverpool office to introduce him to the remaining staff. From the outset the office, with David as manager, continued to do well. It was a help that the office had been effectively run by Richard Davies, but none-the-less three good fee earners had left together with a few clients which left the office in need of restoration.

3.116 David made the right move from the outset in recruiting some very good fee earners; the main leading lights being Terry Clarke, Brian Calardine and Brian Pierpoint, all older than David but very experienced. Terry Clarke and Brian Calardine were engineers steeped in civil engineering, which enabled work to be secured from the engineering industry in general and civil engineering industry in particular. At a fairly early stage David began to take an interest in securing work from overseas clients; the early 1990s being a time of recession in the construction industry in the UK. I recall standing on Westminster Bridge in London and having searched the skyline through 360 degrees, hadn't seen a single tower crane. David recruited Rachel Vaughan as an international co-ordinator and serious marketing of potential international clients began in earnest. In 1995 we set up a formal International Division based at an office in Gadbrook Park in Northwich. We had a team of four comprising David who was transferred from the Liverpool office, Reg Thomas who had returned from Cyprus, Cathy Jones, who by then had replaced Rachel Vaughan and Anne Custerson the office secretary.

3.117 We had, by the mid-1990s, twenty offices in the UK, comprising Glasgow, Edinburgh and Stirling in Scotland, Cardiff and Colwyn Bay in Wales and Newcastle, Leeds, Sheffield, Nottingham, Sutton Coldfield, Manchester, Liverpool, Knutsford, Bristol, Cheltenham, Winchester, Weybridge, Crawley, London and Cambridge in England. I felt that there could be no justification for any more offices in the UK, as we had full coverage and therefore I should put my full weight behind the development of overseas markets. We used our tried and tested seminars to provide leads for new clients and I made regular overseas trips with David. The first international seminar we did was for Interbeton, an international firm of building contractors and civil engineers, who engaged us to present a two day course in Holland for their overseas staff, the subject matter being the international construction contract FIDIC. The in-house organiser of the course was Evert-Jan Van Der Berg. He was a lovely man and really appreciated the course we ran. It was also very popular with overseas based staff, who could return to Holland for a few days to attend the course and naturally visit their families. This course was held for eight years on the trot until Evert-Jan retired and the course seemed to retire with him. Interbeton were part of HBG a much larger organisation which provided David with a good introduction.

3.118 David had been chasing opportunities with Skanska, a major international construction company based in Sweden. A three day course was organised in February 1994 by Agne Sandberg, head of Skanska's legal department and held in Stockholm. My main memory of the trip was the freezing weather. Once this course had finished we went direct to Sao Paulo in Brazil where the weather was a very humid 100 degrees plus, to deliver a three day seminar to CBPO, who were part of Odebrecht. My abiding memory of this trip was the advice given by the staff at the hotel where we were staying, which was not to venture out of the hotel unless accompanied by an armed guard.

CHAPTER NINETEEN

WORKING IN KOREA AND THE LATHAM REPORT

3.119 During the summer of 1996 David got wind of a major dispute on a bridge project in Bangladesh involving Hyundai, the contractor. It seems one of their vice presidents, Mr Kong, was due to visit London and David managed to arrange for us to take him out for lunch. Mr Kong explained that they were in dispute with the Architect they had engaged to design the scheme. It seems he was based in California and whilst the specification had called for British Standards to be applied in the design of the work, the Architect had in error used USA standards. The error had been discovered partway through the construction process and as a result a substantial amount of remedial work became necessary which resulted in a great deal of associated additional cost. David and I applied the hard sell for which we received some encouragement from Mr Kong. It was left that if we were really interested in representing Hyundai we should at our own expense visit the site at Jamuna Bridge in Bangladesh and then travel on to Seoul to meet the Hyundai in-house team and they would then make a decision whether or not to appoint us. I felt that Mr Kong was genuine and being confident of our own abilities at securing work, I accepted the risk of time and money being spent to no avail. I didn't bother to calculate what those abortive costs would be if we didn't secure the commission, as it might have proved off-putting.

3.120 We arrived at Manchester Airport on 13th September 1996 on the first leg of our trip. We both had fairly sizable amounts of luggage and having placed mine in position and had it checked in, as a friendly gesture I did the same with David's, but due to the weight of his cases it felt that my arm was about to be ripped out of its socket. David, assuming the water in Bangladesh would not be fit to drink or the food in any way edible, had packed a suitcase full of bottles of water and apples. In reality the water turned out to be eminently drinkable and the Chinese chefs as good as any to be found in upmarket London Chinese restaurants. Jamuna Bridge connects Bhagalpur on the east bank of the Jamuna River with Sinajganj on the west bank. The bridge is 4.8 km long and carries a dual two-lane highway; dual gauge (broad and metre) railway; high voltage (230KV) electrical interconnector; telecommunication cable and 750 diameter high pressure natural gas pipe. Prior to the completion of the bridge in 1998, people and goods crossed the river by way of the ferries. The cost of construction was $699 million and the bridge at the time of building was the eleventh longest in the world. Following completion in 1998 cracks appeared in the structure which in 2008 resulted in the Government threatening to bring an action against Hyundai for faulty design. When we arrived at the airport in Korea, it was decided that we would need some local currency and so converted £400 into takas. We were met at the airport by representatives of Hyundai and driven to the site, where we were due to stay for the next three days and then returned from site to the airport in a similar manner. This meant at the end of the trip, with nothing on site for which a payment from us was required we still had the equivalent of £400 in takas when we arrived home. When we attempted to convert the takas into sterling, we were told the money was worthless other than in Bangladesh, we therefore donated the money to an airlines charity. Life on site for the Korean workforce was no picnic. They worked a 12 hour day, 13 days out of 14 with the final day off. There were little or no recreational facilities apart from a golf driving range and the nearest town was two hours' drive. The accommodation on site was, by Western standards, very poor and that included ours which were the equivalent of officer's quarters. Hyundai employed on site a bridge engineer Mr E. B. Lee, who was given the nickname of Leapy after the pop singer Leapy Lee who was a one hit wonder with his recording of Little Arrows. Leapy had been delegated to show us round and generally make us feel at home. When we asked him how Hyundai managed to retain personnel on site, his response was to inform us that in Korea they had for their young men the equivalent of our post war National Service which had operated in the UK between 1945 and 1963 and required all eighteen year old males to serve two years in the armed forces. In the case of the young male Korean, the choice was either two years in the armed forces, or two years working on an international construction site.

3.121 The morning after we arrived in Seoul, we were invited by Mr Kong to attend a meeting at which we could address those present as to the services we were able to offer in respect of Hyundai's case against the American Architect who had designed the bridge. When we had made our presentation, we were allowed to stay whilst those at the meeting discussed whether to appoint us or not. There were six Koreans at the meeting including the company lawyer. We had become very friendly with Leapy, who advised us that the in-house lawyer had opposed our appointment, no doubt he considered that a firm of lawyers would be preferable. We couldn't understand what was being said as they all spoke in Korean, however it became obvious that the lawyer was not getting things his own way. When the meeting came to an end Mr Kong, who acted as the chairman, informed us that they intended to appoint us subject to a suitable fee being agree with Mr E B Lee. It was approaching lunchtime by then and Leapy, David and I were dispatched to another room to effect the agreement. We explained that as we were not familiar with the details of the case, it would be impossible to agree a lump sum fee for our services and it would be a matter of setting out our hourly rates for various levels of staff plus expenses. We quickly produced a list of hourly rates at which point Leapy informed us that he would have to discuss the matter with Mr Kong. He returned some three hours later to say that Mr Kong wasn't happy with the rates we had proposed and that we would have to reduce them if we were to secure the appointment. It was by then the end of the working day and Leapy suggested the meeting should be reconvened the following morning. David and I had included a bit of fat in the rates and so we were not too worried about offering a reduction. When we met the following morning we advised Leapy of the revised rates and he informed us that he would have to discuss the matter with Mr Kong. He returned just prior to lunch time to inform us that Mr Kong didn't like the revised rates and that we would have to reduce them further to secure the appointment. David and I discussed the matter over lunch and anxious not to return home empty handed, reduced the rates down to the bone. The same old routine applied after lunch with Leapy disappearing to discuss the matter with Mr Kong. We both realised that as it was Friday and as the following week was a public holiday in Korea, if we didn't reach agreement before close of play that day then our chances of securing the commission were virtually nil. On his return Leapy advised us that Mr Kong was prepared to accept the rates but required some assurances as to the level of expenses we were intending to charge. Our firm had never been in the habit of uplifting the sums expended on expenses and we assured Leapy we only charge out of pocket expenses. We left Korea very pleased and much wiser with the commission in the bag. The work on the commission was undertaken by Danny Atkinson, a civil engineer/ barrister who worked on the project for a couple of years spending some time in California negotiating with lawyers acting for the

Architect and also lawyers acting for the Architect's Insurers. Finally a deal was struck which pleased Hyundai. We were also more than happy as our fees for the commission exceeded £1m. The relationship with Hyundai blossomed and they were still using the firm's services on other projects nearly twenty years later.

3.122 Hyundai put us in touch with the International Contractors Association of Korea, who asked us to present a seminar to its members. We thought this would be an introduction to a few more Korean contractors with problems similar to those of Hyundai and so we gladly accepted. This was popular with the Koreans and we were asked back on two subsequent occasions. It was during the trip made in August 1997 that I heard of the death of Princess Diana. I had arrived at the Lotte Hotel in Seoul before David and when he turned up asked if I had heard the news concerning Princess Diana, which up to that point in time I hadn't. She had died as a result of injuries sustained in a car crash in the Pont de l'Alma road tunnel in Paris. Her boyfriend Dodi Fayed and the driver Henri Paul were also pronounced dead at the scene; the bodyguard Trevor Rees-Jones was the only survivor. Although the media pinned the blame on the paparazzi, the crash was found by the French judicial investigation held in 1999 to have been caused by the reckless actions of the chauffeur, who was head of security at the Ritz Hotel and had earlier goaded the paparazzi who were waiting outside the hotel. The judicial investigation found that the crash was due to Henri Paul having lost control of the car at high speed whilst drunk. The deaths were held to have been contributed to by the deceased not wearing seat belts. We delivered our last seminar in Korea in 1998 and as no work opportunities arose from the visits we handed the contact over to Mike Charlton who was based in Hong Kong, only a short flight from Seoul.

3.123 Our main sources of work came from disputes arising on building projects. Work which arrived from engineering projects was not so frequent. We employed at least three members of staff with great experience in the engineering business, Danny Atkinson, Terry Clarke and Tim McGoldrick and I thought that if they worked together the number of commissions on engineering projects would increase; this led to the start of the Engineering Division. I would with hindsight judge it as a qualified success as all three were good as either solo artists or team players, but their day to day commitments left little time for working together to secure more engineering work. I did become involved in the work of the Engineering Division through Terry, who had made his mark among dredging contractors. One of his disputes involved Zanen Dredging, who were contracted to undertake dredging work in connection with the River Conway crossing which had become the subject of a dispute regarding payment in respect of a casting basin; the dispute didn't settle and was referred to arbitration. Terry had become our dredging expert with a few dredging contractors forming part of his portfolio of clients and this was one of his cases. I am not sure how it happened, but I was appointed as the quantum expert representing Zanen at the arbitration. I hoped with reasonable expectation that it would settle as I dreaded having to give evidence as an expert regarding the cost relating to dredging as my knowledge of all matters relating thereto was nil. The dispute wasn't settled and all too quickly the day of the hearing arrived. The arbitrator was Douglas Stephenson who was well known and very experienced. Richard Fernyhough QC was the barrister acting for Costain Tarmac, the opposition. Richard was a friend, but all friendships are suspended when it comes to cross examination. I expected Richard's first question would require me to outline my experience of dredging which would place me in trouble from the outset. If asked this question I intended to admit that my experience was limited but considered dredging to be part of the civil engineering industry of which my experience was quite extensive. Not much of an answer but the best I could come up with. Richard in addressing me, much to my amazement and relief, at the outset asked if I considered that dredging was a civil engineering process and didn't bother to probe into my dredging experience. As an old friend he must have realised my dilemma and taken pity on me. Our client was awarded a substantial sum of money and so I managed to keep my reputation intact. Danny Atkinson was involved in a major dispute relating to the design and manufacture of two tunnel boring machines used on the Storebelt Project in Denmark under Danish law. The tunnel boring machines, which were each about 100 metres long, broke down in the early part of the project. Was it the fault of the manufacturer, or the operator which caused the problem? We acted for the manufacturer and were able to prove some fault on the part of the operator which had the effect of significantly reducing the settlement sum.

3.124 By the early 1990s the construction industry in the UK was engulfed in a crisis. There had been a recession in the country in the late 1980s and early 1990s which had caused a drop in orders and a great deal of unemployment. Prices were at rock bottom and contractors and subcontractors in large numbers were experiencing cash-flow problems which often led to insolvency. Despite the shortage of work, costs due to inefficiencies in the UK construction industry were far higher when compared with other countries in Europe and the USA. Disputes were rife and often were referred to arbitration or litigation which proved extremely time-consuming and very costly. It was felt in Parliament that something had to be done. On 5th July 1993 it was announced in the House of Commons that there was to be a Joint Review of Procurement and Arrangements in the United Kingdom Construction Industry. The Review was to be conducted by Sir Michael Latham who produced an interim report entitled Trusting the Team which was published in December 1993. The Final Report entitled Constructing the Team was published in July 1994. The

Report made a number of recommendations the principle ones being:

Partnering should be used to encourage the establishment of long-term contracting arrangements

The New Engineering Contract (NEC) should be adopted more widely as a less adversarial form of contract.

A specific duty to deal fairly with each other and the supply chain in an atmosphere of mutual co-operation

Firm duties of teamwork with shared financial motivation

Risk allocation to the party best able to manage, estimate and carry it

Steps should be taken to avoid disputes

Dispute where unavoidable should be resolved quickly by referral to an adjudicator.

Sir Michael suggested that if the full range of measures described in the report were adopted, savings of 30% could be achieved over five years.

He also expressed the opinion that unless his recommendations were backed up by statute very little in the industry would change.

CHAPTER TWENTY

THE CONSTRUCTION ACT

3.125 As a result of the publication of The Latham Report, a major event occurred with the coming into law of The Housing Grants, Construction and Regeneration Act, commonly referred to as the Construction Act, which received the Royal Assent in July 1996, but did not come into force until 1st May 1998 and only applied to contracts entered into after that date. The intention of the delay was to give the industry time to digest the contents of the Act and to take whatever steps were necessary for its implementation. As far as we were concerned the adjudication provisions lit a bonfire under the existing methods of resolving disputes. Prior to the Act coming into force, if there was no arbitration clause in the contract, all unresolved disputes would be referred to the court for a final decision. This was almost without exception, a long and costly process. Where the contract provided for disputes to be referred to an independent arbitrator the process would be quicker and cheaper, or at least that was the intention, as the arbitrator would normally be a technical person who fully understood the industry and hearings would not be delayed awaiting a time slot in the court calendar. This was the theory, but in practice the legal profession, who were often appointed by the parties, went at the same pace as they did when cases were referred to the courts, incurring similar costs.

The adjudication process, as provided for in the Act, allows either party to commence an adjudication at any time. The adjudicator would be the person named in the contract, or if none is named an application must be made to the adjudicating nominating body named in the contract to make the appointment and if none is stated, the party who served the adjudication notice may request any adjudicating nominating body to make the appointment. The referring party must send to the adjudicator, within 7 days of its Notice of Adjudication, its case accompanied by all supporting documentation. A decision must then be made within a further 28 days. This period can be extended by 14 days with the approval of the referring party.

The parties must abide by the adjudicator's decision. However at a later stage the matter may be referred to court, where the case can be heard, but in the meantime the adjudicator's decision must be implemented.

3.126 The Act also includes provisions intended to deal with payment abuse and covers the following matters:

Entitlement to and amount of stage payments

Dates for payment

Final date for payment

Notice specifying the amount of payment to be made

Notice of an intention to withhold payment

3.127 There was a period of just short of two years from the Royal Assent to the date the Act came into force. We realised that there would be a great deal of interest and requirement for knowledge from within the industry and therefore swung into action in putting on a seminar roadshow round the country which dealt with the provisions of the Act and how it would affect companies involved in construction. Realising that Professional Bodies, Trade Associations and others would be putting on seminars to explain the provisions of the Act, on the basis of the early bird gets the worm, I was determined to be the first in the field. I wrote the programme and course notes and Suzanne Cash got on with all the arrangements and in no time we were up and running. The seminars were very successful and they also gave us an opportunity of selling our services relating to adjudication.

3.128 We became interested in the provisions of the Act with regard to the appointment of an adjudicator. Rather strangely there are no requirements as to who could class themselves as an adjudicator nominating body. We therefore decided to start one of our own. Mike Milne was very much involved in the idea of setting up an adjudicator nominating body and with Penny, the Cheltenham office administrator, went about establishing the Academy of Construction Adjudicators which was to be based in the Cheltenham office. We held a spectacular opening at the House of Commons and then Mike ran an adjudication roadshow round the country which was aimed at adjudicators and those with ambitions to become adjudicators, and was very successful. It provided an opportunity for publicising the ACA as the Academy became known. I attended the seminar held in Salford which I found both enjoyable and instructive. Penny had been dealing with applications for the appointment of adjudicators and after two years the ACA had made more appointments than any of the other appointing bodies, which included the Royal Institution of Chartered Surveyors and the Royal Institute of British Architects. Unfortunately all good things come to an end. We received several complaints that in respect of some adjudications, we had appointed the adjudicator through the ACA and also represented one of the parties and hence a conflict of interest existed. With great reluctance we came to the conclusion that we would have to find others to run the ACA. After due consideration, Mike Milne, Penny and I decided to make a present of it to the National Specialist Contractors Council, which represents subcontractors. This proved to be a good home for the ACA which was restyled The Association of Independent Construction Adjudicators and named in all the JCT contracts as one of a list of four nominating bodies.

3.129 Our biggest fee earner in the UK was representing parties who had referred their dispute to arbitration. The advent of adjudication hit arbitration hard. Contractors and subcontractors who had submitted claims which were getting nowhere were very excited at the prospect of referring it to adjudication and getting a decision in less than two months. This being the case arbitration was a non-starter. There was no history of how to put together documents for referral to adjudication. It was intended to be a stopgap to keep the money flowing and not the final decision on any disputed matter. However it soon became in the majority of disputes, the first and last stop in the dispute resolution process. We soon developed a procedure and all offices in no time were offering a service. The legal profession was slow at getting off the mark, as in most cases the referral document usually was a contractor or subcontractor's loss and expense claim which solicitors had no expertise in preparing. If a loss and expense claim had already been prepared, it was a simple matter for the contractor or subcontractor to undertake the referral itself.

3.130 We were concerned, with regard to the recommendation in the Latham Report that partnering should be used to encourage the establishment of long-term relationships, the objective being the avoidance of disputes. If this caught on in all probability there would be a major downturn in disputes and as a result our business would be adversely affected. Could we offer a service relating to partnering? Nigel Barr, who was based in our Sheffield office, suggested that we offer a service and that it would be implemented by himself and Sharron Taylor, one of his colleagues in Sheffield. With this in mind we set up a subsidiary company which offered the following services:

Partnering training, advice and facilitation

Procurement

Risk management

Supply chain management

Facilitated problem resolution

Open book accounting

3.131 We were the first in the field to offer consultancy services relating to Partnering and it wasn't long before we were securing a significant amount of work in the public sector. In particular Local Authorities and Housing Associations were very interested in adopting Partnering in their relationships with contractors and consultants, but they lacked the know-how. Nigel built up a team comprising himself and Sharron, plus Adrian Smith, Helen Garnett-Spence, Sarah Morgan, Lynne Margett and Liam Keane who toured the country providing Partnering advice. In some instances it took the form of inter-active training sessions; on other occasions written or verbal advice was provided. The uptake of Partnering was mainly in the public sector, the private sector embracing adjudication with open arms. Within four years of the Act coming into force we had represented parties in over 1,000 adjudications. The main beneficiaries of adjudication were subcontractors who being at the end of the food chain were apt to suffer most with regard to payment issues.

3.132 Nigel and Sharron, in their involvement in seeking out clients, came into contact with the Federation of Property

Societies (FPS) formed in 1988, being an umbrella organisation of Local Authorities which has a number of objectives including bringing consistency to the approach of Local Authorities to property matters in the public sector and the spread of best practice. The FPS also disseminates information it receives to its members relating to all property matters. They became interested in Partnering and how it could be adopted by its members. It was suggested that there was a need for:

A website which contained comprehensive advice and support on Partnering

Process maps of Partnering and Procurement

A new contract designed for Partnering in the Public Sector

I volunteered to draft the contract which I completed with the help of Mike Wills. I gave the contract the title of Public Sector Partnering Contract (PSPC) which has ten options, dependent upon the procurement method adopted. The website, process maps and contract were styled Perform 21. A launch of the contract took place in Birmingham in 2004 and is used by a number of Local Authorities which includes Manchester City Council and a number of Local Authorities who grouped themselves together and were styled North West Construction Hub.

CHAPTER TWENTY-ONE

SOUTH AFRICAN TOUR AND NORTH AMERICAN EXPANSION

3.133 I had just finished presenting a seminar at a hotel near Heathrow when I was approached by a man who introduced himself as Chris Binnington. He explained that he lived in Johannesburg and one of his reasons for visiting the UK was to attend the seminar. It seems one of our booking forms had dropped out of a construction magazine which had landed on his desk. He along with his partner Bill Copeland ran a firm, Binnington Copeland, which provided a similar service to ourselves, but in South Africa. Chris liked the seminar and asked if I would be prepared to go to South Africa and run one there, sharing the lecturing duties with him. I knew nothing about Chris, his partner or any matter relating to South Africa. However we all arrive in this life with an instinct, which if we listen to carefully enough will usually provide us with good guidance. Mine advised me to express an interest in Chris' proposal and so it was left that he would produce a programme with suggested dates and contact me after he had returned home. The programme when it arrived looked fine to me. The proposal was that we would go on a tour with the seminar starting at Johannesburg and then move on to Durban and Capetown followed by Gaborone in Botswana and finish up with a repeat in Johannesburg. This all seemed good and the suggested dates didn't clash with anything else I had planned.

3.134 My wife Wendy fancied the trip and so on a fine day in March 1996 we set off for Johannesburg. I met Chris very soon after I had arrived along with Bill, his partner. I took to them both and knew I was on to a good thing. They had gone out to South Africa some years earlier to set up a dispute resolution firm which had gone well. The standard forms of contract and contractual systems were based upon those used in the UK and so the problems which arose from the use of these contracts were very similar to ours. Johannesburg was a dangerous place in which to live and work. The hotel staff warned us not to leave the hotel without a guard to accompany us. There were even areas within the city where it wasn't even safe to stop at traffic lights. However none of this affected us in any way. There was a full house at the seminar and it went extremely well. We then moved on to Durban which is on the coast and very pleasant, where again we were performing before a full house. It was then time to move on to Cape Town. Cape Town certainly has the wow factor, with stunning scenery and idyllic weather. Wendy and I would have been more than pleased to have stayed there for a few weeks. Again the seminar was well attended and so off we went to Gaborone in Botswana. I am not sure why Chris chose this venue. The airport was to say the least quaint, the departure and arrive lounges being accommodated in a large hut. The number of delegates was considerably less when compared with the three previous venues. However I was more than pleased that we had visited the country as what we were able to see in the short time we were there was very interesting. Finally it was back to Johannesburg for the final seminar. It was not as well attended as the first one, but Chris was happy with the numbers. Chris and Bill were delighted with the success of the tour and I thought it a lovely gesture for them to hand me a sizable cheque when we said our goodbyes at the airport on the way home. Reg Thomas, a seasoned international lecturer, also undertook a seminar tour in South Africa with Chris and Bill, which was very successful.

3.135 Geoff Brewer, who had managed the London office very successfully, handed in his notice and left in the spring of 1997. He had done a first class job in building up the size and profits of the office and I was sorry to see him go. Following his departure he started his own company and took a few of his colleagues with him. There was a tendency at the time to have restrictive clauses in employee's conditions of employment; when employed by LC Wakeman and Partners such clauses appeared in my terms of employment. The purpose of these clauses was to make it difficult for employees to leave the firm and set up in opposition. They normally stated a timescale during which the employee could not start a rival business and a minimum distance from the employer's place of work, within which the former employee could not operate a new business. This type of clause is difficult to enforce, as it is legally regarded as being in restraint of trade. I was also against such a clause on moral grounds. Whilst it is morally right to lay down rights and wrongs which govern employees' actions during their period of employment, in my opinion it is morally wrong to attempt to do so following their departure.

I had to make a decision as to who I would appoint to succeed Geoff. The stand out candidate was Danny Atkinson who had been with the company since 1989. During his time with us Danny had gained an LLB (Hons) and been called to the Bar. He was still fresh from his triumph in successfully settling the Hyundai dispute in California and had no hesitation in accepting the position.

3.136 Wardle House in Knutsford was getting crowded and if we were to carry on expanding some additional premises would be required. There was spare space in the

Liverpool and Manchester offices and we could have transferred some of the fee earners to one or both of these locations. This would have created some disruption and diluted the Knutsford branch which was running well as a team and would, in all probability have been unpopular with Mike Wills and the rest of the Knutsford staff and so the idea never progressed. The problem was solved when a building at Gadbrook Park Northwich, became available to rent. It was a well-appointed building and due to its location wouldn't create too much additional travelling time for those required to move. We transferred the usual head office functions such as accounts, H.R. and marketing plus the seminars and staff placements divisions leaving the fee earning staff at Wardle House. The International Division staff who were already based in other premises at Gadbrook Park were relocated into the new offices. I found myself a room, although it was not my intention to spend much time there. It proved to be quite an expensive exercise but I considered it worthwhile. Shortly after moving in I was reading an article concerning a consultancy which had gone out of business. The chief executive remarked that the rot set in when the company opened an expensive head office with its own flag and flag pole. I looked out of the window and noticed a flag emblazoned with our name fluttering at the top of a flag pole. I thought mmm.

3.137 I felt that I was fast approaching a business crossroads and had to make a decision as to which road to take. We had offices all around the UK plus ones in the Middle East and East Asia, but where do we go from there? I had passed the age of 60 and common sense may well have suggested that it was put your feet up time. This thought did not even reach the "to be considered" list, but I did need a new challenge. It seemed either we could continue expanding abroad or diversify. I had dabbled with the idea of diversifying and whilst Knowles Loss Adjusters was doing well and Staff Placements was successful, I didn't have any other bright ideas. We had, using Frank Hall, Brian Crabtree and Robert Evans, three employee Architects, tried promoting a full Architectural service but it hadn't caught on to any great extent. Further expansion overseas seemed the logical direction in which we should travel, however from our experiences in the Middle East I realised this could come at a price. I had been reading about small to medium companies floating on the Alternative Investment Market (AIM), a sort of small firms' stock exchange. I discussed the matter with Patrick, who warmed to the idea. He pointed out the drawbacks such as accountability to outside investors. However the idea of a substantial investment of money was a major factor and in my mind an AIM listing would be part of a succession plan for when my time for departure finally arrived. To cut a long story short we decided to go ahead with the idea. I say we, as I wouldn't have proceeded with the plan if Patrick had not been fully behind it. We appointed stockbrokers, Wise Speke, who guided us through the process. The system involves issuing shares in the firm; a major portion of shares came to me being the original owner, and a smaller but significant portion of shares to Mike Charlton, based in Hong Kong, in recognition of the large amount of profit made there each year. A significant number of shares were sold to the general public, the money from which was for use by the firm. The big moment when we were accepted on AIM, was midnight of 2nd June 1998. The previous financial year's record for the firm, ending 30th August 1997, was £20.7m in fees, with a net profit of £1.47m, which was an influencing factor for prospective investors. The flotation was a success and the company received a sum of £4.5m from the shares it sold to the general public, which was to be used to fund the expansion. Mike Charlton and I were entitled to sell our shares through the stockbroker on the AIM market at any time, except during the close season, which covered the three months prior to the year ending. This is a legal requirement, as it is considered that during this period directors of the company would have inside knowledge as to the likely year-end profit, which normally affects the share price.

3.138 It was necessary to elect a board of directors and arrange regular board meetings. First and foremost it was a legal requirement to appoint a Company Secretary. Christine Hulley joined the company in 1990, working in the accounts department in Knutsford. In her time with us she had qualified as a Company Secretary and was therefore an obvious choice. I appointed myself as Chairman and CEO and Patrick as the Finance Director. We were advised by our stockbroker, Wise Speke, that we should appoint two non-executive directors who would represent the external shareholders and fix the remunerations of Patrick, Christine and myself. In deciding who to invite to act as non-executive directors, Patrick had an inspired moment and suggested we invite Sir Michael Latham to become one of the non-executive directors. Sir Michael was, at the time, following the publication of the Latham Report, one of the biggest names in the construction industry. I was pleasantly surprised when he responded to the effect that he was interested in taking up the position. Patrick and I met him at the office in Knutsford and the deal was done. Rod Sellers an accountant was appointed as the second non-executive director as the result of a recommendation. We held board meetings quarterly which comprised mainly of bringing the non-executive directors up to date with any developments such as opening new offices and also working through Patrick's financial report, which he produced for every meeting. Rod, being an accountant by profession, always had questions which went into the fine detail of the figures. The other members of the board were apt to spend time looking out of the window whilst Patrick produced the appropriate explanations which often involved a trip to the accounts department for clarification. Sir Michael was a good appointment as he was instrumental in opening a few doors for us which proved very helpful. It is the norm for non-executive directors to resign after a few years. Following the resignations of Sir Michael and Rod, we appointed John Lee, who later became Lord Lee, as one of our non-executive directors. John was a former minister in the John Major government and columnist in the Financial Times. The other non-executive director was Peter Bates, a former merchant banker.

3.139 We didn't have any distinct written plan for expansion overseas as that wasn't my style. I had in mind that as Europe was close at hand, this seemed as good a place as any in which to start. I decided to appoint David Price as Managing Director of James R Knowles (Europe) Ltd with the idea of expanding into Europe. David decided that as we had Siemens as an existing client, an office in Munich where they were based would be a good location in which to start. He placed an advertisement for a manager and carried out interviews at Munich Airport. Juergen Usselmann and Helmut Fanger had run a small consultancy and were looking for employment with a bigger firm. David offered both of them jobs which they accepted. The Munich office opened on 1st November 1998 and became very successful in making profits each and every year thereafter.

3.140 I received a call from Roger Bridges who ran the Toronto office of Pinnacle One. They offered a similar service to ourselves and Roger was keen to meet me. It seemed that a new CEO had been appointed at the Pinnacle One headquarters in Los Angeles and he and Roger hadn't hit it off. Roger, who is English born and bred, came to see us in 1999 and I liked the look of him. Most of his work was for insurance companies, who had received claims from policy-holders, in respect of which they engaged Roger and his team to respond. I hadn't given any thought to expanding into North America but my interest was aroused having received contact from Roger. Brian Quinn, who by then was CEO of James R Knowles in the UK, showed a particular interest in Roger Bridges and what he had to offer. Having satisfied myself that we should engage Roger Bridges I left Brian to sort out the details

3.141 Brian went to Toronto and after a while informed me that the plan was to employ Roger there where he would set up a Knowles office. A series of advertisements would be placed in the press for consultancy staff by Roger and it was anticipated that members of the Pinnacle One staff would apply, attend interviews and be appointed. The plan was to surreptitiously take onto James R Knowles staff in Toronto consultancy staff employed there by Pinnacle One. This approach would be legal in the UK, provided the staff left the current employer by giving notice in accordance with the terms of their conditions of employment. However I felt it to be morally dubious, but despite my reservations the plan went ahead. It worked in that sufficient members of Pinnacle One staff applied to ensure that the office became successful. Roger Bridges was a first class manager and the profits he secured were good and consistent.

3.142 A couple of years later, an opportunity for expansion came when I was informed by Brian that a company named BBCG, based in Toronto and run by Ted Baker, wished to be taken over. Roger Bridges who knew Ted Baker well was keen, but the company would come at a price. Patrick became involved and as we were all agreed that BBCG was a good company to acquire, he would go to Canada to undertake due diligence. BBCG's main office was in Toronto with small branch offices in Vancouver and Montreal. Patrick was satisfied and BBCG was purchased. Without a great deal of effort on our part, the North American end of the business was on a steep rise. Gene Bennett, a former Pinnacle One's president, was currently looking for an opportunity and made contact with me. To cut a long story short we engaged Gene, who opened an office for us in Los Angeles. Within the space of three years we had gone from zero to having a successful business in North America comprising four offices.

CHAPTER TWENTY-TWO

EXPANSION IN EUROPE AND START UP IN AUSTRALIA

3.143 It was the year 2000 and since the flotation in 1998 and the influx of funds to enable us to expand our overseas operations, matters had gone pretty well, with Munich and North America making good progress and so I considered it was time for further expansion. We had been working in France with Graham Dick located in Brest working on a claim relating to two semi-submersible drilling rigs. We had a Frenchman, Frederic Mativat, working in our Bristol office and if we were interested in opening an office in Paris then he may be of some assistance. Discussions took place with David Price as Managing Director of James R Knowles (Europe), Malcolm Roberts, who was responsible for the Bristol office and Frederic himself. It was agreed that we would open a Paris office with Frederic as manager and the Bristol office providing liaison, as we didn't wish to leave Frederic feeling isolated. Having established an office in 2002 we followed our usual procedure and organised a seminar which took place at Le Bristol Hotel with Malcolm Roberts and me undertaking the lecturing duties. I was amazed when Malcolm announced that he intended to deliver his lectures in French. I didn't know how fluent he was in speaking French but he was convinced he would gain more respect from the delegates if his lecture was delivered in their own language. I am unable to comment on the quality of his French, mine being limited to "O" Level, failed. I didn't notice anybody nodding off during Malcolm's lecture and therefore assumed it had been well received.

3.144 After we had been established a few weeks, Frederic dropped the bombshell by advising Malcolm that, due to restrictive trade practice laws which applied in France, it was illegal for any person or organisation, other than a registered company of French lawyers, to provide a service offering legal or contractual advice to its clients. As this was our main service, we would be left in no man's land if this was correct. David Price consulted a French lawyer, who advised him that this was not a legal requirement although it was common practice. Frederic however was not convinced, which left us with a problem. In an effort to escape from our dilemma we decided to send Graham Dick, whose work in Brest was coming to an end, to assist Frederick. This overcame the problem but Frederick remained convinced that under French law we were prevented from providing legal and contractual advice to our clients. Frederick decided his future career would be better served working for another company and so tendered his resignation. Graham Dick took over as manager and was assisted by four French consultants. The office however struggled to make a profit on a regular basis and so we decided to close it down in 2006. This proved to be an expensive exercise as the restrictive practice and employment laws which apply in France are very onerous for employers. Despite our experience in Paris I was not deterred and consequently we opened further offices in Milan and Madrid but unfortunately the results were no better than those we had experienced in Paris. I came to the conclusion that Munich was a one-off and abandoned any ideas of expansion in Europe by opening offices. David Price however was successful in marketing and securing work from European contractors which we serviced from the UK. The Europe expansion plan is a good example of how my "play it by ear, don't bother with a business plan and research" proved to be very costly. In my own inadequate defence I would argue that we dipped our toe in the water in opening an office in Munich which was very successful and tried to repeat the process in Paris, Madrid and Milan with disastrous results.

3.145 Mike Charlton had on several occasions mentioned the possibility of opening an office in Australia. I usually showed some interest but nothing had come along which gave the suggestion any urgency. John Donnelly had worked in our Knutsford office and subsequently emigrated to Australia. John was well regarded and Mike suggested we contact him and enquire if he would like to join us and set up an office in Melbourne which is where he lived. We decided that Mike would be in the best position to supervise matters in Australia due to his location, experience and general admiration for the country. In no time at all we had an office operating in Melbourne and in 2000 John Donnelly was appointed as manager. Charles Elliott, another former James R Knowles employee, surfaced in Australia and was engaged to open an office in Sydney. The building methods and construction contracts were very similar to those which applied in the UK and so we had a fair wind behind us. I decided that the time had arrived for me to make a visit which occurred in April 2003. Within a week or two of my announcement I was informed that seminars had been arranged in Sydney, Melbourne, Brisbane, Perth and Adelaide. There was a rush of bookings; Sydney and Melbourne with 150 delegates each were soon booked up and some of the disappointed applicants decided to fly to Brisbane to attend the seminar to be held there. We had a full house at all five seminars which was entitled 50 Contractual Problems and Their Solutions, a subject we had used in many places with great success. I fell for Australia in a big way; the weather, the go for it and can do attitudes and business opportunities were all to my liking and I made several return visits. The offices in Sydney and Melbourne were built up over a period of two to three years and whilst the profits were a bit thin, the prospects were, in my opinion, excellent.

3.146 European sailors had entered Australian waters in the early 1600s. Between 1606 and 1770 more than 50 ships landed on Australian soil which was inhabited solely by indigenous people and called Terra Australis. England was anxious to find new territories having recently lost the American colonies and in Captain Cook they had probably the foremost explorer in the world. Cook was a great surveyor and mapped coastlines in greater detail and on a scale not previously achieved. His legacy was to influence his successors well into the twentieth century. It was decided to send Captain Cook to colonise Terra Australis. During his journey on HMS Endeavour he mapped New Zealand and the east coast of Australia. He landed in what was named by him and his crew as Botany Bay, in which Sydney now lies, on 22nd August 1770, planted the flag and claimed the whole of Eastern Australia for England. He named Eastern Australia as New South Wales due to it reminding him of Glamorgan. Joseph Banks, a botanist, accompanied Captain Cook on his voyage of discovery and collected 1,330 new plants which made a massive contribution to our horticultural knowledge. At the time of this discovery there are estimated to have been 250 separate tribes of aborigines each with its own language, laws and territorial boundaries. Captain Cook and his crew arrived back home on 10th July 1771.

3.147 In the late 1700s the jails in England were full but the courts continued to send people found guilty of criminal offences to prison. It was considered by the upper and ruling classes in England at the time, that criminals were inherently defective and couldn't be rehabilitated. In view of the lack of accommodation in the jails and the general attitude to the criminal classes, the government decided that the answer to the problem was to deport criminals to the new colony in Australia. The deportation of the first criminals occurred in 1797 when eleven ships containing 736 criminals set sail for Australia. The criminals were kept in chains below deck during the day but released to allow them a breath of fresh air in the evenings. The journey took 252 days, the final head count showing that 48 had died on the journey, 40 of them being convicts. Many were young or old who had committed very minor crimes. Elizabeth Buckworth was 70 years of age and had stolen 12 lbs of cheese; James Grace was 11 years old and had stolen some ribbons and silk stockings, whilst John Wisehammer aged 15 had snatched some snuff from a shop counter. Some women who were transported on the boat became friendly with members of the crew and as a result sexual relationships became rampant. Women were in short supply in the colony and so more were sent out with the result that the ships became known as floating brothels. Captain Arthur Phillips, the captain of the first ship, was instructed to set up the first penal colony. The convicts were not kept behind bars but none-the-less had a tough life. Most of the guards had volunteered to go to the penal colony and were in the main sadistic, delighting in inflicting severe punishment for minor violation of the rules. Those with skills and education did better that the rest. Those who behaved themselves often could qualify for a Ticket for Leave, Certificate of Freedom, Conditional Pardon or even an Absolute Pardon. All Australians now celebrate Australia Day, which takes place on 26th January to commemorate the first landing on that day in 1788.

3.148 In 2000 Danny Atkinson suggested we set up a company which specialised in providing legal services and styled it Knowles Law Ltd with him to be appointed as Managing Director, to which I agreed. Danny took temporary offices in Westminster Tower and then moved to some premises in Bedford Row which also housed Knowles Loss Adjusters. We were able to fit Knowles Law in as it was not the intention to employ many permanent staff. The new firm got off to a good start and finally they employed three legally qualified staff in addition to Danny and a secretary. The service was aimed at clients employing their own staff who could prepare claims of a sort. Danny's team provided the expertise and guidance to enable the client's staff to produce high value complex claims. The fees charged were much higher than we normally charged and the profits extremely good.

3.149 I had given some thought to further expansion in the Middle East. A large number of UK consultants had, in the 1970s and 1980s, achieved success in Iraq and this had been a possibility. In view of events which were to take place in later times, namely war against Iran and also battles with Kurdish civilians, this was soon crossed off my mental list. The Iraqi forces were alleged to have used chemical weapons, which was met with hostility from the United Nations, who condemned outright their use. United Nations' inspectors located large stocks of chemical weapons in 1991 and had them destroyed. Certain levels of co-operation took place between the UN inspectors and Iraqi officials, concerning the manufacture and storage of chemical weapons. The USA and UK governments however alleged that despite these inspections, Iraq possessed large quantities of what were described as WMDs (weapons of mass destruction) a very emotive description for chemical weapons. The United Nations Security Council issued Resolution 1441 which demanded that Saddam Hussein give immediate, unconditional and active support to UN inspectors. Hans Blix, one of those inspectors charged with carrying out the task, reported that he had received limited co-operation. The Bush administration declared that Saddam Hussein would not be disarmed by peaceful means. Tony Blair in his part published dossier unequivocally indicated that Saddam Hussein possessed WDMs. This document was later regularly referred to as the dodgy dossier, due to alleged inaccuracies contained therein. The UN however declined to pass a resolution authorising the use of force. This was not acceptable to George Bush and Tony Blair, the latter stating "the assessed intelligence has established beyond doubt that Saddam has continued to produce chemical weapons and will continue efforts to produce nuclear weapons". George Bush was under pressure in the USA following the attack on the Twin Towers, which occurred on 11th September 2001, to take some reciprocal action and removing Saddam Hussein seemed an ideal opportunity.

3.150 The war against Iraq commenced on 19th March 2003 with the bombing of Baghdad by the US Air Force. Troops had been assembled in nearby Kuwait and moved into Iraq the following day. The forces involved in the war comprised 148,000 from the USA, 45,000 from the UK, 2,000 from Australia and 194 from Poland. Saddam's forces were defeated and surrendered on 1st May 2003. The multi-national force installed an interim administration which held an election on 30th January 2005 considered by international groups and formerly excluded factions to be the first election in Iraq's history to be free and fair. Opponents of the occupation such as various insurgent groups claimed the elections were not free and fair citing flaws in the process. The UN adviser to Iraq's election commission, Craig Jenness, said the matters complained of were not significant. Iraq, like many other Muslim countries, is divided on religious grounds with the Shias on one side and the Sunnis on the other, the great majority of which are Sunnis. Saddam Hussein's administration were all Sunnis, whilst its replacement were all Shias. Once the Saddam regime had been replaced by Shias, the battle continued, with the new government. Shiite forces lined up against the Sunnis, which included Saddam's Ba'athists, who had been driven out of office, together with Al Qaeda, ISIS and other disaffected organisations. The multi-national forces acted on the side of the new government and continued to do so until they withdrew in 2011. In the aftermath of the invasion, the USA Senate Intelligence Committee found that the Bush administration misrepresented the threat from Iraq. It was also said later that the intelligence which led to the invasion was based upon fabrications, wishful thinking and lies. The decision not to open an office in Iraq proved to be one of my better ones.

CHAPTER TWENTY-THREE

NEW VENTURES

3.151 David "The Eagle" Barker joined our staff in Sutton Coldfield in 1990 where he worked as a member of the team until moving home to Devon in 2002. There was no office within reasonable commuting distance from his new home and so he worked for us on a freelance basis, becoming a go anywhere person. One of his commissions was for a German client, Preussagl Noell, which had acquired Whessoe, a firm based in Darlington, and a leading designer and constructor of water, oil and LNG tanks which were exported to all parts of the globe. David found himself leading a team in Taiwan to investigate a delay in relation to a tank farm. The team were accommodated in what became known as the "shop house" as it consisted of a shop on the ground floor and accommodation above. Unfortunately the whole area was prone to earthquakes which, when one occurred, involved a very quick relocation to a place of safety away from all buildings. During one earthquake, which measured 6.4 on the Richter Scale a member of the team was missing at the place of assembly, which caused considerable concern. It seems that at the time he was attending to matters in the toilet and having emerged to find everywhere deserted couldn't understand where everybody had gone. His later explanation for not making a quick exit was that he didn't feel the tremors.

3.152 We considered that with the Olympic Games due to take place in Athens in 2002 and reported to be well behind programme, there would be possibilities for us to sell our services. I asked The Eagle to take himself off to Greece to try his hand at unearthing some work. As UK contractors were involved in some of the construction work, we felt that opportunities would present themselves. However this was not to be the case, as it seems that when a prestigious government project such as the Olympic Games gets behind programme, money is thrown at it to overcome the problem. One can only imagine what would happen if the start of the Games had to be delayed due to the stadium not being ready. However all wasn't lost as Whessoe required a claim to be prepared in respect of two underground tanks, each the size of the Albert Hall, located at the LNG Terminal located on Revithoussa Island which is just west of Athens. The Eagle decided to use a freelance claims consultant to undertake the majority of the work. The gentleman in question had a proclivity toward dressing in women's clothes. In an effort to look professional we had at the time a dress code; all the men were required to wear suits, shirt and tie and the ladies dresses or skirts, no trousers. There was no provision in the dress code for men to wear dresses. There was a problem regarding the dress code, as far as it applied to our freelance consultant. His passport photograph had been taken with him wearing women's clothes and so to overcome this difficulty meant arriving at Heathrow dressed as a woman to conform with his passport photograph. On arrival at Athens Airport a quick change to men's clothing was required to comply with the company dress code, before hailing a taxi. This presented a problem as the changeover was undertaken in the Athens Airport toilets. Did the change take place in the Gents or Ladies? The freelance consultant, when asked the question by The Eagle, refused to provide an answer.

3.153 I liked to indulge myself in new ventures which were usually speculative, expected to provide publicity for the firm, and which may or may not make a profit. We were approached in the late 1980s by Alan Gale and Marion Pope. They had both been made redundant whilst working in the publishing business and were keen to set up their own magazine. It was their expressed wish that we should become involved in a 50/50 partnership. We had some discussions and I concluded that as our only expertise was in construction, if we were to become involved, then it would have to be a construction-related magazine. It was agreed that we would jointly produce a monthly magazine entitled Constructional Law. We would provide all the copy and Alan and Marion would organise the printing and distribution. Alan and Marion had experience of producing large numbers of copies of a magazine and mailing them on a speculative basis, inviting those on the receiving end to subscribe. Alan and Marion undertook to seek out companies willing to have advertisements placed in the magazine and we would provide the copy together with a mailing list. Working capital was required to get the magazine underway, the money being provided in equal share by Alan and Marion and ourselves. Alan and Marion produced a business plan and our venture got off to a good start with sufficient numbers of advertisers and subscribers to accord with the plan. However the good progress was short-lived. Construction unfortunately is cyclical and when the magazine got underway the construction industry was healthy, however within a short time there was a downturn in the industry. The advertising dried up almost overnight and the take-up of new subscriptions was severely reduced. Each month there was a short-fall between income and expenditure which we funded. Eventually we decided that enough was enough and the magazine was sold to Eclipse. It is pleasing to note that some twenty years later that the magazine is still being published.

3.154 At no time did I ever consider I had time on my hands, but I always felt at the back of my mind that for the company to continue being successful, in addition to general marketing and seminars, we needed regular focal points to provide us with publicity. It crossed my mind that publishing a book would be helpful in this respect. The seminars based on the 50 Contractual Nightmares had been an unqualified success wherever it had been presented and so I considered a book by the same title would sell well. As I had available ample material for the seminars, producing a book should not be too onerous a task. I contacted Blackwell Science, the publishers, who expressed an interest. The book finished up as 100 Contractual Problems and Their Solutions which was published in 2000; Blackwell Science didn't care much for the Nightmares bit. It sold well and so in 2006 I produced a second edition entitled 150 Contractual Problems and Their Solutions, with a third edition published in 2012 entitled 200 Contractual Problems and Their Solutions

3.155 Sometime during 1995, my attention was drawn to The Lord Chancellor's Advisory Committee on Legal Education and Conduct (ACLEC) whose duty was to assist in "the maintenance and development of standards in the education, training and conduct of those offering legal services". The composition of the committee was the chairman, seven legal and nine lay members. Solicitors who hold a practising certificate and barristers operating from chambers have a monopoly of representing parties in courts of law and arguably were the most effective closed shop in the country. However ACLEC was charged with breaking the closed shop by allowing rights of court representation to other suitable organisations. I considered it would be a nice diversion if we set up an organisation and applied to ACLEC to allow its members to have court representation. I approached a number of Quantity Surveying firms, inviting them to join me in forming the Institute of Commercial Litigators (ICL). There were six firms in all who were responsible for establishing the ICL, we were the leading firm and spokesperson. The intention was for members of the ICL to be allowed to represent clients in courts of law where the matter in dispute related to construction. We completed the necessary forms and were asked to appear before ACLEC, whose chairman was Lord Stein. The full committee was present and Patrick Lineen and I made our pitch. It was difficult to judge when addressing the Committee as to whether they were favourably disposed to the ICL. However when Lord Stein launched into us with his questions, I felt like a prisoner in the dock under cross examination. Some days later, when a letter arrived from ACLEC both Patrick and I expected a rejection and that is what we received. In addition to rejecting the current application, his Lordship stated in the letter that, were we to restructure the organisation and reapply, it would be a waste of time, as any further application would receive a rejection. This should have come as no surprise, as whilst the committee had a majority of one in favour of non-lawyers, many members of the committee had little experience of court proceedings or construction and no doubt would have been influenced by the legal representatives on the committee. We did receive some consolation in the form of a letter which expressed the minority view which stated that they liked our presentation and were sorry that it had been unsuccessful. I am not aware of any organisation who managed to secure a thumbs up from ACLEC.

3.156 I didn't give up on the idea of forming a legal practice. Brian Quinn came up with the suggestion that we could start a company styled Knowles Solicitors and have the ownership in the hands of practising solicitors but to have our name on the letter heading and for us to underwrite all the costs. This seemed a reasonable suggestion and it was put into operation by Brian, with him acting as the practice manager. We engaged a few solicitors the most prominent being Julian Ives and Neil Hunter and operated the practice from premises in Liverpool. This allowed us to promote ourselves as providing a full service including access to Courts of Law. Mike Charlton had similar ideas for Australia, where he took on board Brett Vincent and Sonya Kroon, both Australian registered solicitors. Whilst the services offered by both these organisations were satisfactory the lack of profits was disappointing.

3.157 In the dim and distant past there existed The Institute of Quantity Surveyors, which was much revered by its members. However they were absorbed into the RICS which in my opinion left a void. The RICS no longer spoke for quantity surveyors, as they had ceased to recognise the job title and on inspection of the RICS website I could find no reference whatsoever to quantity surveyors. I decided in 2004 to start a new Quantity Surveyors Institute which I called Quantity Surveyors International (QSi) as I didn't wish it to be seen as solely a UK organisation, but one which operated on a global scale. Securing publicity presented no difficulty, as the construction press were pleased to give coverage to something controversial such as the QSi. The publicity caused something of a stir at the RICS and I was invited to meet the President and Chief Executive for discussions, which were very cordial, but didn't result in me altering my intentions. Suzanne Cash was appointed as the Administrator and we were soon open for business. We appointed a General Council and produced a set of rules and regulations. A Quarterly magazine styled QSEyc was produced which attracted some excellent contributors and was very successful. Soon the number of applications for membership began to grown. As I had hoped, there were large numbers of applications from overseas countries which helped to justify our title of Quantity Surveyors International. Ten years later and the QSi is still going strong.

CHAPTER TWENTY-FOUR

NIGERIA AND MY LAST DAYS WITH THE COMPANY

3.158 I received a letter from Femi Onashile, the Chairman of The Nigerian Institute of Quantity Surveyors, Lagos Chapter, requesting that we meet. He was due to travel to London in the near future and we arranged a get together, the most convenient place being a coffee shop. He explained that the Institute would like me to present a seminar to its members in Lagos and as Femi seemed a decent sort of person, I agreed. In making the necessary arrangements to deliver the seminar on 7th February 2006, I was advised that, Nigeria being a dangerous country, I should take out kidnap insurance before travelling, which was duly arranged. When I arrived at Lagos airport it was obvious there was a double standards approach to most matters which applied to individuals. There was a long queue at passport control, but I, together with a few others, was ushered through without delay. A car had been sent to meet me at the airport and seated in the front passenger seat was a man with a large gun in his lap. It was a bit late for me to have reservations and in any event, nothing untoward occurred on the trip. A dinner in my honour had been arranged for the evening before the seminar which was well attended. Femi gave a short introductory talk in which he mentioned that I had been advised to take out kidnap insurance, which brought a peal of laughter from those present. It seems that kidnapping only takes place in Port Harcourt, which is the centre of the Nigerian oil industry. There exists a sort of consensual affair between the locals, who consider they derive no benefit from the oil wealth and the oil companies. The locals from time to time kidnap a representative of the oil business, and the oil companies pay the ransom without too much fuss. The seminar was entitled 50 Common Contractual Problems and Their Adjudged Solutions and once I got underway there was a constant stream of people who came into the room and shortly after left, which was a little off-putting at the start, but I soon got used to the system. Another odd factor was that there was a series of short power cuts throughout the day, as the lights from time to time went out and after a few seconds came back on again and, as there was no natural lighting, this left us all in the dark. None-the-less all went well and I enjoyed the experience as it appears did all those who attended. This trip reminded me of an invitation I received in 1994 from the RICS representative in Barbados, to present a one day seminar to its local members. It was referred to by my colleagues as Roger's Day Trip to Barbados. I flew out to Barbados on the day prior to the day of the seminar and returned in the evening after presenting the seminar. Unfortunately on most of my overseas travels I rarely left myself time to visit the local places of interest.

3.159 I was approached after the seminar in Nigeria had concluded by a gentleman who represented ITB Nigeria Ltd, a local contractor. It seems they were in dispute on one of their projects and would like my assistance. The next day I visited their offices and spent half a day reading though all the relevant correspondence. I gave them my opinion and promised to send a written report after I had returned home. As a follow up we received a commission to prepare a claim in respect of the project for which I had provided the opinion. Harold Jepson undertook the task and as a result ITB Nigeria became a regular client. I returned to Lagos later in 2006 to present a one day seminar to ITB Nigeria which went well. Some months later I was asked to present a one day seminar to the employees of an oil company in Port Harcourt, an invitation which I politely declined. Some eight years later Harold was still providing consultancy services to ITB Nigeria and some five other Nigerian companies, all of which resulted from the original contact.

3.160 To be successful as a publicly quoted company, whether on AIM, or the Stock Exchange, its profits need to increase year on year. The share price usually rises when profits are on the increase and falls when profits drop. Investors purchase shares in the expectation of a share price increase which allows them to sell at a profit. Our company's performance over the years was for the profits to rise and then in subsequent years to fall and then rise again which continued after flotation. This resulted in our share price regularly moving from 70p down to 30p and then back to 70p which, from an investor's point of view, wasn't what they were hoping for. After some years of the yo-yo performance in terms of profits and share price Sir Michael Latham took me to one side and suggested I stand down as CEO, but retain the position as Executive Chairman, which he considered was a prerequisite to a more consistent performance by the company. I had a great deal of respect for Sir Michael and having passed retirement age agreed to his suggestion. It was left to me to decide on my successor as CEO and there were two who, in my opinion, were fully capable of undertaking the role successfully. Brian Quinn had been CEO of James R Knowles in the UK and Mike Charlton performed a similar role in East Asia, either of whom would in my opinion make a good CEO. I decided that the best solution was to appoint them both as Joint CEO and this was acceptable to Brian and Mike and also received the approval of the two non-executive members of James R Knowles Holdings Board, Sir Michael and Rod Sellers; I retained the position of full time Executive Chairman.

3.161 After three years as Executive Chairman my enthusiasm for the company had started to wane. Since relinquishing my position as CEO, my role had changed dramatically and comprised devoting myself full-time to promoting the company and selling its services. Leading the team from the front was the job of the CEO and I missed the regular contact with the management and involvement with the day to day running of the company. Many of our stalwarts who had been responsible for building up significant parts of the business had left to start their own business, join other companies, or retire. I was also experiencing irreconcilable differences with the other members of the Holding Board. It is said that there is a right time for everything and as I was approaching 70, it was clearly the right time for me to sell up and leave. Our stockbroker indicated that with such a large shareholding on offer it would be the normal procedure to delist from AIM and sell the whole company. Hill International made a bid which was accepted. I was pleased that the company was to be bought by a consultancy, and Hill International being project managers and dispute resolution specialists seemed ideal. I had met Irv Richter, their founder and major shareholder, on a previous occasion and I was happy to pass ownership over to him. I was asked if I would like to stay on after the company had been acquired, but politely declined. I had been my own boss for over 30 years and the idea of working for somebody else held no attractions whatsoever. My last day was 31st August 2006, having commenced in February 1973. My first office comprised three rooms; I left behind fourteen offices in the UK and thirteen overseas; my first year's fee income was £12,500 compared with over £30m when I left and in thirty-three years of our existence we had made a profit each and every year. I was able to look back with pride. They say that the success of a business depends upon the quality of its employees. I was blessed by being able to recruit such marvellous people who made the company so successful and provided me with thirty three wonderful years.

CHAPTER TWENTY-FIVE

POSTSCRIPT

3.162 A week or two following my departure, I rang Patrick Lineen to inform him that I had an idea with which he may wish to become involved. Patrick rather liked me to have ideas, however he wasn't always so enthusiastic when the idea was explained to him. My idea was to form a new professional firm of Quantity Surveyors made up of a few medium sized companies and go for an AIM flotation. One of the difficulties of being a partner or director/shareholder in a private company is to arrange an exit route on retirement, whereby you are able to sell your stake holding in the company for a decent financial consideration. It usually comes down to a sale to an existing member of the firm often for a very modest sum. If a number of medium sized companies were joined together to form a much larger company which secured an AIM listing, the shares could be sold at any time in any quantity to the public at large. Alternatively, as in my case where some shares were held by Knowles staff and also by the public, the whole company could be sold for a reasonable sum.

3.170 Being well known in the Quantity Surveying world, I suggested contacting a few firms and set out our ideas. We arrived at a list of just over 20 firms and I wrote a personal letter to the head of each firm. The majority responded, most of which showed an interest. We then asked for information concerning recent profits, on receipt of which we selected ten firms for further consideration. Meetings were held with them all and we subsequently reduced the list to five. The final task before the introductions were made, was to allocate the shareholding in the newly formed firm between the five companies, which was accomplished based upon the recent profits of each of them. The largest firm by far had only a modest profit record and objected to their proposed share allocation and withdrew. One of the other firms decided not to proceed, as one of its directors was against the whole idea and the company's policy was to proceed with major changes only when all the directors' views were in accord. The remaining firms were Boxall Sayer, Denley King and Fletcher McNeill, whose directors all attended a meeting at which introductions were made and a programme outlined leading to an AIM listing. The initial process began in late 2006 but it took until the autumn of 2007 before the firms were in place ready to proceed. Patrick's task was to appoint and liaise with the stockbroker and accountants, whilst mine was to bring together the three companies' representatives, being Clive Sayer, Tom Denley and Rob McNeill. It was necessary to fix a date when the flotation was to take place. We were advised not to choose a date in December, as due to its proximity to Christmas, activity in the investment market is at a low ebb. However we were coming to the end of 2007 and the international financial black clouds were in evidence. Patrick and I thought that if we left the flotation until 2008 it may be too late and so, against all advice, we opted for a flotation date of 14th December 2007, on which day the shares in the company became available for sale to the general public. For a flotation to be regarded as successful, all the shares offered for sale need to be sold on the date of flotation, at the price fixed in advance by the stockbroker; it was touch and go however. We needed a name for the company and somebody suggested Baqus. This being the only name on the table, it was unanimously accepted. We were faced at James R Knowles on several occasions over many years with financial exocets heading our way, which miraculously became diverted without hitting the target. Patrick's response when this occurred was usually to remark that "Somebody Up There Likes Us" which was his comment when we received the news from our stockbroker that all the shares in Baqus had been sold on the day of the flotation.

THE END